Getting Started
with Spartan
3rd Edition

Wavefunction, Inc.
18401 Von Karman Avenue, Suite 370
Irvine, CA 92612 U.S.A.
www.wavefun.com

Wavefunction, Inc., Japan Branch Office
Level 14 Hibiya Central Building, 1-2-9 Nishi-Shinbashi
Minato-ku, Tokyo, Japan 105-0003
+81-3-5532-7335 • +81-3-5532-7373 fax
japan@wavefun.com • www.wavefun.com/japan

ISBN 1-890661-25-2

Printed in the United States of America

Preface

Over the last decade, molecular modeling has evolved from a specialized research tool of limited availability, to an important means with which to explore chemistry. The obvious catalyst has been the explosion in computer technology. Today's personal computers are as powerful as yesterday's supercomputers, and computer-based models are now routinely able to supply quantitative information about the structures, stabilities and reactivities of molecules. Computer graphics has made modeling easy to learn and easy to do.

It is inevitable that molecular modeling play a significant role in the teaching of chemistry. It offers a natural companion to both traditional lecture/textbook and laboratory approaches. Modeling, like lectures and textbooks, not only facilitates communication of both concepts and content, but also allows for the discovery of "new chemistry" very much in the same way as a laboratory. Molecular models offer an incredibly rich source of visual and quantitative information. They can be used by instructors to enhance and liven traditional lectures and classroom discussions, and by students on both personal and school computers to learn and explore chemistry.

These opportunities have prompted the development of a version of the Spartan molecular modeling program for use in teaching chemistry. While reduced in functionality and complexity from the full "research" version of Spartan, this program offers students access to state-of-the-art molecular modeling tools. This guide is intended to help teachers and students get started. Following a brief introduction, it provides two series of "tutorials", one for Windows Spartan and the other for Macintosh Spartan. These illustrate the way in which molecules are built, calculations specified and results analyzed. Although the focus is on using Spartan as a molecular modeling tool, a number of the tutorials touch on interesting chemistry. A series of "essays" follows. These describe the origins of the molecular mechanics and quantum chemical methods available in Spartan and assess their ability to calculate important chemical quantities. They also provide guidelines for determining equilibrium and transition-state geometries, for "interpreting" conformational preferences and using Spartan's graphical analysis tools. Next is a series of "hands-on" activities where the focus is on chemistry and not on the molecular models or modeling techniques. These span a variety of topics from general and organic chemistry to both inorganic chemistry and biochemistry. Each activity stands on its own, but many refer back to the essays in the previous section. Some activities require only a few minutes to complete while others may demand several hours. The guide concludes with a glossary of terms and acronyms common to molecular modeling.

The development of Spartan for use in teaching chemistry has been influenced by many individuals. Special mention goes to Wim Buijs of DSM Corporation and of the Technical University of Delft (The Netherlands), Richard Johnson and Barbara Hopkins of the University of New Hampshire, Tom Gardner of Muhlenberg College, Alan Shusterman of Reed College and Philip Bays of St. Mary's College.

Table of Contents

Section A

Introduction

Why does computer-based molecular modeling play an increasingly important role in chemical research? Is it that, at the same time that the cost of experimental laboratory science has skyrocketed, the cost of modeling has sharply decreased? Is it that computational methods, and the software and hardware needed to implement these methods, have matured to the point where useful results can be obtained for real systems in a practical time period? Could it be that the famous quote,

> *The underlying physical laws necessary for the mathematical theory of a large part of physics and the whole of chemistry are thus completely known, and the difficulty is only that the exact application of these laws leads to equations much too complicated to be soluble.*

> P.A.M. Dirac 1902-1984

made by one of the founders of quantum mechanics at a time when that science was still in its infancy, is now only half true? Could it be that "the whole of chemistry" is now open to computation?

All of these factors contribute, but together they have a cumulative effect that is considerably greater than the sum of their separate contributions. Effective and accurate theoretical models, combined with powerful and "user friendly" software, and inexpensive, powerful computer hardware, have made molecular modeling an affordable and widely accessible tool for solving real chemical problems. The time is now at hand for modeling tools to be used on a par with experimental methods, as a legitimate and practical means for exploring chemistry. What is needed now is for mainstream chemists to be trained in the practical use of modeling techniques. Only then will they adopt molecular modeling in the same way that they have adopted other research tools, NMR, GC-MS, X-ray crystallography, once deemed the exclusive province of highly trained "experts."

Molecular modeling offers two major benefits over experiment as a tool for exploration of chemistry. First, modeling tools can be used to investigate a much wider variety of chemical species than are normally accessible to the experimental chemist. Different conformers of a flexible molecule, reactive intermediates, and even transition states for chemical reactions, can all be easily investigated using computational models. Moreover, the computational effort required to identify and characterize each of these species is essentially the same. This contrasts with experiment, where procedures for isolating and characterizing a molecule become increasingly more difficult as its lifetime and/or concentration decreases. And, because transition states "do not exist" in the sense that sizeable populations may be established, they are not subject to direct experimental characterization.

Even more important, molecular modeling allows chemists to think more clearly about issues that are really central to chemistry, structure, stability and reactivity, than would normally be possible using experiments. To see why this is so, consider the "most important" tool conventionally used by chemists to describe molecular structure, that is, two-dimensional line drawings. While these are easy for an "expert" to understand and produce, two-dimensional drawings do not look at all like the molecules they are intended to depict. Even worse, students learning chemistry must spend considerable time mastering the creation and interpretation of these drawings, and this turns out to be a major educational hurdle. Computer-generated models, by contrast, "look" and "behave" much more like "real molecules". Good models can be produced even when a student is unable to make an accurate drawing, and the resulting model is more than a symbol or representation of a molecule as it also conveys quantitative information (geometry, volume, contact area, symmetry, etc.) about the molecular structure. Thus, a chemistry student or a research chemist, working with a computer, can explore "new areas of chemistry". Finally, computer models can also be constructed for molecules that cannot be represented by simple line drawings. Such molecules appear throughout chemistry, and include molecules containing delocalized charges, many unstable molecules, and, perhaps most important, reaction transition states.

The advantages of computer modeling over conventional representational tools are not limited to molecular structure. Models based on quantum mechanics such as those produced by Spartan can be easily and routinely used to calculate and display a myriad of chemical and physical observables, among them, stability ("thermodynamics"), reactivity ("kinetics"), spectra and charge distribution. And, as already mentioned, these properties can be studied and compared for a much wider range of molecules than can be investigated experimentally. Therefore, computer modeling can provide both students and research chemists with a firm grasp of both sides of the structure-property relationship.

This edition of Spartan is intended to provide a realistic impression of the capabilities and limitations of molecular modeling as a tool for exploring chemistry. While the program restricts the choice of theoretical models and limits the size of the systems which can be treated (relative to Spartan'04, the full version of Spartan), it is well suited to supplement both the lecture and laboratory components of general chemistry and elementary organic chemistry courses, to extend problem solving central to advanced physical organic and synthetic organic courses, or to form the basis of an "advanced" course in computational chemistry.

Features and capabilities of the program relative to Spartan'04 are provided below.

available tasks: energies and wavefunctions
                       equilibrium and transition-state geometries
                       energy profiles

missing from Spartan'04: conformational searching
                              intrinsic reaction coordinates

available theoretical models: MMFF molecular mechanics
                                 PM3 semi-empirical
                                 3-21G and 6-31G* Hartree-Fock

missing from Spartan'04: SYBYL molecular mechanics model
                              MNDO and AM1 semi-empirical models
                              density functional models
                              Møller-Plesset models

CCSD and higher-order correlated models
CIS, CISD and density functional models for excited states
basis sets larger than 6-31G*
pseudopotentials

available properties and spectra: dipole moments
electrostatic charges
infrared spectra

missing from Spartan'04: Mulliken and NBO charges
NMR spectra
UV/visible spectra

size limitations: PM3 50 atoms
3-21G and 6-31G* 30 atoms

This guide takes a very pragmatic approach. The focus is almost entirely on the use of molecular modeling to solve problems in chemistry. An analogy might be made between "computational chemistry" and "spectroscopy". Most chemists think of the latter in terms of the identification and characterization of compounds using spectroscopic techniques, and not of the quantum mechanical description of the interaction of "light" with matter or of the construction and repair of spectrometers. Readers who are interested in treatment of the theories underlying molecular models, or the algorithms used to construct these models, should consult one of the many texts that have been written on these topics.

Section B

Tutorials

This section comprises two "identical" series of "tutorials" for Spartan, the first for the Windows version (1W to 9W) and second for the Mac OS X version (1M to 9M). These are intended to provide a first exposure to the workings of the program, as well as to illustrate use of its various calculation and analysis tools including graphical modeling tools. Their focus is not on the chemistry but rather on the basic workings of Spartan's interface and on the use of its diverse modeling tools.

The first tutorial does not involve either molecule building or calculation, but rather works off of "prebuilt" and "precalculated" models. It is primarily intended to acquaint the first-time user with the "basics"... molecule display and manipulation, molecular structure, energy and property query and display, manipulation and query of graphical models. This tutorial should be completed first. The next seven tutorials involve both molecule building and calculation. Each brings focus to a particular aspect of molecular modeling, for example, construction and interpretation of electrostatic potential maps. The last tutorial, like the first, does not involve molecule building or calculation. It is intended to showcase models appropriate for display of large molecules, specifically proteins and nucleotides, as well as to further illustrate the display of hydrogen bonds.

Spartan files associated with the tutorials are grouped in the "tutorials" directory on the CD-ROM. File names are those specified in the individual tutorials. Only for the first and the last tutorials are these files needed. The remainder have been provided only to show the "proper outcome".

Basic Operations

This tutorial introduces a number of basic operations in the Windows version of Spartan required for molecule manipulation and property query. Specifically it shows how to: i) open molecules, ii) view different models and manipulate molecules on screen, iii) measure bond distances, angles and dihedral angles, iv) display energies, dipole moments, atomic charges and infrared spectra, and v) display graphical surfaces and property maps. Molecule building is not illustrated and no calculations are performed.

1. Start Spartan. *Click* on the **Start** button, then *click* on **Programs** and finally *click* on **Spartan**. Spartan's window will appear with a menu bar at the top of the screen.

    File Edit Model Geometry Build Setup Display Search   Options Help

File	Allows you to create a new molecule or read in a molecule which you have previously created.
Model	Allows you to control the style of your model.
Geometry	Allows you to measure bond lengths and angles.
Build	Allows you to build and edit molecules.
Setup	Allows you to specify the task to be performed and the theoretical model to be employed, to specify graphical surfaces and property maps and to submit jobs for calculation.
Display	Allows you to display text output, molecular and atomic properties, surfaces and property maps and infrared spectra. Also allows data presentation in a spreadsheet and plots to be made from these data.
Search	Allows you to "guess" a transition-state geometry based on a library of reactions. This guess may then be used as the basis for a quantum chemical calculation of the actual reaction transition state.

2. *Click* with the left mouse button on **File** from the menu bar.

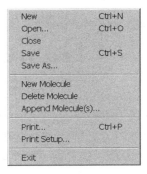

Click on **Open....** Alternatively, *click* on the 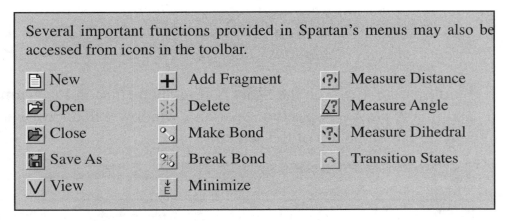 icon in the toolbar.

Several important functions provided in Spartan's menus may also be accessed from icons in the toolbar.

New	Add Fragment	Measure Distance
Open	Delete	Measure Angle
Close	Make Bond	Measure Dihedral
Save As	Break Bond	Transition States
View	Minimize	

Locate the "tutorials" directory in the dialog which appears, *click* on "*tutorial 1*" and *click* on **Open** (or *double click* on "*tutorial 1*"). Ball-and-spoke models for *ethane*, *acetic acid dimer*, *propene*, *ammonia*, *hydrogen peroxide*, *acetic acid*, *water*, *cyclohexanone*, *ethylene*, *benzene* and *aniline* appear on screen. You can select a molecule by *clicking* on it with the left mouse button. Once selected, a molecule may be manipulated (rotated, translated and scaled).

select molecule	*click* (left mouse button)
rotate molecule	*press* the left button and *move* the mouse
translate molecule	*press* the right button and *move* the mouse
scale molecule	*press* both the **Shift** key and the right button and *move* the mouse "up and down"

3. Identify *ethane* on the screen, and *click* on it (left button) to make it the selected molecule. Practice rotating (*move* the mouse while *pressing* the left button) and translating (*move* the mouse while *pressing* the right button) *ethane*. *Click* on a different molecule, and then rotate and translate it.

4. Return to *ethane*. *Click* on **Model** from the menu bar.

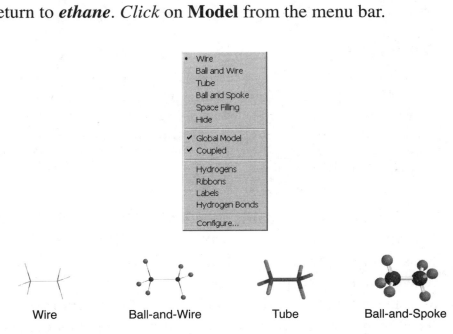

| Wire | Ball-and-Wire | Tube | Ball-and-Spoke |

One after the other, select **Wire, Ball and Wire, Tube** and finally **Ball and Spoke** from the **Model** menu. All four models for *ethane* show roughly the same information. The wire model looks like a conventional line formula, except that all atoms, not just the carbons, are found at the end of a line or at the intersection of lines. The wire model uses color to distinguish different atoms, and one, two and three lines between atoms to indicate single, double and triple bonds, respectively.

The ball-and-wire model is identical to the wire model, except that atom positions are represented by small spheres. This makes it easy to identify atom locations. The tube model is identical to the wire model, except that bonds, whether single, double or triple, are represented by solid cylinders. The tube model is better than the wire model in conveying the three-dimensional shape of a molecule. The ball-and-spoke model is a variation on the tube model; atom positions are represented by colored spheres, making it easy to see atom locations.

Select **Space Filling** from the **Model** menu.

Space-Filling

This model is different from the others in that bonds are not shown. Rather, each atom is displayed as a colored sphere that represents its approximate "size". Thus, the space-filling model for a molecule provides a measure of its size. While lines between atoms are not drawn, the existence (or absence) of bonds can be inferred from the amount of overlap between neighboring atomic spheres. If two spheres substantially overlap, then the atoms are almost certainly bonded, and conversely, if two spheres hardly overlap, then the atoms are not bonded. Intermediate overlaps suggest "weak bonding", for example, hydrogen bonding (see the activity "*Water*").

Select *acetic acid dimer*. Switch to a space-filling model and look for overlap between the (OH) hydrogen on one acetic acid molecule and the (carbonyl) oxygen on the other. Return to a ball-and-spoke model and select **Hydrogen Bonds** from the **Model** menu.

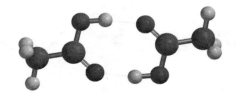

Ball-and-Spoke model for acetic acid dimer
with hydrogen bonds displayed

The two hydrogen bonds, which are responsible for holding the acetic acid molecules together, will be drawn.

Use the **3** key to toggle between stereo 3D and regular display. To view in 3D you will need to wear the red/blue glasses provided with Spartan.

5. Distances, angles, and dihedral angles can easily be measured with Spartan using **Measure Distance**, **Measure Angle**, and **Measure Dihedral**, respectively, from the **Geometry** menu.

Alternatively, the measurement functions may be accessed from the ⟨?⟩, ⟨?⟩ and ⟨?⟩ icons in the toolbar.

a) **Measure Distance**: This measures the distance between two atoms. First select ***propene*** from the molecules on screen, and then select **Measure Distance** from the **Geometry** menu (or *click* on the ⟨?⟩ icon in the toolbar). *Click* on a bond or on two atoms (the atoms do not need to be bonded). The distance (in Ångstroms) will be displayed at the bottom of the screen. Repeat the process as necessary. When you are finished, select **View** from the **Build** menu.

Alternatively, *click* on the V icon in the toolbar.

b) **Measure Angle**: This measures the angle around a central atom. Select ***ammonia*** from the molecules on screen, and then select **Measure Angle** from the **Geometry** menu (or *click* on the ⟨?⟩ icon in the toolbar). *Click* first on H, then on N, then on another H. Alternatively, *click* on two NH bonds. The HNH angle (in degrees) will be displayed at the bottom of the screen. *Click* on V when you are finished.

c) **Measure Dihedral**: This measures the angle formed by two intersecting planes, the first containing the first three atoms selected and the second containing the last three atoms selected. Select ***hydrogen peroxide*** from the molecules on screen, then select **Measure Dihedral** from the **Geometry** menu (or *click* on the ⟨?⟩ icon in the toolbar) and then *click* in turn on the four atoms (HOOH) which make up hydrogen peroxide. The HOOH dihedral angle will be displayed at the bottom of the screen. *Click* on V when you are finished.

6. Energies, dipole moments and atomic charges among other calculated properties, are available from **Properties** under the **Display** menu.

a) **Energy:** Select *acetic acid* from the molecules on screen and then select **Properties** from the **Display** menu. The **Molecule Properties** dialog appears.

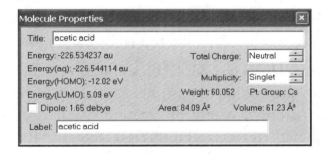

This provides the total energy for acetic acid in atomic units (au). See the essay *"Total Energies and Thermodynamic and Kinetic Data"* for a discussion of energy units.

b) **Dipole Moment:** The magnitude of the dipole moment (in debyes) is also provided in the **Molecule Properties** dialog. A large dipole moment indicates large separation of charge. You can attach the dipole moment vector, "⊦→" where the lefthand side "+" refers to the positive end of the dipole, to the model on the screen, by *checking* **Dipole** near the bottom of the dialog. The vector will not be displayed if the magnitude of the dipole moment is zero, or if the molecule is charged.

c) **Atomic Charges:** To display the charge on an atom, *click* on it with the **Molecule Properties** dialog on the screen. The **Atom Properties** dialog replaces the **Molecule Properties** dialog.

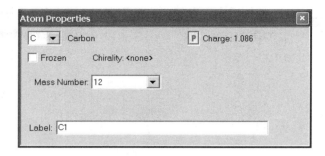

Atomic charges are given in units of electrons. A positive charge indicates a deficiency of electrons on an atom and a negative charge, an excess of electrons. Repeat the process as necessary by *clicking* on other atoms. Confirm that the positively-charged atom(s) lie at the positive end of the dipole moment vector. When you are finished, remove the dialog from the screen by *clicking* on the ⊠ in the top right-hand corner.

d) **Infrared Spectra:** Molecules vibrate (stretch, bend, twist) even if they are cooled to absolute zero. This is the basis of infrared spectroscopy, where absorption of energy occurs when the frequency of molecular motions matches the frequency of the "light". Infrared spectroscopy is important in organic chemistry as different functional groups vibrate at noticeably different and characteristic frequencies.

Select *water* from the molecules on screen. To animate a vibration, select **Spectra** from the **Display** menu. This leads to the **Spectra** dialog.

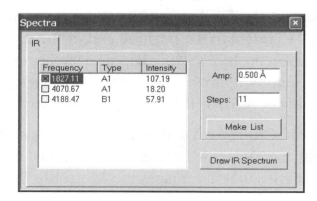

This displays the three vibrational frequencies for the water molecule, corresponding to bending and symmetric and antisymmetric stretching motions. One after the other, *double click* on each frequency and examine the motion. Turn "off" the animation when you are finished.

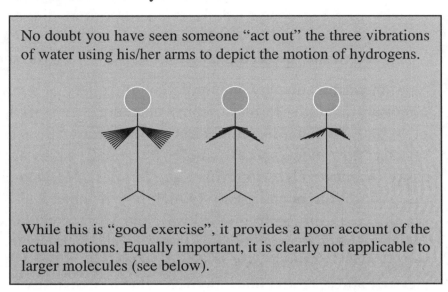

No doubt you have seen someone "act out" the three vibrations of water using his/her arms to depict the motion of hydrogens.

While this is "good exercise", it provides a poor account of the actual motions. Equally important, it is clearly not applicable to larger molecules (see below).

Select *cyclohexanone*. The **Spectra** dialog now lists its 45 vibrational frequencies. Examine each in turn (*double click* on the entry in the dialog) until you locate the frequency corresponding to the CO (carbonyl) stretch. Next, *click* on **Draw IR Spectrum** at the bottom of the dialog. The infrared spectrum of cyclohexanone will appear.

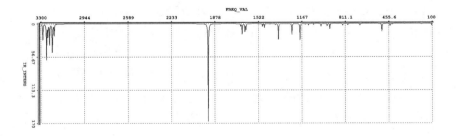

You can move the spectrum around the screen by first *clicking* on it to select it and then *moving* the mouse while *pressing* the right button. You can size it by *moving* the mouse "up and down" while *pressing* both the **Shift** key and the right button.

15

Identify the line in the spectrum associated with the CO stretch (a small gold ball moves from line to line as you step through the frequencies in the **Spectra** dialog). Note that this line is separated from the other lines in the spectrum and that it is intense. This makes it easy to find and is the primary reason why infrared spectroscopy is an important diagnostic for carbonyl functionality. When you are finished, *click* on ✕ at the top of the **Spectra** dialog to remove it from the screen.

7. Spartan permits display, manipulation and query of a number of important quantities resulting from a quantum chemical calculation in "visual" format. Most important are the electron density (which reveals "how much space" a molecule actually takes up; see the essay "***Electron Densities: Sizes and Shapes of Molecules***" for a discussion), the bond density (which reveals chemical "bonds"; see the essay on electron densities), and key molecular orbitals (which provide insight both into bonding and chemical reactivity; see the essay "***Atomic and Molecular Orbitals***"). In addition, the electrostatic potential map, an overlaying of a quantity called the electrostatic potential (the attraction or repulsion of a positive charge for a molecule) onto the electron density, is valuable for describing overall molecular charge distribution as well as anticipating sites of electrophilic addition. Further discussion is provided in the essay "***Electrostatic Potential Maps: Charge Distributions***". Another indicator of electrophilic addition is provided by the local ionization potential map, an overlaying of the energy of electron removal ("ionization") onto the electron density. Finally, the likelihood of nucleophilic addition can be ascertained using a LUMO map, an overlaying of the lowest-unoccupied molecular orbital (the LUMO) onto the electron density. Both of these latter graphical models are described in the essay "***Local Ionization Potential Maps and LUMO Maps***".

Select *ethylene* from among the molecules on screen, and then select **Surfaces** from the **Display** menu. The **Surfaces** dialog appears.

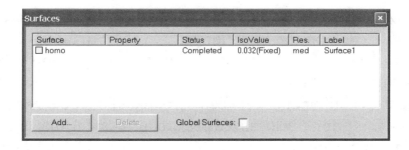

Surface	Property	Status	IsoValue	Res.	Label
☐ homo		Completed	0.032(Fixed)	med	Surface1

Add... Delete Global Surfaces: ☐

Double click on the line "homo..." inside the dialog. This will result in the display of ethylene's highest-occupied molecular orbital as a solid. This is a π orbital, equally concentrated above and below the plane of the molecule. The colors ("red" and "blue") give the sign of the orbital. Changes in sign often correlate with bonding or antibonding character. You can if you wish, turn "off" the graphic by again *double clicking* on the line "homo . . .".

Next, select **benzene** from among the molecules on screen and *double click* on the line "density potential..." inside the **Surfaces** dialog. An electrostatic potential map for benzene will appear. *Click* on the map. The **Style** menu will appear at the bottom right of the screen. Select **Transparent** from this menu to present the map as a translucent solid. This will allow you to see the molecular skeleton underneath. The surface is colored "red" in the π system (indicating negative potential and the fact that this region is attracted to a positive charge), and "blue" in the σ system (indicating positive potential and the fact that this region is repelled by a positive charge).

Select **aniline** from the molecules on screen, and *double click* on the line "density ionization..." inside the **Surfaces** dialog. The graphic which appears, a so-called local ionization potential map, colors in red regions on the density surface from which electron removal (ionization) is relatively easy, meaning that they are subject to electrophilic attack. These are easily distinguished from regions where ionization is relatively difficult (colored in blue). Note that the *ortho* and *para* ring carbons are more red than the *meta* carbons, consistent with the known directing ability of the amino substituent.

Finally, select *cyclohexanone* from the molecules on screen , and *double click* on the line "lumo..." in the **Surfaces** dialog. The resulting graphic portrays the lowest-energy empty molecular orbital (the LUMO) of cyclohexanone. This is a so-called π^* orbital which is antibonding between carbon and oxygen. Note that the LUMO is primarily localized on carbon, meaning that this is where a pair of electrons (a nucleophile) will "attack" cyclohexanone.

A better portrayal is provided by a LUMO map, which displays the (absolute) value of the LUMO on the electron density surface. Here, the color blue is used to represent maximum value of the LUMO and the color red, minimum value. First, remove the LUMO from your structure (*double click* on the line "lumo..." in the **Surfaces** dialog) and then turn on the LUMO map (*double click* on the line "density lumo..." in the dialog). Note that the blue region is concentrated directly over the carbonyl carbon. Also, note that the so-called *axial* face shows a greater concentration of the LUMO than the *equatorial* face. This is consistent with the known stereochemistry of nucleophilic addition (see the activity "*Molecular Shapes V. Which Conformer Leads to Product?*").

8. When you are finished, close all the molecules on screen by selecting **Close** from the **File** menu or alternatively by *clicking* on 🖃.

Acrylonitrile: Building an Organic Molecule

This tutorial illustrates use of the organic model kit, as well as the steps involved in examining and querying different molecular models and in carrying out a quantum chemical calculation.

The simplest building blocks incorporated into Spartan's organic model kit are "atomic fragments". These constitute specification of atom type, e.g., carbon, and hybridization, e.g., sp^3. The organic model kit also contains libraries of common functional groups and hydrocarbon rings, the members of which can easily be extended or modified. For example, the carboxylic acid group in the library may be modified to build a carboxylate anion (by deleting a free valence from oxygen), or an ester (by adding tetrahedral carbon to the free valence at oxygen).

carboxylic acid   carboxylate anion   ester

Acrylonitrile provides a good first opportunity to illustrate the basics of molecule building, as well as the steps involved in carrying out and analyzing a simple quantum chemical calculation.

acrylonitrile

1. *Click* on **File** from the menu bar and then *click* on **New** from the menu which appears (or *click* on the 📄 icon in the **File** toolbar). The "organic" model kit appears.

Click on trigonal planar sp² hybridized carbon  from the library of atomic fragments. The fragment icon is shown in reverse video, and a model of the fragment appears at the top of the model kit. Bring the cursor anywhere on screen and *click*. Rotate the carbon fragment (*move* the mouse while holding down the left button) so that you can clearly see both the double free valence ("=") and the two single free valences ("-").

> Spartan's model kits connect atomic fragments (as well as groups, rings and ligands) through free valences. Unless you "use" them or delete them, free valences will automatically be converted to hydrogen atoms.

2. sp² carbon is still selected. *Click* on the double free valence. The two fragments are connected by a double bond, leaving you with ethylene.

> Spartan's model kits allows only the same type of free valences to be connected, e.g., single to single, double to double, etc.

3. *Click* on **Groups** in the model kit, and then select **Cyano** from among the functional groups available from the menu.

Click on one of the free valences on ethylene, to make acrylonitrile.*
If you make a mistake, you can select **Undo** from the **Edit** menu
to "undo" the last operation or **Clear** (**Edit** menu) to start over.

4. Select **Minimize** from the **Build** menu (or *click* on the ![E icon] icon in
   the toolbar). The "strain energy" and symmetry point group (C_s)
   for acrylonitrile are provided at the bottom right of the screen.

5. Select **View** from the **Build** menu (or *click* on the ![V] icon in the
   toolbar). The model kit disappears, leaving only a ball-and-spoke
   model of acrylonitrile on screen.

6. Select **Calculations**... from the **Setup** menu.

   The **Calculations** dialog appears. This will allow you to specify
   what task is to be done with your molecule and what theoretical
   model Spartan will use to accomplish this task.

---

*   You could also have built acrylonitrile without using the **Groups** menu. First, clear the screen
  by selecting **Clear** from the **Edit** menu. Then build ethylene from two sp^2 carbons (as above),
  select sp hybridized carbon ![-C≡] from the model kit and then *click* on the tip of one of the free
  valences on ethylene. Next, select sp hybridized nitrogen ![≡N] from the model kit and *click* on
  the triple free valence on the sp carbon. Alternatively, you could have built the molecule
  entirely from groups. First, clear the screen. Then *click* on **Groups**, select **Alkene** from the
  menu and *click* anywhere on screen. Then select **Cyano** from the same menu and *click* on
  one of the free valences on ethylene. In general, molecules can be constructed in many ways.

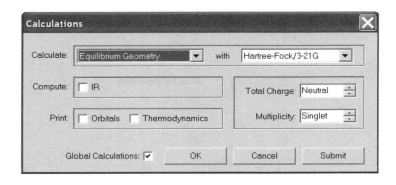

Select **Equilibrium Geometry** from the menu to the right of "Calculate". This specifies optimization of equilibrium geometry. Next, select **Hartree-Fock/3-21G** from the menu to the right of "with". This specifies a Hartree-Fock calculation using the 3-21G basis set (referred to as an HF/3-21G calculation). This method generally provides a reliable account of geometries (see the essay *"Choosing a Theoretical Model"*).

7. *Click* on **Submit** at the bottom of the dialog. The **Calculations** dialog is replaced by a file browser.

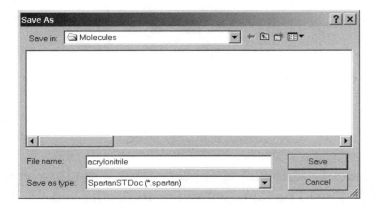

Type "acrylonitrile" in the box to the right of "File name", and *click* on **Save**[*]. You will be notified that the calculation has been submitted. *Click* on **OK** to remove the message.

---

[*] You can use default names (spartan1, spartan2, . . .) simply by *clicking* on **Save**.

After a molecule has been submitted, and until the calculation has completed, you are not permitted to modify information associated with it. You can monitor your calculation as well as abort it if necessary using **Monitor** under the **Options** menu.

8. You will be notified when the calculation has completed. *Click* **OK** to remove the message. Select **Output** from the **Display** menu. A window containing "text output" for the job appears.

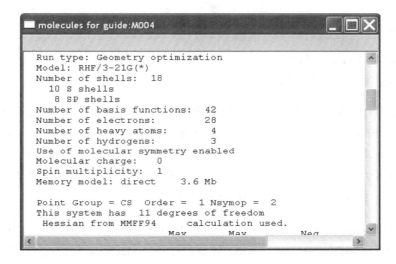

```
molecules for guide:M004

   Run type: Geometry optimization
   Model: RHF/3-21G(*)
   Number of shells:   18
     10 S shells
      8 SP shells
   Number of basis functions:   42
   Number of electrons:        28
   Number of heavy atoms:       4
   Number of hydrogens:         3
   Use of molecular symmetry enabled
   Molecular charge:   0
   Spin multiplicity:  1
   Memory model: direct     3.6 Mb

   Point Group = CS  Order =  1 Nsymop =  2
   This system has  11 degrees of freedom
    Hessian from MMFF94     calculation used.
                    Max         Max         Neg
```

You can scan the output from the calculation by using the scroll bar at the right of the window. Information provided includes the task, basis set, number of electrons, charge and multiplicity, as well as the point group of the molecule. A series of lines, each beginning with "Cycle no:", tell the history of the optimization process. Each line provides results for a particular geometry; "Energy" gives the energy in atomic units (1 atomic unit = 2625 kJ/mol) for this geometry, "Max Grad." gives the maximum gradient ("slope"), and "Max Dist." gives the maximum displacement of atoms between cycles. The energy will monotonically approach a minimum value for an optimized geometry, and Max Grad. and Max Dist. will each approach zero. Near the end of the output is the final total energy (-168.82040 atomic units). *Click* on ⊠ in the top right-hand corner of the dialog to remove the dialog from the screen.

9. You can obtain the final total energy and the dipole moment from

the **Molecule Properties** dialog, without having to go through the text output. Select **Properties** from the **Display** menu. You can "see" the dipole moment vector (indicating the sign and overall direction of the dipole moment), by *checking* **Dipole** near the bottom of this dialog. (A tube model provides the clearest picture.)

When you are finished, turn "off" display of the dipole moment vector by *unchecking* the box.

10. *Click* on an atom. The (**Molecule Properties**) dialog will be replaced by the **Atom Properties** dialog. This gives the charge on the selected atom. To obtain the charge on another atom, simply *click* on it. *Click* on ⊠ at the top right of the **Atom Properties** dialog to remove it from the screen.

11. Atomic charges can also be attached as "labels" to your model. Select **Configure...** from the Model menu, and *check* **Charge** under "Atom" in the **Configure** dialog which appears.

Click **OK** to remove the dialog.

12. *Click* on 🖼 to remove "*acrylonitrile*" from the screen. Also, close any dialogs which may still be open.

Sulfur Tetrafluoride: Building an Inorganic Molecule

This tutorial illustrates the use of the inorganic model kit for molecule building. It also shows how molecular models may be used to quantify concepts from more qualitative treatments.

Organic molecules are made up of a relatively few elements and generally obey conventional valence rules. They may be easily built using the organic model kit. However, many molecules incorporate other elements, or do not conform to normal valence rules, or involve ligands. They cannot be constructed using the organic model kit. Sulfur tetrafluoride is a good example.

sulfur tetrafluoride

The unusual "see-saw" geometry observed for the molecule is a consequence of the fact that the "best" (least crowded) way to position five electron pairs around sulfur is in a trigonal bipyramidal arrangement. The lone pair assumes an *equatorial* position so as to least interact with the remaining electron pairs. The rationale behind this is that a lone pair is "bigger" than a bonding electron pair.

Sulfur tetrafluoride provides the opportunity to look at the bonding and charges in a molecule which "appears" to have an excess of electrons around its central atom (ten instead of eight), as well as to look for evidence of a lone pair. Further attention is given to sulfur tetrafluoride in the activity "***Beyond VSEPR Theory***" later in this guide.

1. Bring up the inorganic model kit by *clicking* on  and then *clicking* on the **Inorganic** tab at the top of the organic model kit.

The inorganic model kit comprises a *Periodic Table* followed by a selection of "atomic hybrids" and then bond types. Further down the model kit are the **Rings, Groups** and **Ligands** menus, the first two of which are the same as found in the organic model kit.

2. Select (*click* on) **S** in the *Periodic Table* and the five-coordinate trigonal bipyramid structure ⌖ from the list of atomic hybrids. *Click* anywhere in the main window. A trigonal bipyramid sulfur will appear.

3. Select **F** in the *Periodic Table* and the one-coordinate entry ⌖ from the list of atomic hybrids. One after the other, *click* on both *axial* free valences of sulfur, and two of the three *equatorial* free valences.[*]

4. It is necessary to delete the remaining free valence (on an *equatorial* position); otherwise it will become a hydrogen upon leaving the builder. Select **Delete** from the **Build** menu (or *click*

---

[*] This step and the following two steps could also be accomplished from the organic model kit. To bring it up, *click* on the **Organic** tab at the top of the inorganic model kit.

on the 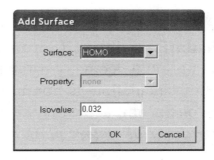 icon in the toolbar) and then *click* on the remaining *equatorial* free valence.

5. *Click* on ⬛. Molecular mechanics minimization will result in a structure with C_{2v} symmetry. *Click* on ✓.

6. Select **Calculations...** from the **Setup** menu. Specify calculation of equilibrium geometry using the HF/3-21G model. *Click* on **OK**.

7. Select **Surfaces** from the **Setup** menu. *Click* on **Add...** at the bottom of the **Surfaces** dialog and select **HOMO** from the **Surface** menu in the (**Add Surface**) dialog which appears.

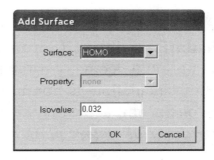

Click on **OK**. Leave the **Surfaces** dialog on screen.

8. Select **Submit** from the **Setup** menu, and supply the name "*sulfur tetrafluoride see-saw*".

9. After the calculations have completed, select **Properties** from the **Display** menu to bring up the **Molecule Properties** dialog. Next, *click* on sulfur to bring up the **Atom Properties** dialog. Is sulfur neutral or negatively charged, indicating that more than the normal complement of (eight) valence electron surrounds this atom, or is it positively charged, indicating "ionic bonding"?

10. *Click* on the line "homo..." inside the **Surfaces** dialog to examine the highest-occupied molecular orbital. Does it "point" in the

expected direction? It is largely localized on sulfur or is there significant concentration on the fluorines? If the latter, is the orbital "bonding" or "antibonding"? (For a discussion of non-bonding, bonding and antibonding molecular orbitals, see the essay "*Atomic and Molecular Orbitals*".)

11. Build square planar SF_4 as an alternative to the "see-saw" structure. Bring up the inorganic model kit (📄), select **S** from the *Periodic Table* and the four-coordinate square-planar structure ⋈ from the list of atomic hybrids. *Click* anywhere on screen. Select **F** in the *Periodic Table* and the one-coordinate entry -- from the list of atomic hybrids. *Click* on all four free valences on sulfur. *Click* on ⬇E and then on V.

12. Enter the **Calculations** dialog (**Setup** menu) and specify calculation of equilibrium geometry using the HF/3-21G model (the same level of calculation as you used for the "see-saw" structure*). *Click* on **Submit** at the bottom of the dialog, with the name "*sulfur tetrafluoride square planar*".

13. After the calculation has completed, bring up the **Molecule Properties** dialog (**Properties** from the **Display** menu) and note the energy. Is it actually higher (more positive) than that for the "see-saw" structure?

14. Close both molecules as well as any remaining dialogs.

---

* You need to use exactly the same theoretical model in order to compare energies or other properties for different molecules.

Infrared Spectrum of Acetone

This tutorial illustrates the steps required to calculate and display the infrared spectrum of a molecule.

Molecules vibrate in response to their absorbing infrared light. Absorption occurs only at specific wavelengths, which gives rise to the use of infrared spectroscopy as a tool for identifying chemical structures. The vibrational frequency is proportional to the square root of a quantity called a "force constant" divided by a quantity called the "reduced mass".

$$\text{frequency} \quad \alpha \quad \sqrt{\frac{\text{force constant}}{\text{reduced mass}}}$$

The force constant reflects the "flatness" or "steepness" of the energy surface in the vicinity of the energy minimum. The steeper the energy surface, the larger the force constant and the larger the frequency. The reduced mass reflects the masses of the atoms involved in the vibration. The smaller the reduced mass, the larger the frequency.

This tutorial shows you how to calculate and display the infrared spectrum of acetone, and explore relationships between frequency and both force constant and reduced mass. It shows why the carbonyl stretching frequency is of particular value in infrared spectroscopy.

1. *Click* on 🖹 to bring up the organic model kit. Select sp² carbon (🔲) and *click* anywhere on screen. Select sp² oxygen (🔲) and *click* on the double free valence on carbon to make the carbonyl group. Select sp³ carbon (🔲) and, one after the other, *click* on the two single free valences on carbon. *Click* on 🔲 and then on 🔽.

2. Enter the **Calculations** dialog (**Setup** menu) and request calculation of an equilibrium geometry using the HF/3-21G model.

Check **IR** to the right of "Compute" to specify calculation of vibrational frequencies. Finally, *click* on the **Submit** button at the bottom of the dialog, and provide the name "*acetone*".

3. After the calculation has completed, bring up the **Spectra** dialog (**Display** menu). This contains a list of vibrational frequencies for acetone. First *click* on the top entry (the smallest frequency) and, when you are done examining the vibrational motion, *click* on the bottom entry (the largest frequency).

> The smallest frequency is associated with torsional motion of the methyl rotors. The largest frequency is associated with stretching motion of CH bonds. Methyl torsion is characterized by a flat potential energy surface (small force constant), while CH stretching is characterized by a steep potential energy surface (large force constant).

Display the IR spectrum (*click* on **Draw IR Spectrum** at the bottom of the dialog). Locate the frequency corresponding to the CO stretch. The experimental frequency is around 1740 cm^{-1}, but the calculations will yield a higher value (around 1940 cm^{-1}).

> The CO stretching frequency is a good "chemical identifier" because it "stands alone" in the infrared spectrum and because it is "intense".

4. Change all the hydrogens in acetone to deuteriums to see the effect which increased mass has on vibrational frequencies. First make a copy of "*acetone*" (**Save As...** from the **File** menu or *click* on the 🖫 icon in the toolbar). Name the copy "*acetone d6*" Select **Properties** from the **Display** menu and *click* on one of the hydrogens. Select **2 deuterium** from the **Mass Number** menu. Repeat for the remaining five hydrogens.

5. Submit for calculation. When completed, examine the vibrational frequencies. Note that the frequencies of those motions which involve the hydrogens (in particular, the six vibrational motions corresponding to "CH stretching") are significantly reduced over those in the non-deuterated system.

6. Close all molecules on screen in addition to any remaining dialogs.

Electrophilic Reactivity of Benzene and Pyridine

This tutorial illustrates the calculation, display and interpretation of electrostatic potential maps. It also illustrates the use of "documents" comprising two or more molecules.

While benzene and pyridine have similar geometries and while both are aromatic, their "chemistry" is different. Benzene's chemistry is dictated by the molecule's π system, while the chemistry of pyridine is a consequence of the lone pair on nitrogen. This tutorial shows how to use electrostatic potential maps to highlight these differences.

1. Build benzene. *Click* on 📄. Select **Benzene** from the **Rings** menu and *click* on screen. *Click* on ⌊Ė⌋.

2. Build pyridine. In order to put both benzene and pyridine into the same "document", select **New Molecule** (not **New**) from the **File** menu. **Benzene** (**Rings** menu) is still selected. *Click* anywhere on screen. Select aromatic nitrogen ⌊ℕ⌋ from the model kit and *double click* on one of the carbon atoms (not a free valence). *Click* on ⌊Ė⌋ and then *click* on ⌊V⌋. To go between the two molecules in your document, use the ⌊◁⌋ and ⌊▷⌋ keys at the bottom left of the screen (or use the slider bar).

3. Select **Calculations...** (**Setup** menu) and specify calculation of equilibrium geometry using the HF/3-21G model. *Click* on **OK** to dismiss the dialog. Select **Surfaces** (**Setup** menu). *Click* on **Add...** at the bottom of the **Surfaces** dialog to bring up the **Add Surface** dialog. Select **density** from the **Surface** menu and **potential** from the **Property** menu. *Click* on **OK**. Leave the **Surfaces** dialog on screen. Select **Submit** (**Setup** menu) and supply the name *"benzene and pyridine"*.

4. When completed, bring up the spreadsheet (**Spreadsheet** under the **Display** menu) and *check* the box to the right of the molecule "Label" (leftmost column) for both entries. This allows benzene and pyridine to be displayed simultaneously. However, the motions of the two molecules will be "coupled" (they will move together). Select (*uncheck*) **Coupled** from the **Model** to allow the two molecules to be manipulated independently. In turn, select (*click* on) each and orient such that the two are side-by-side.

5. *Double click* on the line "density potential..." inside the **Surfaces** dialog. Electrostatic potential maps for both benzene and pyridine will be displayed. Change the scale so that the "neutral" color is "green". Select **Properties** (**Display** menu) and *click* on one of the maps to bring up the **Surface Properties** dialog.

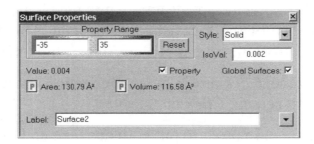

Type "-35" and "35" inside the boxes underneath "Property Range" (*press* the **Enter** key following each data entry). The "red" regions in benzene, which are most attractive to an electrophile, correspond to the molecule's π system, while in pyridine they correspond to the σ system in the vicinity of the nitrogen. Note that the π system in benzene is "more red" than the π system in pyridine (indicating that it is more susceptible to electrophilic attack here), but that the nitrogen in pyridine is "more red" than the π system in benzene (indicating that pyridine is overall more susceptible to attack by an electrophile).

Further discussion of the use of such maps is provided in the essay "*Electrostatic Potential Maps: Charge Distributions*".

6. Remove "*benzene and pyridine*" and any dialogs from the screen.

Weak vs. Strong Acids

This tutorial shows how electrostatic potential maps may be used to distinguish between weak and strong acids, and quantify subtle differences in the strengths of closely-related acids. It also shows how information can be retrieved from Spartan's database.

Chemists know that nitric acid and sulfuric acids are strong acids, acetic acid is a weak acid, and that ethanol is a very weak acid. What these compounds have in common is their ability to undergo heterolytic bond fracture, leading to a stable anion and a "proton". What distinguishes a strong acid from a weak acid is the stability of the anion. NO_3^- and $HOSO_3^-$ are very stable anions, $CH_3CO_2^-$ is somewhat less stable and $CH_3CH_2O^-$ is even less so.

One way to reveal differences in acidity is to calculate the energy of deprotonation for different acids, e.g., for nitric acid.

$$HONO_2 \longrightarrow H^+ + NO_3^-$$

This involves calculations on both the neutral acid and on the resulting anion (the energy of a proton is zero). An alternative approach, illustrated in this tutorial, involves comparison of electrostatic potential maps for different acids, with particular focus on the potential in the vicinity of the "acidic hydrogen". The more positive the potential, the more likely will dissociation occur, and the stronger the acid.

1. Build nitric acid. *Click* on 📄 to bring up the organic model kit. Select **Nitro** from the **Groups** menu and *click* anywhere on screen. Add sp³ oxygen ᵒ⁻ to the free valence on nitrogen. *Click* on ⬇ᴇ. Build sulfuric acid. Select **New Molecule** (not **New**) from the **File** menu. Select **Sulfone** from the **Groups** menu and *click* anywhere on screen. Add sp³ oxygen to both free valences on sulfur. *Click* on ⬇ᴇ. Build acetic acid. Again select **New Molecule**. Select **Carboxylic Acid** from the **Groups** menu and *click*

anywhere on screen. Add sp³ carbon ⌐ᴄ- to the free valence at carbon. *Click* on ⌶. Finally, build ethanol. Select **New Molecule** and construct from two sp³ carbons and an sp³ oxygen. *Click* on ⌶, and then on ⋁.

2. Bring up the **Calculations** dialog and specify calculation of equilibrium geometry using the HF/6-31G* model. *Click* on **OK**. Bring up the **Surfaces** dialog and *click* on **Add...** (at the bottom of the dialog). Select **density** from the **Surface** menu and **potential** from the **Property** menu in the **Add Surface** dialog which appears. *Click* on **OK**. Leave the **Surfaces** dialog on screen. Submit for calculation with the name "*acids*".

3. When completed, bring up the spreadsheet and *check* the box immediately to the right of the molecule label for all four entries. The four molecules will now be displayed simultaneously on screen. Select (*uncheck*) **Coupled** from the **Model** menu so that they may be independently manipulated, and arrange on screen such that the "acidic" hydrogens are visible.

> Manipulations normally refer only to the selected molecule. To rotate or translate all molecules together, hold down the **Ctrl** (**Control**) key in addition to the left or right buttons, respectively, while moving the mouse.

4. *Double click* on the line "density potential ..." inside the **Surfaces** dialog. Electrostatic potential maps for all four acids will be displayed. Examine the potential in the vicinity of the acidic hydrogen (one of the two equivalent acidic hydrogens for sulfuric acid). Change the scale (color) to highlight differences in this region. Select **Properties** (**Display** menu) and *click* on one of the maps. Type "0" and "90" inside the boxes underneath "Property Range" in the **Surface Properties** dialog. *Press* the **Enter** key following each data entry.

"Blue" regions identify acidic sites, the more blue the greater the acidity. On this basis, rank the acid strength of the four compounds.

5. Remove "*acids*" and any open dialogs from the screen.

6. One after the other, build trichloroacetic, dichloroacetic, chloroacetic, formic, benzoic, acetic and pivalic acids (structural formulae are provided in the table below). Put all into the same document (**New Molecule** instead of **New** following the first molecule). *Click* on $\boxed{\lor}$ when you are finished.

acid	pK$_a$	acid	pK$_a$
trichloroacetic (Cl_3CCO_2H)	0.7	benzoic ($C_6H_5CO_2H$)	4.19
dichloroacetic (Cl_2CHCO_2H)	1.48	acetic (CH_3CO_2H)	4.75
chloroacetic ($ClCH_2CO_2H$)	2.85	pivalic ((CH_3)$_3CCO_2H$)	5.03
formic (HCO_2H)	3.75		

7. Note that the name of the presently selected molecule in the document appears at the bottom of the screen. This indicates that a HF/3-21G calculation is available in Spartan's database. *Click* on $\blacktriangle$ to the left of the name, and then *click* on **Replace All** in the dialog which results. Structures obtained from HF/3-21G calculations will replace those you have built.

8. Enter the **Calculations** dialog and specify a single-point-energy HF/3-21G calculation. *Click* on **OK**. Enter the **Surfaces** dialog. *Click* on **Add...**, select **density** from the **Surface** menu and **potential** from the **Property** menu in the **Add Surface** dialog which appears and then *click* on **OK**. Leave the **Surfaces** dialog on screen. Submit for calculation. Name it "*carboxylic acids*".

9. Bring up the spreadsheet. Expand it so that you can see all seven molecules, and that three data columns are available. *Click* inside the header cell for a blank column. *Click* on **Add...** at the bottom of the spreadsheet, select **Name** from the list of entries and *click* on **OK**. The name of each molecule will appear. Next, *click* inside the header cell of an available data column, *type* "pKa" and *press* the **Enter** key. Enter the experimental pK$_a$'s (see above) into the appropriate cells under this column. *Press* the **Enter** key following each entry. Finally, *click* inside the header cell of the next available data column and *type* "potential". *Press* the **Enter** key.

10. After all calculations have completed, arrange the molecules such that the "acidic hydrogen" is visible. You need to *check* the box to the right of the "Label" column in the spreadsheet for each entry, and select (*uncheck*) **Coupled** from the **Model** menu.

11. *Double click* on the line "density . . ." inside the **Surfaces** dialog to turn on the electrostatic potential map for each molecule. Bring up the **Properties** dialog, remove the checkmark from **Global Surfaces**, and *click* on the **Reset** button at the top of the dialog. The property range will now apply to the individual molecules. Enter the maximum value (most positive electrostatic potential) into the appropriate cell of the spreadsheet (under "potential"), and *press* the **Enter** key.

12. Plot experimental pK_a vs. potential. Bring up the **Plots** dialog (**Display** menu), select **pKa** under the **X Axis** menu and **potential** from the **Y Axes** list, and *click* on **OK**. The data points are connected by a cubic spline. For a least squares fit, select **Properties** from the **Display** menu, *click* on the curve, and select **Linear LSQ** from the **Fit** menu in the **Curve Properties** dialog.

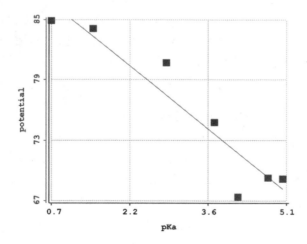

13. Close "***carboxylic acids***" and remove any remaining dialogs from the screen.

Internal Rotation in *n*-Butane

This tutorial illustrates the steps required to calculate the energy of a molecule as a function of the torsion angle about one of its bonds, and to produce a conformational energy diagram.

Rotation by 180⁰ about the central carbon-carbon bond in *n*-butane gives rise to two distinct "staggered" structures, *anti* and *gauche*.

CH₃ ... anti   CH₃ ... gauche

Both of these should be energy minima (conformers), and the correct description of the properties of *n*-butane is in terms of a Boltzmann average of the properties of both conformers (for discussion see the essay "***Total Energies and Thermodynamic and Kinetic Data***").

This tutorial shows you how to calculate the change in energy as a function of the torsion angle in *n*-butane, place your data in a spreadsheet and make a conformational energy diagram.

1. *Click* on ▤ to bring up the organic model kit. Make *n*-butane from four sp³ carbons. *Click* on Ⅴ to dismiss the model kit.

2. Set the CCCC dihedral angle to 0⁰ (*syn* conformation). *Click* on ⁇ then, one after the other, *click* on the four carbon atoms in sequence. *Type* "0" (0⁰) into the text box to the right of "dihedral..." at the bottom right of the screen and *press* the **Enter** key.

3. Select **Constrain Dihedral** from the **Geometry** menu. *Click* again on the same four carbons you used to define the dihedral angle, and then *click* on ▦ at the bottom right of the screen. The icon will change to ▣ indicating that a dihedral constraint is to be

imposed. Select **Properties** (**Display** menu) and *click* on the constraint marker on the model on screen. This leads to the **Constraint Properties** dialog.

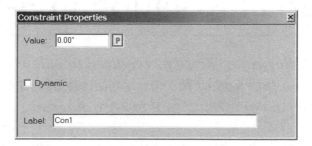

4. *Check* **Dynamic** inside the dialog. This leads to an extended form of the **Constraint Properties** dialog which allows the single (dihedral angle) constraint value to be replaced by a "range" of constraint values.

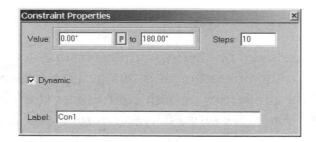

Leave the value of "0" (0°) in the box to the right of **Value** as it is, but change the contents of the box to the right of **to** to "180" (180⁰). Be sure to *press* the **Enter** key after you type in the value. The box to the right of **Steps** should contain the value "10". (If it does not, *type* "10" in this box and *press* the **Enter** key.) What you have specified is that the dihedral angle will be constrained first to 0°, then to 20°*, etc. and finally to 180°. *Click* on ⊠ to dismiss the dialog.

5. Bring up the **Calculations** dialog and select **Energy Profile** from the menu to the right of "Calculate", and **Semi-Empirical** from the menu to the right of "with". *Click* on **Submit** at the bottom of the dialog and provide the name "*n-butane*".

---

* The difference between constraint values is given by: (final-initial)/(steps-1).

6. When the calculations on all conformers have completed, they will go into a document named "*n-butane.Profile1*". Open this document (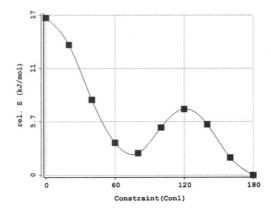). (You might wish to first close "*n-butane*" to avoid confusion.) Align the conformers to get a clearer view of the rotation. Select **Align Molecules** from the **Geometry** menu and, one after the other, *click* on either the first three carbons or the last three carbons. Then *click* on the **Align** button at the bottom right of the screen, and finally *click* on V. Bring up the spreadsheet (**Display** menu), and enter both the energies relative to the 180° or *anti* conformer, and the CCCC dihedral angles. First, *click* on the label ("M010") for the bottom entry in the spreadsheet (this should be the *anti* conformer), then *click* on the header cell for the left most blank column, and finally, *click* on **Add...** at the bottom of the spreadsheet. Select **rel. E** from among the selections in the dialog which results, **kJ/mol** from the **Energy** menu and *click* on **OK**. To enter the dihedral angle constraints, *click* on ⬛, *click* on the constraint marker and *click* on P at the bottom of the screen (to the right of the value of the dihedral angle constraint). Finally, *click* on V.

7. Select **Plots...** (**Display** menu). Select **Dihedral (Con1)** from the items in the **X Axis** menu and **rel. E(kJ/mol)** from the **Y Axes** list. *Click* on **OK** to dismiss the dialog and display a plot.

The curve (a so-called "cubic spline") smoothly connects the data points. You can see that it contains two minima, one at 180° (the *anti* form) and one around 60° (the *gauche* form). The former is lower in energy.

Further discussion of the potential energy surface for *n*-butane among other systems is provided in the essay "***Potential Energy Surfaces***".

8. Remove any molecules and any remaining dialogs from the screen.

8W

Ene Reaction

This tutorial illustrates the steps involved in first guessing and then obtaining a transition state for a simple chemical reaction. Following this, it shows how to produce a "reaction energy diagram".

The ene reaction involves addition of an electrophilic double bond to an alkene with an allylic hydrogen. The (allylic) hydrogen is transferred and a new carbon-carbon bond is formed, e.g.

The ene reaction belongs to the class of pericyclic reactions which includes such important processes as the Diels-Alder reaction and the Cope and Claisen rearrangements.

Spartan may be used to locate the transition-state for the ene reaction of ethylene and propene and then show the detailed motions which the atoms undergo during the course of reaction. It is easier to start from 1-pentene, the product of the ene reaction, rather than from the reactants.

1. Build 1-pentene. Click on 🗎 to bring up the organic model kit. *Click* on the **Groups** button, select **Alkene** from the menu and *click* anywhere on screen. Select sp³ carbon (x-) and build a three-carbon chain onto one of the free valences on ethylene. Adjust the conformation of the molecule such that all five carbons and one of the "hydrogens" (free valences) on the terminal methyl group form a "6-membered ring." You can rotate about a bond by first *clicking* on it (a red torsion marker appears on the bond) and then *moving* the mouse "up and down" while holding down on both the left button and the **Alt** key. ***Do not minimize.*** *Click* on ⩒.

41

2. Select **Transition States** from the **Search** menu (or *click* on the
   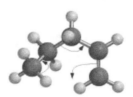 icon in the toolbar). Orient the molecule such that both the CH
   bond involving the hydrogen which will "migrate" and the C_4-C_5
   bond are visible (see figure on previous page for numbering). *Click*
   on the CH bond and then on the C_4-C_5 bond. An "arrow" will be
   drawn.* Orient the molecule such that both the C_3-C_4 and the C_2-
   C_3 bonds are visible. *Click* on the C_3-C_4 bond and then on the C_2-
   C_3 bond. A second arrow will be drawn. Orient the molecule such
   that the C_1=C_2 bond, C_1 and the hydrogen (on C_5) which will
   migrate are all visible. *Click* on the C_1=C_2 bond and, while holding
   down on the **Shift** key, *click* on C_1 and then on the hydrogen. A
   third arrow will be drawn.

   If you make a mistake, you can delete an arrow by *clicking* on it
   while holding down on the **Delete** key. Alternatively, select **Delete**
   from the **Build** menu (or *click* on the ⋇ icon in the toolbar), then
   click on the arrow and finally *click* on ⌃. When all is in order,
   click on ⟳ at the bottom right of the screen. Your structure will
   be replaced by a guess at the transition state.

3. Select **Calculations...** (**Setup** menu). Select **Transition State
   Geometry** from the menu to the right of "Calculate" and **Semi-
   Empirical** from the menu to the right of "with". *Check* **IR** to the
   right of "Compute" and *click* on **Submit** with the name "*ene
   transition state*".

4. When the calculation has completed animate the motion of atoms
   along the reaction coordinate. Select **Spectra** under the **Display**
   menu. *Click* on the top entry of the list in the **Spectra** dialog. It
   corresponds to an imaginary frequency, and will be designated

---

* Formally, this corresponds to migration of a pair of electrons from the tail of the arrow to
the head. However, Spartan treats arrows simply as a convenient and familiar nomenclature
with which to search its database of transition states.

with an "i" in front of the number*. Make certain that the associated vibrational motion is consistent with the reaction of interest and not with some other process.

5. Controls at the bottom of the **Spectra** dialog allow for changing both the amplitude of Vibration (**Amp**) and the number of steps which make up the motion (**Steps**). The latter serves as a "speed control". Change the amplitude to "0.3" (*type* "0.3" in the box to the right of **Amp** and *press* the **Enter** key). Next, *click* on **Make List** at the bottom of the dialog. This will give rise to a document containing a series of structures which follow the reaction coordinate down from the transition state both toward reactant and product. To avoid confusion, it might be better to remove original molecule from the screen. *Click* on "***ene transition state***" (the vibrating molecule) and close it. Also remove the **Spectra** dialog by *clicking* on ☒.

6. Enter the **Calculations** dialog (**Setup** menu) and specify a single-point energy calculation using the semi-empirical model (the same theoretical model used to obtain the transition state and calculate the frequencies). Make certain that **Global Calculations** at the bottom of the dialog is *checked* before you exit the dialog. Next, enter the **Surfaces** dialog and specify evaluation of two surfaces: a bond density surface and a bond density surface onto which the electrostatic potential has been mapped. *Click* on **Add . . .**, select **density (bond)** for **Surface** and **none** for **Property** and *click* on **OK**. *Click* on **Add . . .** again, select **density (bond)** for **surface** and **potential** for **Property** and *click* on **OK**. Make certain that **Global Surfaces** at the bottom of the dialog is *checked*. Leave the **Surfaces** dialog on screen.

7. Submit for calculation (**Submit** from the **Setup** menu). Name it "***ene reaction***". Once the calculations have completed, enter the

---

*   Recall from the tutorial "***Infrared Spectrum of Acetone***", that frequency is proportional to the square root of the force constant divided by the reduced mass. The force constant associated with the reaction coordinate is negative because the energy "curves downward" at the transition state (see the essay "***Potential Energy Surfaces***"). Since the reduced mass is positive, the ratio of force constant to reduced mass is a negative number, meaning that its square root is an imaginary number.

Surfaces dialog and, one after the other, select the surfaces which you have calculated. For each, step through the sequence of structures (▶ and ◀) keys at the bottom of the screen) or animate the reaction (▶). Note, in particular, the changes in bonding revealed by the bond density surface. Also pay attention to the "charge" on the migrating atom as revealed by the sequence of electrostatic potential maps. Is it best described as a "proton" (blue color), hydrogen atom (green color) or "hydride anion" (red color)?

Further discussion of the use of electrostatic potential maps to investigate charge distributions is provided in the essay "***Electrostatic Potential Maps: Charge Distributions***".

9. Close "***ene reaction***" as well as any remaining dialogs.

Proteins and Nucleotides

This tutorial illustrates models appropriate to large biomolecules, in particular, ribbon displays of protein and nucleotide "backbones" and display of hydrogen bonds. Biomolecule building is not illustrated and no calculations are performed.

Treatment of very large molecules, proteins and nucleotides ("biopolymers") most important among them, requires models which are simpler than those which are appropriate for small organic and inorganic molecules. This refers both to display and manipulation, where much detail needs to be eliminated, and to the calculation of structure and properties, where molecular mechanics needs to replace quantum mechanics.

This tutorial uses an unusual "protein-RNA complex" to illustrate a variety of models for the display of biopolymers, including ribbon displays to elucidate the "backbone" and hydrogen-bond displays to show how the structure is "held together".

1. Open "***tutorial 9***" in the "tutorials" directory. This contains a PDB (Protein Data Bank) file[*] of a protein-RNA complex. Note that a simple ribbon display, demarking the backbones of the protein and RNA chains has replaced the usual structure models ("tube", "ball-and-spoke", etc.). To see why this is necessary, turn "on" (select) one of these models from the **Model** menu. The detail has completely obliterated the most important structure feature, that the molecule is made up of two "intertwined" segments. Note, however, that a space-filling model (**Space Filling** under the **Model** menu) does provide indication of overall size and shape of the complex. When you are done, select **Hide** from the **Model** menu.

---

[*]   PDB designation 1A1T. R.N. de Guzman, Z.R. Wu, C.C. Stalling, L. Pappalardo, P.N. Borer and M.F. Summers, Science, **279**, 384 (1998).

2. The structure of this complex has been determined by NMR spectroscopy which gives several alternative conformers. Step through them (▶ and ◀ at the bottom left of the screen) to see where they are similar and where they differ. In particular, notice that a large portion of the overall structure remains basically the same from one conformer to another.

3. Select **Configure...** from the **Model** menu and *click* on the **Ribbons** tab in the dialog which results. Select **By Residue** under "Coloring" in the **Configure Ribbons** dialog and *click* on **OK**. The model is now colored according to amino acid/nucleotide base. *Click* on the various "color bands" to see what they are (labels are provided at the bottom right of the screen).

Hydrogen bonding is known to be a decisive factor in determining the three-dimensional structures of biopolymers. The base pairs in complementary strands which make up DNA are "held together" by hydrogen bonds. Helical structures in proteins are also maintained by hydrogen bonds as are neighboring strands in so-called β sheets.

4. Select **Hydrogen Bonds** (**Model** menu). Single "dotted lines" represent hydrogen bonds throughout the "protein part" of the complex, and "sets" of two or three dotted lines in the "RNA" part. The latter form the connections between nucleotide bases and the number of lines in each set actually allows you to identify what the bases are.

5. Select **Tube** (**Model** menu). Also, select (*uncheck*) **Hydrogens** from this menu. You can now see in greater detail the structure of the complex and the positions of the hydrogen bonds.

6. Close "*tutorial 9*".

Basic Operations

This tutorial introduces a number of basic operations in the Macintosh (OS X) version of Spartan required for molecule manipulation and property query. Specifically it shows how to: i) open molecules, ii) view different models and manipulate molecules on screen, iii) measure bond distances, angles and dihedral angles, iv) display energies, dipole moments, atomic charges and infrared spectra, and v) display graphical surfaces and property maps. Molecule building is not illustrated and no calculations are performed.

1. Start Spartan. *Double click* on the icon on the desktop. Spartan's window will appear with a menu bar at the top of the screen.

🍎   **Spartan**   File   Edit   Model   Geometry   Build   Setup   Display   Search   Help

File	Allows you to create a new molecule or read in a molecule which you have previously created.
Model	Allows you to control the style of your model.
Geometry	Allows you to measure bond lengths and angles.
Build	Allows you to build and edit molecules.
Setup	Allows you to specify the task to be performed and the theoretical model to be employed, to specify graphical surfaces and property maps and to submit jobs for calculation.
Display	Allows you to display text output, molecular and atomic properties, surfaces and property maps and infrared spectra. Also allows data presentation in a spreadsheet and plots to be made from these data.
Search	Allows you to "guess" a transition-state geometry based on a library of reactions. This guess may then be used as the basis for a quantum chemical calculation of the actual reaction transition state.

2. *Click* with the left mouse button on **File** from the menu bar.

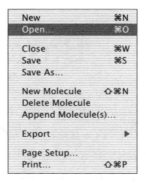

Click on **Open....** Alternatively, *click* on the 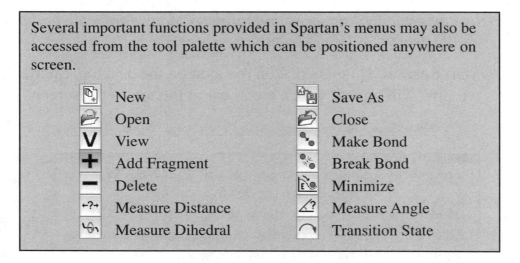 icon in the toolbar.

Several important functions provided in Spartan's menus may also be accessed from the tool palette which can be positioned anywhere on screen.

	New			Save As
	Open			Close
V	View			Make Bond
+	Add Fragment			Break Bond
−	Delete			Minimize
	Measure Distance			Measure Angle
	Measure Dihedral			Transition State

Locate the "tutorials" directory in the dialog which appears, *click* on "*tutorial 1*" and *click* on **Open** (or *double click* on "*tutorial 1*"). Ball-and-spoke models for ***ethane***, ***acetic acid dimer***, ***propene***, ***ammonia***, ***hydrogen peroxide***, ***acetic acid***, ***water***, ***cyclohexanone***, ***ethylene***, ***benzene*** and ***aniline*** appear on screen. You can select a molecule by *clicking* on it with the (left) mouse button. Once selected, a molecule may be manipulated (rotated, translated and scaled). You may use either the Mac's "traditional" one-button mouse or a two-button mouse (as on Windows' machines). This and the following tutorials assume use of a two-button mouse.

One-Button Mouse

select molecule	*click*
rotate molecule	*press* the button and *move* the mouse
translate molecule	*press* the button and the **option** key and *move* the mouse
scale molecule	*press* both the ⌘ and **option** keys in addition to the button and *move* the mouse "up and down"

Two-Button Mouse

select molecule	*click* (left mouse button)
rotate molecule	*press* the left button and *move* the mouse
translate molecule	*press* the right button and *move* the mouse
scale molecule	*press* both the ⌘ key and the right button and *move* the mouse "up and down"

If available, the scroll wheel on your mouse may be used to scale the molecule.

3. Identify *ethane* on the screen, and *click* on it (left button) to make it the selected molecule. Practice rotating (*move* the mouse while *pressing* the left button) and translating (*move* the mouse while *pressing* the right button) *ethane*. *Click* on a different molecule, and then rotate and translate it.

4. Return to *ethane*. *Click* on **Model** from the menu bar.

| Wire | Ball-and-Wire | Tube | Ball-and-Spoke |

One after the other, select **Wire**, **Ball and Wire**, **Tube** and finally **Ball and Spoke** from the **Model** menu. All four models for *ethane* show roughly the same information. The wire model looks like a conventional line formula, except that all atoms, not just the carbons, are found at the end of a line or at the intersection of lines. The wire model uses color to distinguish different atoms, and one, two and three lines between atoms to indicate single, double and triple bonds, respectively.

Atoms are colored according to type:

Hydrogen	white		
Lithium	tan	**Sodium**	yellow
Beryllium	green	**Magnesium**	dark blue
Boron	tan	**Aluminum**	violet
Carbon	black	**Silicon**	grey
Nitrogen	blue-gray	**Phosphorous**	tan
Oxygen	red	**Sulfur**	sky blue
Fluorine	green	**Chlorine**	tan

Atom colors (as well as bond colors, the color of the background, etc.) may be changed from their defaults using **Colors** under the **Edit** menu. An atom may be labelled with a variety of different quantities using **Configure...** under the **Model** menu. Labels are then automatically turned "on" and may be turned "off" by selecting **Labels** under the **Model** menu.

The ball-and-wire model is identical to the wire model, except that atom positions are represented by small spheres. This makes it easy to identify atom locations. The tube model is identical to the wire model, except that bonds, whether single, double or triple, are represented by solid cylinders. The tube model is better than the wire model in conveying the three-dimensional shape of a molecule. The ball-and-spoke model is a variation on the tube model; atom positions are represented by colored spheres, making it easy to see atom locations.

Select **Space Filling** from the **Model** menu.

Space-Filling

This model is different from the others in that bonds are not shown. Rather, each atom is displayed as a colored sphere that represents its approximate "size". Thus, the space-filling model for a molecule provides a measure of its size. While lines between atoms are not drawn, the existence (or absence) of bonds can be inferred from the amount of overlap between neighboring atomic spheres. If two spheres substantially overlap, then the atoms are almost certainly bonded, and conversely, if two spheres hardly overlap, then the atoms are not bonded. Intermediate overlaps suggest "weak bonding", for example, hydrogen bonding (see the activity "*Water*").

Select *acetic acid dimer*. Switch to a space-filling model and look for overlap between the (OH) hydrogen on one acetic acid molecule and the (carbonyl) oxygen on the other. Return to a ball-and-spoke model and select **Hydrogen Bonds** from the **Model** menu.

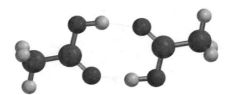

Ball-and-Spoke model for acetic acid dimer
with hydrogen bonds displayed

The two hydrogen bonds, which are responsible for holding the acetic acid molecules together, will be drawn.

Use the **3** key to toggle between stereo 3D and regular display. To view in 3D you will need to wear the red/blue glasses provided with Spartan.

5. Distances, angles, and dihedral angles can easily be measured with Spartan using **Measure Distance**, **Measure Angle**, and **Measure Dihedral**, respectively, from the **Geometry** menu.

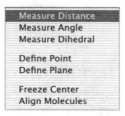

Alternatively the measurement functions may be accessed from the ⟶, ∠? and ⤾ icons in the tool palette.

a) **Measure Distance**: This measures the distance between two atoms. First select *propene* from the molecules on screen, and then select **Measure Distance** from the **Geometry** menu (or *click* on the ⟶ icon in the tool palette). *Click* on a bond or on two atoms (the atoms do not need to be bonded). The distance (in Ångstroms) will be displayed at the bottom of the screen. Repeat the process as necessary. When you are finished, select **View** from the **Build** menu.

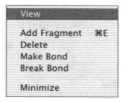

Alternatively, *click* on the V icon in the toolbar.

b) **Measure Angle**: This measures the angle around a central atom. Select *ammonia* from the molecules on screen, and then select **Measure Angle** from the **Geometry** menu (or *click* on the ∠? icon in the toolbar). *Click* first on H, then on N, then on another H. Alternatively, *click* on two NH bonds. The HNH angle (in degrees) will be displayed at the bottom of the screen. *Click* on V when you are finished.

c) **Measure Dihedral**: This measures the angle formed by two intersecting planes, the first containing the first three atoms selected and the second containing the last three atoms selected. Select *hydrogen peroxide* from the molecules on screen, then select **Measure Dihedral** from the **Geometry** menu (or *click* on the  icon in the tool palette) and then *click* in turn on the four atoms (HOOH) which make up hydrogen peroxide. The HOOH dihedral angle will be displayed at the bottom of the screen. *Click* on **V** when you are finished.

6. Energies, dipole moments and atomic charges among other calculated properties, are available from **Properties** under the **Display** menu.

Output
Properties
Surfaces
Spectra
Spreadsheet
Plots...

a) **Energy:** Select *acetic acid* from the molecules on screen and then select **Properties** from the **Display** menu. The **Molecule Properties** dialog appears.

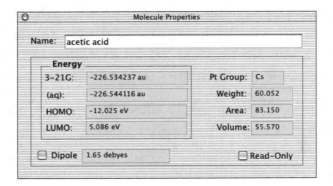

This provides the total energy for acetic acid in atomic units (au). See the essay "*Total Energies and Thermodynamic and Kinetic Data*" for a discussion of energy units.

b) **Dipole Moment:** The magnitude of the dipole moment (in debyes) is also provided in the **Molecule Properties** dialog. A large dipole moment indicates large separation of charge. You can attach the dipole moment vector, "+——▸" where the lefthand side "+" refers to the positive end of the dipole, to the model on the screen, by *checking* **Dipole** near the bottom of the dialog. The vector will not be displayed if the magnitude of the dipole moment is zero, or if the molecule is charged.

c) **Atomic Charges:** To display the charge on an atom, *click* on it with the **Molecule Properties** dialog on the screen. The **Atom Properties** dialog replaces the **Molecule Properties** dialog.

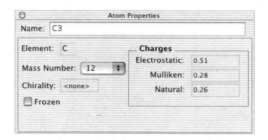

Atomic charges are given in units of electrons. A positive charge indicates a deficiency of electrons on an atom and a negative charge, an excess of electrons. Repeat the process as necessary by *clicking* on other atoms. Confirm that the positively-charged atom(s) lie at the positive end of the dipole moment vector. When you are finished, remove the dialog from the screen by *clicking* on the ◉ in the top left-hand corner.

d) **Infrared Spectra:** Molecules vibrate (stretch, bend, twist) even if they are cooled to absolute zero. This is the basis of infrared spectroscopy, where absorption of energy occurs when the frequency of molecular motions matches the frequency of the "light". Infrared spectroscopy is important in organic chemistry as different functional groups vibrate at noticeably different and characteristic frequencies.

Select *water* from the molecules on screen. To animate a vibration, select **Spectra** from the **Display** menu. This leads to the **Spectra** dialog.

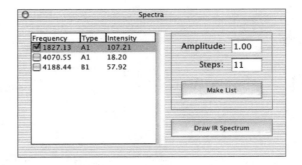

This displays the three vibrational frequencies for the water molecule, corresponding to bending and symmetric and antisymmetric stretching motions. One after the other, *double click* on each frequency and examine the motion. Turn "off" the animation when you are finished.

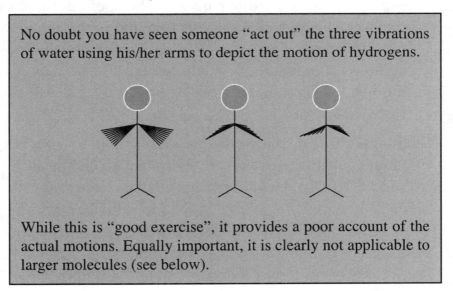

No doubt you have seen someone "act out" the three vibrations of water using his/her arms to depict the motion of hydrogens.

While this is "good exercise", it provides a poor account of the actual motions. Equally important, it is clearly not applicable to larger molecules (see below).

Select *cyclohexanone*. The **Spectra** dialog now lists its 45 vibrational frequencies. Examine each in turn (*double click* on the entry in the dialog) until you locate the frequency corresponding to the CO (carbonyl) stretch. Next, *click* on **Draw IR Spectrum** at the bottom of the dialog. The infrared spectrum of cyclohexanone will appear.

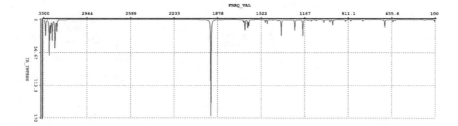

You can move the spectrum around the screen by first *clicking* on it to select it and then *moving* the mouse while *pressing* the right button. You can size it by using the scroll wheel on the mouse or by *moving* the mouse "up and down" while *pressing* both the key and the right button. Identify the line in the spectrum associated with the CO stretch. Note that this line is separated from the other lines in the spectrum and that it is intense. This makes it easy to find and is the primary reason why infrared spectroscopy is an important diagnostic for carbonyl functionality. When you are finished, *click* on at the top left-hand corner of the **Spectra** dialog to remove it from the screen.

7. Spartan permits display, manipulation and query of a number of important quantities resulting from a quantum chemical calculation in "visual" format. Most important are the electron density (which reveals "how much space" a molecule actually takes up; see the essay "*Electron Densities: Sizes and Shapes of Molecules*" for a discussion), the bond density (which reveals chemical "bonds"; see the essay on electron densities), and key molecular orbitals (which provide insight both into bonding and chemical reactivity; see the essay "*Atomic and Molecular Orbitals*"). In addition, the electrostatic potential map, an overlaying of a quantity called the electrostatic potential (the attraction or repulsion of a positive charge for a molecule) onto the electron density, is valuable for describing overall molecular charge distribution as well as anticipating sites of electrophilic addition. Further discussion is provided in the essay "*Electrostatic Potential Maps: Charge Distributions*". Another indicator of electrophilic addition is provided by the local ionization potential map, an overlaying of

the energy of electron removal ("ionization") onto the electron density. Finally, the likelihood of nucleophilic addition can be ascertained using a LUMO map, an overlaying of the lowest-unoccupied molecular orbital (the LUMO) onto the electron density. Both of these latter graphical models are described in the essay *"**Local Ionization Potential Maps and LUMO Maps: Electrophilic and Nucleophilic Reactivity**"*.

Select *ethylene* from among the molecules on screen, and then select **Surfaces** from the **Display** menu. The **Surfaces** dialog appears.

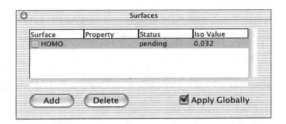

Double click on the line "homo..." inside the dialog. This will result in the display of ethylene's highest-occupied molecular orbital as a solid. This is a π orbital, equally concentrated above and below the plane of the molecule. The colors ("red" and "blue") give the sign of the orbital. Changes in sign often correlate with bonding or antibonding character. You can if you wish, turn "off" the graphic by again *double clicking* on the line "homo . . .".

Next, select *benzene* from among the molecules on screen and *double click* on the line "density potential..." inside the **Surfaces** dialog. An electrostatic potential map for benzene will appear. Position the cursor over the map while holding down either the left or right button. Select **Transparent** from the menu which appears to present the map as a translucent solid. This will allow you to see the molecular skeleton underneath. The surface is colored "red" in the π system (indicating negative potential and the fact that this region is attracted to a positive charge), and "blue" in the σ system (indicating positive potential and the fact that this region is repelled by a positive charge).

Select *aniline* from the molecules on screen, and *double click* on the line "density ionization..." inside the **Surfaces** dialog. The graphic which appears, a so-called local ionization potential map, colors in red regions on the density surface from which electron removal (ionization) is relatively easy, meaning that they are subject to electrophilic attack. These are easily distinguished from regions where ionization is relatively difficult (colored in blue). Note that the *ortho* and *para* ring carbons are more red than the *meta* carbons, consistent with the known directing ability of the amino substituent.

Finally, select *cyclohexanone* from the molecules on screen , and *double click* on the line "lumo..." in the **Surfaces** dialog. The resulting graphic portrays the lowest-energy empty molecular orbital (the LUMO) of cyclohexanone. This is a so-called π^* orbital which is antibonding between carbon and oxygen. Note that the LUMO is primarily localized on carbon, meaning that this is where a pair of electrons (a nucleophile) will "attack" cyclohexanone.

A better portrayal is provided by a LUMO map, which displays the (absolute) value of the LUMO on the electron density surface. Here, the color blue is used to represent maximum value of the LUMO and the color red, minimum value. First, remove the LUMO from your structure (*double click* on the line "lumo..." in the **Surfaces** dialog) and then turn on the LUMO map (*double click* on the line "density lumo..." in the dialog). Note that the blue region is concentrated directly over the carbonyl carbon. Also, note that the so-called *axial* face shows a greater concentration of the LUMO than the *equatorial* face. This is consistent with the known stereochemistry of nucleophilic addition (see the activity "*Molecular Shapes V. Which Conformer Leads to Product?*").

8. When you are finished, close all the molecules on screen by selecting **Close** from the **File** menu or alternatively by *clicking* on 🖘.

2M

Acrylonitrile:
Building an Organic Molecule

This tutorial illustrates use of the organic model kit, as well as the steps involved in examining and querying different molecular models and in carrying out a quantum chemical calculation.

The simplest building blocks incorporated into Spartan's organic model kit are "atomic fragments". These constitute specification of atom type, e.g., carbon, and hybridization, e.g., sp³. The organic model kit also contains libraries of common functional groups and hydrocarbon rings, the members of which can easily be extended or modified. For example, the carboxylic acid group in the library may be modified to build a carboxylate anion (by deleting a free valence from oxygen), or an ester (by adding tetrahedral carbon to the free valence at oxygen).

carboxylic acid   carboxylate anion   ester

Acrylonitrile provides a good first opportunity to illustrate the basics of molecule building, as well as the steps involved in carrying out and analyzing a simple quantum chemical calculation.

acrylonitrile

1. *Click* on **File** from the menu bar and then *click* on **New** from the menu which appears (or *click* on the 🗐 icon in the tool palette). The "organic" model kit appears.

Click on trigonal planar sp^2 hybridized carbon ⟩c⟨ from the library of atomic fragments. The fragment icon is highlighted, and a model of the fragment appears at the top of the model kit. Bring the cursor anywhere on screen and *click*. Rotate the carbon fragment (*move* the mouse while holding down the left button) so that you can clearly see both the double free valence ("=") and the two single free valences ("-").

> Spartan's model kits connect atomic fragments (as well as groups, rings and ligands) through free valences. Unless you "use" them or delete them, free valences will automatically be converted to hydrogen atoms.

2. sp^2 carbon is still selected. *Click* on the double free valence. The two fragments are connected by a double bond, leaving you with ethylene.

> Spartan's model kits allows only the same type of free valences to be connected, e.g., single to single, double to double, etc.

3. *Click* on **Groups** in the model kit, and then select **Cyano** from among the functional groups available from the menu.

Click on one of the free valences on ethylene, to make acrylonitrile.*
If you make a mistake, you can select **Undo** from the **Edit** menu
to "undo" the last operation or **Clear** (**Edit** menu) to start over.

4. Select **Minimize** from the **Build** menu (or *click* on the 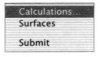 icon in
   the tool palette). The "strain energy" and symmetry point group
   (C_s) for acrylonitrile are provided at the bottom right of the screen.

5. Select **View** from the **Build** menu (or *click* on the V icon in the
   tool palette). The model kit disappears, leaving only a ball-and-
   spoke model of acrylonitrile on screen.

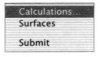

6. Select **Calculations**... from the **Setup** menu.

The **Calculations** dialog appears. This will allow you to specify
what task is to be done with your molecule and what theoretical
model Spartan will use to accomplish this task.

---

* You could also have built acrylonitrile without using the **Groups** menu. First, clear the screen
by selecting **Clear** from the **Edit** menu. Then build ethylene from two sp^2 carbons (as above),
select sp hybridized carbon 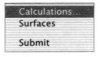 from the model kit and then *click* on the tip of one of the free
valences on ethylene. Next, select sp hybridized nitrogen 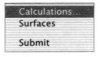 from the model kit and *click* on
the triple free valence on the sp carbon. Alternatively, you could have built the molecule
entirely from groups. First, clear the screen. Then *click* on **Groups**, select **Alkene** from the
menu and *click* anywhere on screen. Then select **Cyano** from the same menu and *click* on
one of the free valences on ethylene. In general, molecules can be constructed in many ways.

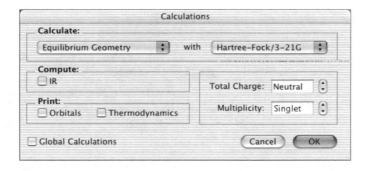

Select **Equilibrium Geometry** from the menu to the right of "Calculate". This specifies optimization of equilibrium geometry. Next, select **Hartree-Fock/3-21G** from the menu to the right of "with". This specifies a Hartree-Fock calculation using the 3-21G basis set (referred to as an HF/3-21G calculation). This method generally provides a reliable account of geometries (see the essay "*Choosing a Theoretical Model*").

7. *Click* on **OK** at the bottom of the **Calculations** dialog and then select **Submit** from the **Setup** menu. A file browser appears.

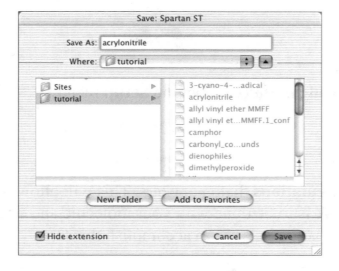

Type "*acrylonitrile*" in the box to the right of "File name", and *click* on **Save***. You will be notified that the calculation has been submitted. *Click* on **OK** to remove the message.

---

*   If the molecule exists in the Spartan Molecular Database, a name will automatically be supplied. You may change this name if desired.

After a molecule has been submitted, and until the calculation has completed, you are not permitted to modify information associated with it. You can monitor your calculation as well as abort it if necessary using **Spartan Monitor** under the **Spartan ST** menu.

8. You will be notified when the calculation has completed. *Click* **OK** to remove the message. Select **Output** from the **Display** menu. A window containing "text output" for the job appears.

```
● ○ ○          Output for "acrylonitrile"
ACRYLONITRILE

Run type: Geometry optimization
Model: RHF/3-21G
Number of shells:  18
   10 S shells
    8 SP shells
Number of basis functions:  42
Number of electrons:        28
Number of heavy atoms:       4
Number of hydrogens:         3
Use of molecular symmetry enabled
Molecular charge:   0
Spin multiplicity:  1
Memory model: direct      3.6 Mb

Point Group = CS  Order =  1 Nsymop =  2
This system has  11 degrees of freedom
```

You can scan the output from the calculation by using the scroll bar at the right of the window. Information provided includes the task, basis set, number of electrons, charge and multiplicity, as well as the point group of the molecule. A series of lines, each beginning with "Cycle no:", tell the history of the optimization process. Each line provides results for a particular geometry; "Energy" gives the energy in atomic units (1 atomic unit = 2625 kJ/mol) for this geometry, "Max Grad." gives the maximum gradient ("slope"), and "Max Dist." gives the maximum displacement of atoms between cycles. The energy will monotonically approach a minimum value for an optimized geometry, and Max Grad. and Max Dist. will each approach zero. Near the end of the output is the final total energy (-168.82040 atomic units). *Click* on ◎ in the top left-hand corner of the dialog to remove the dialog from the screen.

9. You can obtain the final total energy and the dipole moment from the **Molecule Properties** dialog, without having to go through the text output. Select **Properties** from the **Display** menu. You can "see" the dipole moment vector (indicating the sign and overall

direction of the dipole moment), by *checking* **Dipole** near the bottom of this dialog. (A tube model provides the clearest picture.)

When you are finished, turn "off" display of the dipole moment vector by *unchecking* the box.

10. *Click* on an atom. The (**Molecule Properties**) dialog will be replaced by the **Atom Properties** dialog. This gives the charge on the selected atom. To obtain the charge on another atom, simply *click* on it. *Click* on ⊙ at the top left-hand corner of the **Atom Properties** dialog to remove it from the screen.

11. Atomic charges can also be attached as "labels" to your model. Select **Configure...** from the **Model** menu, and *check* **Charge** under "Atom" in the **Configure** dialog which appears.

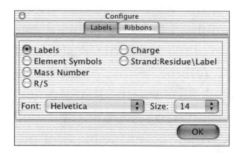

Click **OK** to remove the dialog.

12. *Click* on ✍ to remove "*acrylonitrile*" from the screen. Also, close any dialogs which may still be open.

3M

Sulfur Tetrafluoride: Building an Inorganic Molecule

This tutorial illustrates the use of the inorganic model kit for molecule building. It also shows how molecular models may be used to quantify concepts from more qualitative treatments.

Organic molecules are made up of a relatively few elements and generally obey conventional valence rules. They may be easily built using the organic model kit. However, many molecules incorporate other elements, or do not conform to normal valence rules, or involve ligands. They cannot be constructed using the organic model kit. Sulfur tetrafluoride is a good example.

sulfur tetrafluoride

The unusual "see-saw" geometry observed for the molecule is a consequence of the fact that the "best" (least crowded) way to position five electron pairs around sulfur is in a trigonal bipyramidal arrangement. The lone pair assumes an *equatorial* position so as to least interact with the remaining electron pairs. The rationale behind this is that a lone pair is "bigger" than a bonding electron pair.

Sulfur tetrafluoride provides the opportunity to look at the bonding and charges in a molecule which "appears" to have an excess of electrons around its central atom (ten instead of eight), as well as to look for evidence of a lone pair. Further attention is given to sulfur tetrafluoride in the activity *"Beyond VSEPR Theory"* later in this guide.

1. Bring up the inorganic model kit by *clicking* on 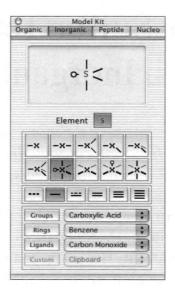 and then *clicking* on the **Inorganic** tab at the top of the organic model kit.

Controls at the top of the model kit allow selection of element, atomic hybrid and bond type. Further down the model kit are the **Rings**, **Groups** and **Custom** menus, which are the same as found in the organic model kit, and a **Ligands** menu. The last is essential for constructing coordination compounds and organometallics.

2. Position the cursor inside the box to the right of "Element" and hold down on the left button to bring up a *Periodic Table*.

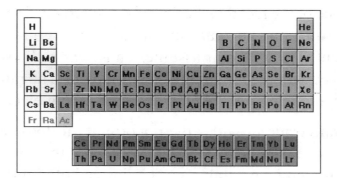

Slide the cursor over **S** in the *Periodic Table* and release the button. Then select the five-coordinate trigonal bipyramid structure from the list of atomic hybrids.

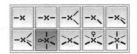

Move the cursor anywhere in the main window and *click*. A trigonal bipyramid sulfur will appear.

3. Select **F** from the *Periodic Table* and the one-coordinate entry 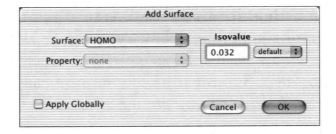 from the list of atomic hybrids. *Click* on both *axial* free valences of sulfur, and two of the three *equatorial* free valences.

4. It is necessary to delete the remaining free valence (on an *equatorial* position); otherwise it will become a hydrogen. *Click* on ▬ and then *click* on the remaining *equatorial* free valence.

5. *Click* on ▣. Molecular mechanics minimization will result in a structure with C_{2v} symmetry. *Click* on **V**.

6. Select **Calculations...** from the **Setup** menu. Specify calculation of equilibrium geometry using the HF/3-21G model. *Click* on **OK**.

7. Select **Surfaces** from the **Setup** menu. *Click* on **Add...** at the bottom of the **Surfaces** dialog and select **HOMO** from the **Surface** menu in the (**Add Surface**) dialog which appears.

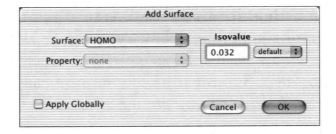

Click on **OK**. Leave the **Surfaces** dialog on screen.

8. Select **Submit** from the **Setup** menu, and supply the name "*sulfur tetrafluoride see-saw*".

9. After the calculations have completed, select **Properties** from the **Display** menu to bring up the **Molecule Properties** dialog. Next, *click* on sulfur to bring up the **Atom Properties** dialog. Is sulfur neutral or negatively charged, indicating that more than the normal

complement of (eight) valence electron surrounds this atom, or is it positively charged, indicating "ionic bonding"?

$$\begin{array}{c}
\text{F} \\
| \\
\underset{|}{\overset{+}{\text{S}}}\text{......}^{\text{||||}}\text{F} \\
| \quad \text{F}^{-} \\
\text{F}
\end{array}$$

10. *Double click* on the line "homo..." inside the **Surfaces** dialog to examine the highest-occupied molecular orbital. Does it "point" in the anticipated direction? It is largely localized on sulfur or is there significant concentration on the fluorines? If the latter, is the orbital "bonding" or "antibonding"? (For a discussion of non-bonding, bonding and antibonding molecular orbitals, see the essay "*Atomic and Molecular Orbitals*".)

11. Build square planar SF_4 as an alternative to the "see-saw" structure. Bring up the inorganic model kit (🔲), select **S** from the *Periodic Table* and the four-coordinate square-planar structure ⧓ from the list of atomic hybrids. *Click* anywhere on screen. Select **F** in the *Periodic Table* and the one-coordinate entry ⊣ from the list of atomic hybrids. *Click* on all four free valences on sulfur. *Click* on 🔲 and then on **V**.

12. Enter the **Calculations** dialog (**Setup** menu) and specify calculation of equilibrium geometry using the HF/3-21G model (the same as you used for the "see-saw" structure[*]). Close the dialog and select **Submit** from the **Setup** menu with the name "*sulfur tetrafluoride square planar*".

13. After the calculation has completed, bring up the **Molecule Properties** dialog (**Properties** from the **Display** menu) Is the energy actually higher (more positive) than that for the "see-saw" structure?

14. Close both molecules as well as any remaining dialogs.

---

[*] You need to use exactly the same theoretical model in order to compare energies or other properties for different molecules.

Infrared Spectrum of Acetone

This tutorial illustrates the steps required to calculate and display the infrared spectrum of a molecule.

Molecules vibrate in response to their absorbing infrared light. Absorption occurs only at specific wavelengths, which gives rise to the use of infrared spectroscopy as a tool for identifying chemical structures. The vibrational frequency is proportional to the square root of a quantity called a "force constant" divided by a quantity called the "reduced mass".

$$\text{frequency} \quad \alpha \quad \sqrt{\frac{\text{force constant}}{\text{reduced mass}}}$$

The force constant reflects the "flatness" or "steepness" of the energy surface in the vicinity of the energy minimum. The steeper the energy surface, the larger the force constant and the larger the frequency. The reduced mass reflects the masses of the atoms involved in the vibration. The smaller the reduced mass, the larger the frequency.

This tutorial shows you how to calculate and display the infrared spectrum of acetone, and explore relationships between frequency and both force constant and reduced mass. It shows why the carbonyl stretching frequency is of particular value in infrared spectroscopy.

1. *Click* on 🔳 to bring up the organic model kit. Select sp^2 carbon (🔳) and *click* anywhere on screen. Select sp^2 oxygen (🔳) and *click* on the double free valence on carbon to make the carbonyl group. Select sp^3 carbon (🔳) and, one after the other, *click* on the two single free valences on carbon. *Click* on 🔳 and then on **V**.

2. Enter the **Calculations** dialog (**Setup** menu) and request calculation of an equilibrium geometry using the HF/3-21G model.

Check **IR** below "Compute" to specify calculation of vibrational frequencies. *Click* on **OK** to remove the **Calculations** dialog and select **Submit** from the **Setup** menu. Provide the name *"acetone"*.

3. After the calculation has completed, bring up the **Spectra** dialog (**Display** menu). This contains a list of vibrational frequencies for acetone. First *click* on the top entry (the smallest frequency) and, when you are done examining the vibrational motion, *click* on the bottom entry (the largest frequency).

> The smallest frequency is associated with torsional motion of the methyl rotors. The largest frequency is associated with stretching motion of CH bonds. Methyl torsion is characterized by a flat potential energy surface (small force constant), while CH stretching is characterized by a steep potential energy surface (large force constant).

Display the IR spectrum (*click* on **Draw IR Spectrum** at the bottom of the dialog). Locate the frequency corresponding to the CO stretch. The experimental frequency is around 1740 cm^{-1}, but the calculations will yield a higher value (around 1940 cm^{-1}).

> The CO stretching frequency is a good "chemical identifier" because it "stands alone" in the infrared spectrum and because it is "intense".

4. Change all the hydrogens in acetone to deuteriums to see the effect which increased mass has on vibrational frequencies. First make a copy of *"acetone"* (**Save As...** from the **File** menu or *click* on the ▣ icon in the tool palette). Name the copy *"acetone d6"* Select **Properties** from the **Display** menu and *click* on one of the hydrogens. Select **2 deuterium** from the **Mass Number** menu. Repeat for the remaining five hydrogens.

5. Submit for calculation. When completed, examine the vibrational frequencies. Note that the frequencies of those motions which involve the hydrogens are significantly reduced over those in the non-deuterated system.

6. Close all molecules on screen in addition to any remaining dialogs.

70

5M

Electrophilic Reactivity of Benzene and Pyridine

This tutorial illustrates the calculation, display and interpretation of electrostatic potential maps. It also illustrates the use of "documents" comprising two or more molecules.

While benzene and pyridine have similar geometries and while both are aromatic, their "chemistry" is different. Benzene's chemistry is dictated by the molecule's π system, while the chemistry of pyridine is a consequence of the lone pair on nitrogen. This tutorial shows how to use electrostatic potential maps to highlight these differences.

1. Build benzene. *Click* on ⊞. Select **Benzene** from the **Rings** menu and *click* on screen. *Click* on ⊠.

2. Build pyridine. In order to put both benzene and pyridine into the same "document", select **New Molecule** (not **New**) from the **File** menu. **Benzene** (**Rings** menu) is still selected. *Click* anywhere on screen. Select aromatic nitrogen ⊠ from the model kit and *double click* on one of the carbon atoms (not a free valence). *Click* on ⊠ and then *click* on **V**. To go between the two molecules in your document, use the ◀ and ▶ keys at the bottom left of the screen (or use the slider bar).

3. Select **Calculations...** (**Setup** menu) and specify calculation of equilibrium geometry using the HF/3-21G model. *Click* on **OK** to dismiss the dialog. Select **Surfaces** (**Setup** menu). *Click* on **Add...** at the bottom of the **Surfaces** dialog to bring up the **Add Surface** dialog. Select **density** from the **Surface** menu and **potential** from the **Property** menu. *Click* on **OK**. Leave the **Surfaces** dialog on screen. Select **Submit** (**Setup** menu) and supply the name "*benzene and pyridine*".

71

4. When completed, *click* on ◉ at the bottom left of the screen (it will become ◙). Bring up the spreadsheet (**Spreadsheet** under the **Display** menu) and *check* the box to the left of the molecule name for both entries. This allows benzene and pyridine to be displayed simultaneously. However, the motions of the two molecules will be "coupled" (they will move together). Select (*uncheck*) **Coupled** from the **Model** menu to allow the two molecules to be manipulated independently. In turn, select (*click* on) each and orient such that the two are side-by-side.

5. *Double click* on the line "density potential..." inside the **Surfaces** dialog. Electrostatic potential maps for both benzene and pyridine will be displayed. Change the scale so that the "neutral" color is "green". Select **Properties** (**Display** menu) and *click* on one of the maps to bring up the **Surface Properties** dialog.

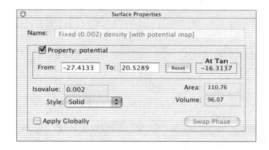

Type "-35" and "35" inside the boxes underneath "Property" (*press* the **return** key following each data entry). The "red" regions in benzene, which are most attractive to an electrophile, correspond to the molecule's π system, while in pyridine they correspond to the σ system in the vicinity of the nitrogen. Note that the π system in benzene is "more red" than the π system in pyridine (indicating that it is more susceptible to electrophilic attack here), but that the nitrogen in pyridine is "more red" than the π system in benzene (indicating that pyridine is overall more susceptible to attack by an electrophile).

Further discussion of the use of such maps is provided in the essay *"Electrostatic Potential Maps: Charge Distributions"*.

6. Remove *"benzene and pyridine"* and any dialogs from the screen.

Weak vs. Strong Acids

This tutorial shows how electrostatic potential maps may be used to distinguish between weak and strong acids, and quantify subtle differences in the strengths of closely-related acids. It also shows how information can be retrieved from Spartan's database.

Chemists know that nitric acid and sulfuric acids are strong acids, acetic acid is a weak acid, and that ethanol is a very weak acid. What these compounds have in common is their ability to undergo heterolytic bond fracture, leading to a stable anion and a "proton". What distinguishes a strong acid from a weak acid is the stability of the anion. NO_3^- and $HOSO_3^-$ are very stable anions, $CH_3CO_2^-$ is somewhat less stable and $CH_3CH_2O^-$ is even less so.

One way to reveal differences in acidity is to calculate the energy of deprotonation for different acids, e.g., for nitric acid.

$$HONO_2 \longrightarrow H^+ + NO_3^-$$

This involves calculations on both the neutral acid and on the resulting anion (the energy of a proton is zero). An alternative approach, illustrated in this tutorial, involves comparison of electrostatic potential maps for different acids, with particular focus on the potential in the vicinity of the "acidic hydrogen". The more positive the potential, the more likely will dissociation occur, and the stronger the acid.

1. Build nitric acid. *Click* on 🖻 to bring up the organic model kit. Select **Nitro** from the **Groups** menu and *click* anywhere on screen. Add sp^3 oxygen 🗝 to the free valence on nitrogen. *Click* on 🖻. Build sulfuric acid. Select **New Molecule** (not **New**) from the **File** menu. Select **Sulfone** from the **Groups** menu and *click* anywhere on screen. Add sp^3 oxygen to both free valences on sulfur. *Click* on 🖻. Build acetic acid. Again select **New Molecule**. Select **Carboxylic Acid** from the **Groups** menu and *click*

anywhere on screen. Add sp^3 carbon ⌊c-⌋ to the free valence at carbon. *Click* on ⌊▨⌋. Finally, build ethanol. Select **New Molecule** and construct from two sp^3 carbons and an sp^3 oxygen. *Click* on ⌊▨⌋, and then on ⌊V⌋.

2. Bring up the **Calculations** dialog and specify calculation of equilibrium geometry using the HF/6-31G* model. *Click* on **OK**. Bring up the **Surfaces** dialog and *click* on **Add...** (at the bottom of the dialog). Select **density** from the **Surface** menu and **potential** from the **Property** menu in the **Add Surface** dialog which appears. *Click* on **OK**. Leave the **Surfaces** dialog on screen. Submit for calculation with the name "*acids*".

3. When completed, bring up the spreadsheet, *click* on ⌊▣⌋ at the bottom left of the screen and *check* the box to the right of the name for all four molecules. They will now be displayed simultaneously on screen. Select (*uncheck*) **Coupled** from the **Model** menu so that they may be independently manipulated. Arrange such that the "acidic" hydrogen in each is visible.

> Manipulations normally refer only to the selected molecule. To rotate and translate all molecules together, hold down the **ctrl** (**control**) key in addition to the left or right buttons, respectively, while moving the mouse.

4. *Double click* on the line "density potential ..." inside the **Surfaces** dialog. Electrostatic potential maps for all four acids will be displayed. Examine the potential in the vicinity of the acidic hydrogen. Change the property range to highlight differences in this region. Select **Properties** (**Display** menu) and *click* on one of the maps. Type "0" and "90" inside the boxes underneath "Property" in the **Surface Properties** dialog. *Press* the **return** key following each data entry.

    "Blue" regions identify acidic sites, the more blue the greater the acidity. On this basis, rank the acid strength of the four compounds.

5. Remove "*acids*" and any open dialogs from the screen.

6. One after the other, build trichloroacetic, dichloroacetic, chloroacetic, formic, benzoic, acetic and pivalic acids (structural formulae are provided in the table below). Put all into the same document (**New Molecule** instead of **New** following the first molecule). *Click* on $\boxed{V}$ when you are finished.

acid	pK$_a$	acid	pK$_a$
trichloroacetic (Cl$_3$CCO$_2$H)	0.7	benzoic (C$_6$H$_5$CO$_2$H)	4.19
dichloroacetic (Cl$_2$CHCO$_2$H)	1.48	acetic (CH$_3$CO$_2$H)	4.75
chloroacetic (ClCH$_2$CO$_2$H)	2.85	pivalic ((CH$_3$)$_3$CCO$_2$H)	5.03
formic (HCO$_2$H)	3.75		

7. Note that the name of the presently selected molecule in the document appears at the bottom of the screen. This indicates that a HF/3-21G calculation is available in Spartan's database. *Click* on $\boxed{\blacktriangle}$ to the left of the name, and then *click* on **Replace** in the dialog which results. Repeat for all seven molecules. Structures obtained from HF/3-21G calculations will replace those you have built.

8. Enter the **Calculations** dialog and specify a single-point-energy HF/3-21G calculation. *Click* on **OK**. Enter the **Surfaces** dialog. *Click* on **Add...**, select **density** from the **Surface** menu and **potential** from the **Property** menu in the **Add Surface** dialog which appears and then *click* on **OK**. Leave the **Surfaces** dialog on screen. Submit for calculation. Name it "*carboxylic acids*".

9. Bring up the spreadsheet. Expand it so that you can see all seven molecules, and that two data columns are available. *Click* inside the header cell of an available data column, *type* "pKa" and *press* the **return** key. Enter the experimental pK$_a$'s (see above) into the appropriate cells under this column. *Press* the **return** key following each entry. Finally, *click* inside the header cell of the next available data column and *type* "potential". *Press* the **return** key.

10. After all calculations have completed, arrange the molecules such that the "acidic hydrogen" is visible. You need to *click* on $\boxed{\bullet}$ at the bottom left of the screen and *check* the box to the right of the

75

molecule name in the spreadsheet for each entry, and finally select (*uncheck*) **Coupled** from the **Model** menu.

11. *Double click* on the line "density . . ." inside the **Surfaces** dialog to turn on the electrostatic potential map for each molecule. Bring up the **Properties** dialog, remove the checkmark from **Apply Globally**, and *click* on the **Reset** button in the center of the dialog. The property range will now apply to the individual molecules. Enter the maximum value (most positive electrostatic potential) into the appropriate cell of the spreadsheet (under "potential"), and *press* the **return** key.

12. Plot experimental pK_a vs. potential. Bring up the **Plots** dialog (**Display** menu), select **pKa** under the **X Axis** menu and **potential** from the **Y Axes** list, and *click* on **OK**. The data points are connected by a cubic spline. For a least squares fit, select **Properties** from the **Display** menu, *click* on the curve, and select **Linear LSQ** from the **Fit** menu in the **Curve Properties** dialog.

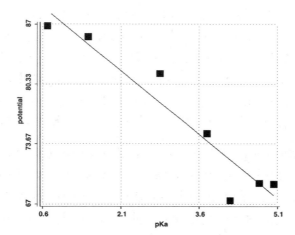

13. Close "*carboxylic acids*" and remove any remaining dialogs from the screen.

Internal Rotation in *n*-Butane

This tutorial illustrates the steps required to calculate the energy of a molecule as a function of the torsion angle about one of its bonds, and to produce a conformational energy diagram.

Rotation by 180^0 about the central carbon-carbon bond in *n*-butane gives rise to two distinct "staggered" structures, *anti* and *gauche*.

CH₃

anti   *gauche*

Both of these should be energy minima (conformers), and the correct description of the properties of *n*-butane is in terms of a Boltzmann average of the properties of both conformers (for discussion see the essay "**Total Energies and Thermodynamic and Kinetic Data**").

This tutorial shows you how to calculate the change in energy as a function of the torsion angle in *n*-butane, place your data in a spreadsheet and make a conformational energy diagram.

1. *Click* on 📑 to bring up the organic model kit. Make *n*-butane from four sp^3 carbons. *Click* on **V** to dismiss the model kit.

2. Set the CCCC dihedral angle to 0^0 (*syn* conformation). *Click* on 🔄 then, one after the other, *click* on the four carbon atoms in sequence. *Type* "0" (0^0) into the text box to the right of "dihedral..." at the bottom right of the screen and *press* the **return** key.

3. *Click* on 🔓 at the bottom right of the screen. The icon will change to 🔒 indicating that a dihedral constraint is to be imposed. Select **Properties** (**Display** menu) and *click* on the constraint marker on

77

the model on screen. This brings up the **Constraint Properties** dialog. Leave the value of "0" (0°) in the box to the right of **Value** as it is, but change the contents of the box to the right of **To** to "180" (180⁰). Enter "10" in the box to the right of **Steps** and *press* the **Return** key.

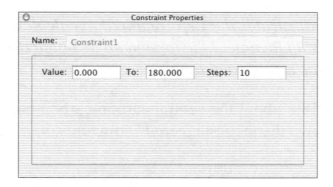

What you have specified is that the dihedral angle will be constrained first to 0°, then to 20°*, etc. and finally to 180°. *Click* on ⊙ to dismiss the dialog.

4. Bring up the **Calculations** dialog and select **Energy Profile** from the menu to the right of "Calculate", and **Semi-Empirical** from the menu to the right of "with". *Click* on **Submit** at the bottom of the dialog and provide the name *"n-butane"*.

5. When the calculations on all conformers have completed, they will go into a document named *"n-butane_prof"* which will be opened for you. (You might wish to first close *"n-butane"* to avoid confusion.) Align the conformers to get a clearer view of the rotation. Select **Align Molecules** from the **Geometry** menu and, one after the other, *click* on either the first three carbons or the last three carbons. Then *click* on the **Align** button at the bottom right of the screen, and finally *click* on **V**. Bring up the spreadsheet (**Display** menu), and enter both the energies relative to the 180° or *anti* conformer, and the CCCC dihedral angles. First, *click* on the label ("P10") for the bottom entry in the spreadsheet (this should be the *anti* conformer), then *click* on the header cell for the

---

*   The difference between constraint values is given by: (final-initial)/(steps-1).

78

left most blank column, and finally, *click* on **Add...** at the bottom of the spreadsheet. Select **rel. E** from among the selections in the dialog which results, **kJ/mol** from the **Energy** menu and *click* on **OK**. To enter the dihedral angle constraints, *click* on 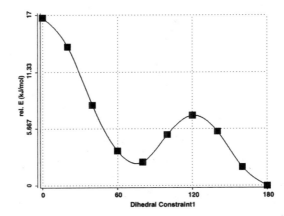, *click* on the constraint marker and *drag* the name of the constraint (Dihedral Contraint 1) at the bottom of the screen into the spreadsheet. Finally, *click* on $\boxed{V}$.

6. Select **Plots...** (**Display** menu). Select **Dihedral Constraint 1** from the items in the **X Axis** menu and **rel. E(kJ/mol)** from the **Y Axes** list. *Click* on **OK** to dismiss the dialog and display a plot.

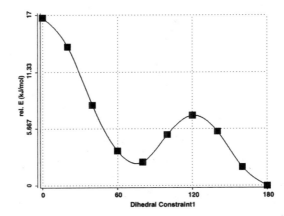

The curve (a so-called "cubic spline") smoothly connects the data points. You can see that it contains two minima, one at 180° (the *anti* form) and one around 60° (the *gauche* form). The former is lower in energy.

Further discussion of the potential energy surface for *n*-butane among other systems is provided in the essay "***Potential Energy Surfaces***".

7. Remove any molecules and any remaining dialogs from the screen.

8M

Ene Reaction

This tutorial illustrates the steps involved in first guessing and then obtaining a transition state for a simple chemical reaction. Following this, it shows how to produce a "reaction energy diagram".

The ene reaction involves addition of an electrophilic double bond to an alkene with an allylic hydrogen. The (allylic) hydrogen is transferred and a new carbon-carbon bond is formed, e.g.

The ene reaction belongs to the class of pericyclic reactions which includes such important processes as the Diels-Alder reaction and the Cope and Claisen rearrangements.

Spartan may be used to locate the transition-state for the ene reaction of ethylene and propene and then show the detailed motions which the atoms undergo during the course of reaction. It is easier to start from 1-pentene, the product of the ene reaction, rather than from the reactants.

1. Build 1-pentene. Click on [📋] to bring up the organic model kit. *Click* on the **Groups** button, select **Alkene** from the menu and *click* anywhere on screen. Select sp³ carbon ($\rangle$c-) and build a three-carbon chain onto one of the free valences on ethylene. Adjust the conformation of the molecule such that all five carbons and one of the "hydrogens" (free valences) on the terminal methyl group form a "6-membered ring." You can rotate about a bond by first *clicking* on it (a red torsion marker appears on the bond) and then *moving* the mouse "up and down" while holding down on both the left button and the **spacebar**. *Do not minimize. Click* on [V].

2. Select **Transition States** from the **Search** menu (or *click* on the ⌃ icon in the tool palette). Orient the molecule such that both the CH bond involving the hydrogen which will "migrate" and the C_4-C_5 bond are visible (see figure on previous page for numbering). *Click* on the CH bond and then on the C_4-C_5 bond. An "arrow" will be drawn.* Orient the molecule such that both the C_3-C_4 and the C_2-C_3 bonds are visible. *Click* on the C_3-C_4 bond and then on the C_2-C_3 bond. A second arrow will be drawn. Orient the molecule such that the C_1=C_2 bond, C_1 and the hydrogen (on C_5) which will migrate are all visible. *Click* on the C_1=C_2 bond and, while holding down on the **Shift** key, *click* on C_1 and then on the hydrogen. A third arrow will be drawn.

If you make a mistake, you can delete an arrow. Select **Delete** from the **Build** menu (or *click* on the ▬ icon in the tool palette), then *click* on the arrow and finally *click* on ⌃. When all is in order, *click* on ⓡ ⓟ at the bottom right of the screen. Your structure will be replaced by a guess at the transition state.

3. Select **Calculations...** (**Setup** menu). Select **Transition State Geometry** from the menu to the right of "Calculate" and **Semi-Empirical** from the menu to the right of "with". *Check* **IR** to the right of "Compute" and *click* on **OK**. Submit for calculation with the name "*ene transition state*".

4. When the calculation has completed animate the motion of atoms along the reaction coordinate. Select **Spectra** under the **Display** menu. *Click* on the top entry of the list in the **Spectra** dialog. It corresponds to an imaginary frequency, and will be designated

---

* Formally, this corresponds to migration of a pair of electrons from the tail of the arrow to the head. However, Spartan treats arrows simply as a convenient and familiar nomenclature with which to search its database of transition states.

with an "i" in front of the number*. Make certain that the associated vibrational motion is consistent with the reaction of interest and not with some other process.

5. Controls at the bottom of the **Spectra** dialog allow for changing both the amplitude of Vibration (**Amplitude**) and the number of steps which make up the motion (**Steps**). The latter serves as a "speed control". Change the amplitude to "0.3" (*type* "0.3" in the box to the right of **Amplitude** and *press* the **return** key). Next, *click* on **Make List** at the bottom of the dialog. This will give rise to a document containing a series of structures which follow the reaction coordinate down from the transition state both toward reactant and product. To avoid confusion, it might be better to remove original molecule from the screen. *Click* on "*ene transition state*" (the vibrating molecule) and close it. Also remove the **Spectra** dialog by *clicking* on ⊗.

6. Enter the **Calculations** dialog (**Setup** menu) and specify a single-point energy calculation using the semi-empirical model (the same theoretical model used to obtain the transition state and calculate the frequencies). Make certain that **Apply Globally** at the bottom of the dialog is *checked* before you exit the dialog. Next, enter the **Surfaces** dialog and specify evaluation of two surfaces: a bond density surface and a bond density surface onto which the electrostatic potential has been mapped. *Click* on **Add . . .**, select **density (bond)** for **Surface** and **none** for **Property** and *click* on **OK**. *Click* on **Add . . .** again, select **density (bond)** for **surface** and **potential** for **Property** and *click* on **OK**. Make certain that **Apply Globally** at the bottom of the dialog is *checked*. Leave the **Surfaces** dialog on screen.

7. Submit for calculation with the name "*ene reaction*". Once the calculations have completed, enter the **Surfaces** dialog and, one

---

* Recall from the tutorial "*Infrared Spectrum of Acetone*", that frequency is proportional to the square root of the force constant divided by the reduced mass. The force constant associated with the reaction coordinate is negative because the energy "curves downward" at the transition state (see the essay "*Potential Energy Surfaces*"). Since the reduced mass is positive, the ratio of force constant to reduced mass is a negative number, meaning that its square root is an imaginary number.

after the other, select the surfaces which you have calculated. For each, step through the sequence of structures ($\blacktriangleright$ and $\blacktriangleleft$) keys at the bottom of the screen) or animate the reaction ($\blacktriangleright$). Note, in particular, the changes in bonding revealed by the bond density surface. Also pay attention to the "charge" on the migrating atom as revealed by the sequence of electrostatic potential maps. Is it best described as a "proton" (blue color), hydrogen atom (green color) or "hydride anion" (red color)?

Further discussion of the use of electrostatic potential maps to investigate charge distributions is provided in the essay *"Electrostatic Potential Maps: Charge Distributions"*.

9. Close *"ene reaction"* as well as any remaining dialogs.

9M

Proteins and Nucleotides

This tutorial illustrates models appropriate to large biomolecules, in particular, ribbon displays of protein and nucleotide "backbones" and display of hydrogen bonds. Biomolecule building is not illustrated and no calculations are performed.

Treatment of very large molecules, proteins and nucleotides ("biopolymers") most important among them, requires models which are simpler than those which are appropriate for small organic and inorganic molecules. This refers both to display and manipulation, where much detail needs to be eliminated, and to the calculation of structure and properties, where molecular mechanics needs to replace quantum mechanics.

This tutorial uses an unusual "protein-RNA complex" to illustrate a variety of models for the display of biopolymers, including ribbon displays to elucidate the "backbone" and hydrogen-bond displays to show how the structure is "held together".

1. Open *"tutorial 9"* in the "tutorials" directory. This contains a PDB (Protein Data Bank) file[*] of a protein-RNA complex. Note that a simple ribbon display, demarking the backbones of the protein and RNA chains has replaced the usual structure models ("tube", "ball-and-spoke", etc.). To see why this is necessary, turn "on" (select) one of these models from the **Model** menu. The detail has completely obliterated the most important structure feature, that the molecule is made up of two "intertwined" segments. Note, however, that a space-filling model (**Space Filling** under the **Model** menu) does provide indication of overall size and shape of the complex. When you are done, select **Hide** from the **Model** menu.

---

[*] PDB designation 1A1T. R.N. de Guzman, Z.R. Wu, C.C. Stalling, L. Pappalardo, P.N. Borer and M.F. Summers, Science, **279**, 384 (1998).

2. The structure of this complex has been determined by NMR spectroscopy which gives several alternative conformers. Step through them (▶ and ◀ at the bottom left of the screen) to see where they are similar and where they differ. In particular, notice that a large portion of the overall structure remains basically the same from one conformer to another.

3. Select **Configure...** from the **Model** menu and *click* on the **Ribbons** tab in the dialog which results. Select **By Residue** under "Coloring" in the **Configure Ribbons** dialog and *click* on **OK**. The model is now colored according to amino acid/nucleotide base.

Hydrogen bonding is known to be a decisive factor in determining the three-dimensional structures of biopolymers. The base pairs in complementary strands which make up DNA are "held together" by hydrogen bonds. Helical structures in proteins are also maintained by hydrogen bonds as are neighboring strands in so-called β sheets.

4. Select **Hydrogen Bonds** (**Model** menu). Single "dotted lines" represent hydrogen bonds throughout the "protein part" of the complex, and "sets" of two or three dotted lines in the "RNA" part. The latter form the connections between nucleotide bases and the number of lines in each set actually allows you to identify what the bases are.

5. Select **Tube** (**Model** menu). Also, select (*uncheck*) **Hydrogens** from this menu. You can now see in greater detail the structure of the complex and the positions of the hydrogen bonds.

6. Close "*tutorial 9*".

Section C

Essays

The following section comprises a series of "Essays" on topics related to the underpinnings of molecular modeling in general and to the methods and procedures available in the Spartan molecular modeling program in particular. They are deliberately brief and non-mathematical and are intended primarily as a first exposure.

The first essay describes what is commonly known as a potential energy surface, and defines clearly the meaning of equilibrium and transition-state structures. The next two essays address the origins of the molecular mechanics and quantum chemical models available in Spartan, and provide broad guidelines for selecting a particular model for the task at hand. The fourth essay discusses the use of energy data which comes out of quantum chemical calculations to provide information about reaction thermochemistry and kinetics. It refers back to the first essay on potential energy surfaces connecting energy with equilibrium and transition-state structure. The fifth essay outlines techniques for locating and verifying transition states and the sixth essay for interpreting preferences in conformationally flexible molecules. The final four essays discuss different graphical models available in Spartan: molecular orbitals, electron densities, electrostatic potential maps, and local ionization potential and LUMO maps. These illustrate how each of the different graphical models can be employed to provide insight in molecular structure and bonding and chemical reactivity.

Associated with Essays 1, 7, 8, 9 and 10 are a series of Spartan files grouped in the "essays" directory on the CD-ROM. File names are specified in the individual essays.

1

Potential Energy Surfaces

One Dimensional Energy Surfaces

Every chemist has encountered a plot depicting the change in energy of ethane as a function of the angle of torsion (dihedral angle) around the carbon-carbon bond.

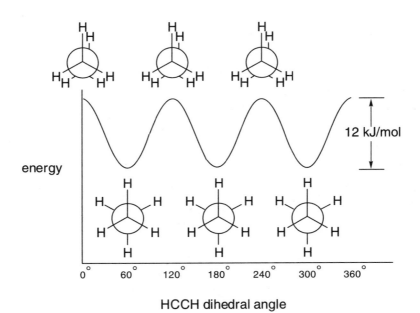

HCCH dihedral angle

Full 360° rotation leads to three identical "staggered" structures which are energy minima, and three identical "eclipsed" structures which are energy maxima. The difference in energy between eclipsed and staggered structures of ethane, termed the barrier to rotation, is known experimentally to be 12 kJ/mol. Note, that any physical measurements on ethane pertain only to its staggered structure, or more precisely the set of three identical staggered structures. Eclipsed ethane "does not exist" in the sense that it cannot be isolated and characterized. Rather, it can only be "imagined" as a structure in between equivalent staggered forms.

Somewhat more complicated but also familiar is a plot of energy vs. the dihedral angle involving the central carbon-carbon bond in *n*-butane (see the tutorial *"Internal Rotation in n-Butane"*).

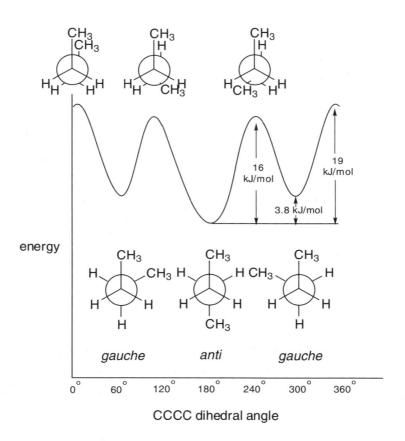

This plot also reveals three energy minima, corresponding to staggered structures, and three energy maxima, corresponding to eclipsed structures. In the case of *n*-butane, however, the three structures in each set are not identical. Rather, one of the minima, corresponding to a dihedral angle of 180° (the *anti* structure), is lower in energy and distinct from the other two *gauche* minima (dihedral angles around 60° and 300°), which are identical. Similarly, one of the energy maxima corresponding to a dihedral angle of 0°, is distinct from the other two maxima (with dihedral angles around 120° and 240°), which are identical. As with ethane, eclipsed forms of *n*-butane do not exist, and correspond only to hypothetical structures in between *anti* and *gauche* minima. Unlike ethane, which is a single compound, any sample of *n*-butane is made up of two distinct compounds, *anti n*-butane and *gauche n*-butane. The relative abundance of the two compounds as a function of temperature is given by the Boltzmann equation (see the essay *"Total Energies and Thermodynamic and Kinetic Data"*).

Open *"n-butane rotation"*. The image which appears is one frame of a sequence depicting rotation about the central carbon-carbon bond in *n*-butane. *Click* on the ⏮ and ⏭ keys at the bottom left of the screen to look at other frames. Verify that the staggered structures correspond to minima on the energy plot and that the eclipsed structures correspond to maxima. Also, verify that the *anti* structure is lower in energy than the *gauche* structure. *Click* on ▶ to animate the sequence. Close *"n-butane rotation"* when you are finished.

The "important" geometrical coordinate in both of the above examples may clearly be identified as a torsion involving one particular carbon-carbon bond. This is an oversimplification, as bond lengths and angles no doubt change during rotation around the carbon-carbon bond.

The molecular models available in Spartan are able to account for the subtle changes in bond lengths and angles which result from changes in conformation. Open *"n-butane geometry changes"*. The two plots depict the variation in central CC bond distance and in CCC bond angle as a function of the CCCC torsional angle. The variation in energy is superimposed on each plot. Note how closely the bond distance and energy changes parallel each other. Note also that the bond angle is insensitive to conformation except in the region of the *syn* (0° torsional angle) structure where it has opened up by several degrees. Close *"n-butane geometry changes"* when you are finished.

Many Dimensional Energy Surfaces

It will usually not be possible to identify a single "simple" geometrical coordinate to designate a chemical transformation. A good example of this is provided by the potential energy surface for "ring inversion" in cyclohexane.

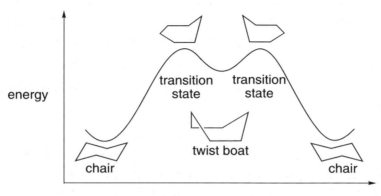

In this case, the geometrical coordinate connecting stable forms is not specified in detail (as it was in the previous two examples), but is referred to simply as the "reaction coordinate". Also the energy maxima have been designated as "transition states" as an indication that their structures may not be simply described (as are the energy maxima for rotation in ethane and *n*-butane).

The energy surface for ring inversion in cyclohexane, like that for *n*-butane, contains three distinct energy minima, two of lower energy identified as "chairs", and one of higher energy identified as a "twist boat" (see the activity "***Molecular Shapes IV. The Other Cyclohexane***"). In fact, the energy difference between the chair and twist boat structures is sufficiently large (around 23 kJ/mol) that only the former can be observed at normal temperatures. For a discussion, see the essay "***Total Energies and Thermodynamic and Kinetic Data***".

All six carbons are equivalent in the chair form of cyclohexane, but the hydrogens divide into two sets of six equivalent "*equatorial*" hydrogens and six equivalent "*axial*" hydrogens.

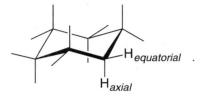

However, only one kind of hydrogen can normally be observed, meaning that *equatorial* and *axial* positions interconvert via some low-energy process. This is the ring inversion process just described, in which one side of the ring is bent upward while the other side is bent downward.

As shown in the potential energy diagram on the previous page, the overall ring inversion process actually occurs in two steps, with a twist boat structure as a midway point (an intermediate). The two (equivalent) transition states leading to this intermediate adopt structures in which five of the ring carbons lie (approximately) in one plane.

The energy profile for ring inversion in cyclohexane may be rationalized given what we have already said about single-bond rotation in *n*-butane. Basically, the interconversion of the reactant into the twist-boat intermediate via the transition state can be viewed as a "rotation" about one of the ring bonds.

Correspondingly, the interconversion of the twist boat intermediate into the product can be viewed as rotation about the opposite ring bond. Overall, two independent "bond rotations", pausing at the high-energy (but stable) twist-boat intermediate effect conversion of one chair structure into another equivalent chair, and at the same time switch *axial* and *equatorial* hydrogens.

Open *"cyclohexane ring inversion"*. The image which appears is one frame in a sequence depicting ring inversion in cyclohexane. *Click* on the ◁ and ▷ keys at the bottom left of the screen to look at other frames. Verify that the three minima on the energy plot correspond to staggered structures and that the two maxima correspond to eclipsed structures. Also, verify that the twist boat structure is higher in energy than the chair structures. *Click* on ▶ to animate the sequence. Note that the overall ring inversion appears to occur in two steps, one step leading up to the twist boat and the other step leading away from it. Close *"cyclohexane ring inversion"* when you are finished.

Ethane, *n*-butane and cyclohexane are all examples of the types of motions which molecules may undergo. Their potential energy surfaces are special cases of a general type of plot in which the variation in energy is given as a function of reaction coordinate.

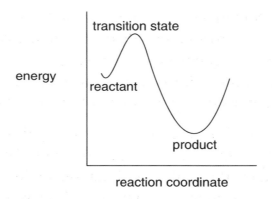

Diagrams like this provide essential connections between important chemical observables - structure, stability, reactivity and selectivity - and energy.

The positions of the energy minima along the reaction coordinate give the equilibrium structures of the reactant and product. Similarly, the position of the energy maximum gives the structure of the transition state. Both energy minima ("stable molecules") and the energy maximum (transition state) are well defined. However, the path connecting them (reaction coordinate) is not well defined, in the sense that there are many possible paths. Liken this to climbing a mountain. The starting and ending points are well defined as is the summit, but there can be many possible routes.

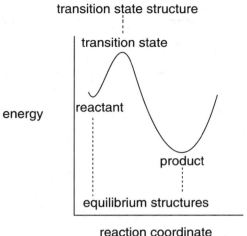

transition state structure

transition state

energy

reactant

product

equilibrium structures

reaction coordinate

As previously commented, the reaction coordinate for some processes may be quite simple. For example, where the "reaction" is rotation about the carbon-carbon bond in ethane, the reaction coordinate may be thought of as the HCCH torsion angle, and the structure may be thought of in terms of this angle alone. Thus, staggered ethane (both the reactant and the product) is a molecule for which this angle is 60° and eclipsed ethane is a molecule for which this angle is 0°.

60°

H
H   H
H   H
H

staggered ethane
"reactant"

0°

H H
H
H   H
H

eclipsed ethane
"transition state"

60°

H
H   H
H   H
H

staggered ethane
"product"

A similar description applies to "reaction" of *gauche n*-butane leading to the more stable *anti* conformer. Again, the reaction coordinate may be thought of as a torsion about the central carbon-carbon bond, and the individual reactant, transition state and product structures in terms of this coordinate.

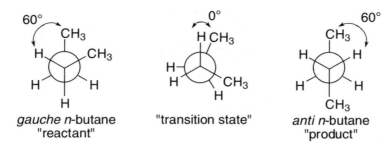

gauche n-butane   "transition state"   anti n-butane
    "reactant"   "product"

Equilibrium structure (geometry) may be determined from experiment, given that the molecule can be prepared and is sufficiently long-lived to be subject to measurement. On the other hand, the geometry of a transition state may not be experimentally established. This is simply because a transition state is not an "energy well" which can serve as a "trap". Therefore, it is impossible to establish a population of molecules on which measurements may be performed.

Both equilibrium and transition-state structures may be determined from quantum chemical calculations. Existence is not a requirement. Equilibrium and transition-state structures can be distinguished from one another not only from a reaction coordinate diagram, but more generally by determining the complete set of vibrational motions and associated vibrational frequencies. (The latter are the same quantities measured by infrared spectroscopy.) Systems for which all frequencies are real numbers are "stable" molecules (energy minima), while transition states are characterized by having one (and only one) vibrational frequency which is an imaginary number. The coordinate (vibrational motion) associated with this imaginary frequency is the reaction coordinate.

2

Theoretical Models

A wide variety of different procedures or "models" have been developed to calculate molecular structure and energetics among other properties. These have generally been broken down into two categories, quantum chemical models, which ultimately derive from the Schrödinger equation, and molecular mechanics models.

The Schrödinger Equation

Practical quantum chemical methods seek an approximate solution to the deceptively simple-looking equation formulated by Schrödinger in the 1920's.

$$\hat{H}\Psi \; = \; \varepsilon\Psi$$

In this equation, $\hat{H}$ is termed the "Hamiltonian operator"; it describes both the kinetic energies of the nuclei and electrons which make up the molecule, as well as the electrostatic interactions felt between the nuclei and electrons. Nuclei, which are positively charged, repel other nuclei, and electrons, which are negatively charged, repel other electrons, but nuclei attract electrons. The quantity ε in the Schrödinger equation is the energy of the system, and Ψ is termed a "wavefunction". While the wavefunction has no particular physical meaning, its square times a small volume element corresponds to the probability of finding the system at a particular set of coordinates.

The Schrödinger equation has been solved exactly for the hydrogen atom (a one-electron system), where its solutions are actually quite familiar to chemists as the s, p, d atomic orbitals, i.e.

s orbital   p orbital   d orbital

They correspond to the ground and various excited states of the hydrogen atom.

Hartree-Fock Molecular Orbital Models

Although the Schrödinger equation may easily be written down for many-electron atoms as well as for molecules, it cannot be solved. Approximations must be made. So-called Hartree-Fock molecular orbital models, or simply, molecular orbital models, start from the Schrödinger equation and then make three approximations:

1. Separation of nuclear and electron motions (the "Born-Oppenheimer approximation"). In effect, what this says is that "from the point of view of the electrons, the nuclei are stationary". This eliminates the mass dependence in what is now referred to as the electronic Schrödinger equation. (For discussion of how mass affects the properties of molecules, see the activity *"Transition States are Molecules Too"*.)

2. Separation of electron motions (the "Hartree-Fock approximation"). What is actually done is to represent the many-electron wavefunction as a sum of products of one-electron wavefunctions, the spatial parts of which are termed "molecular orbitals". This reduces the problem of simultaneously accounting for the motions of several electrons to the much simpler problem of accounting for the motion of a single electron in an environment made up of the nuclei and all the remaining electrons.

3. Representation of the individual molecular orbitals in terms of linear combinations of atom-centered basis functions or "atomic orbitals" (the "LCAO approximation"). This reduces the problem of finding the best functional form for the molecular orbitals to the much simpler problem of finding the best set of linear coefficients. The limit of a "complete" set of basis functions is the so-called "Hartree-Fock limit".

These three approximations lead to a series of equations commonly referred to as the "Roothaan-Hall equations".

Hartree-Fock models differ in the number and kind of atomic basis functions, and their cost increases as the fourth power of the number of basis functions. The simplest models utilize a "minimal basis set" of atomic orbitals, which includes only those functions required to hold all the electrons on an atom and to maintain spherical symmetry. Minimal basis set methods are often too restrictive to properly describe molecular properties, and "split-valence basis sets", which incorporate two sets of valence atomic orbitals, or "polarization basis sets", which, in addition, include atomic orbitals of higher angular type than are occupied in the atom in its ground state, e.g., d-type atomic orbitals in the case of main-group elements, are often employed. Hartree-Fock molecular orbital models using split-valence or polarization basis sets, have become a mainstay for routine and reliable descriptions of the structures, stabilities and other molecular properties.

Semi-Empirical Molecular Orbital Models

The principal disadvantage of Hartree-Fock models is their cost. It is possible to introduce further approximations in order to significantly reduce cost while still retaining the underlying quantum mechanical formalism. "Semi-empirical" molecular orbital models follow in a straightforward way from Hartree-Fock models:

1. Elimination of overlap between functions on different atoms (the "NDDO approximation"). This is rather drastic but reduces the computation effort by more than an order of magnitude over Hartree-Fock models.

2. Restriction to a "minimal valence basis set" of atomic functions. Inner-shell (core) functions are not included explicitly, and because of this, the cost of doing a calculation involving a second-row element, e.g., silicon, is no more than that incurred for the corresponding first-row element, e.g., carbon.

3. Introduction of adjustable parameters to reproduce specific experimental data. This is what distinguishes the various semi-empirical models currently available. Choice of parameters, more than anything else, appears to be the key to formulating successful semi-empirical models.

Molecular Mechanics Models

The alternative to quantum chemical models are molecular mechanics models. These do not start from the Schrödinger equation, but rather from a simple but "chemically reasonable" picture of molecular structure, a so-called "force field". In this picture, just as with a Lewis structure, molecules are made up of atoms (as opposed to nuclei and electrons), some of which are connected ("bonded"). Both crowding ("van der Waals") and charge-charge ("Coulombic") interactions between atoms are then considered, and atom positions are adjusted to best match known structural data (bond lengths and angles).

Molecular mechanics is much simpler than solving the Schrödinger equation, but requires an explicit description of "chemical bonding", as well as a large amount of information about the structures of molecules. This biases results and seriously limits the predictive value of molecular mechanics models. Nevertheless, molecular mechanics has found an important role in molecular modeling as a tool to establish equilibrium geometries of large molecules, in particular, proteins and equilibrium conformations of highly-flexible molecules.

3

Choosing a Theoretical Model

No single method of calculation is likely to be ideal for all applications. A great deal of effort has been expended to define the limits of different molecular mechanics and quantum chemical models, and to judge the degree of success of different models. The latter follows from the ability of a model to consistently reproduce known (experimental) data. Molecular mechanics models are restricted to determination of geometries and conformations of stable molecules. Quantum chemical models also provide energy data, which may in turn be directly compared with experimental thermochemical data, as well as infrared spectra and properties such as dipole moments, which may be compared directly with the corresponding experimental quantities. Quantum chemical models may also be applied to transition states. While there are no experimental structures with which to compare (see the essay "*Potential Energy Surfaces*"), experimental kinetic data may be interpreted to provide information about activation energies (see the essay "*Total Energies and Thermodynamic and Kinetic Data*").

"Success" is not an absolute. Different properties, and certainly different problems may require different levels of confidence to actually be of value. Neither is success sufficient. A model also needs to be "practical" for the task at hand. Were this not the case, there would be no reason to look further than the Schrödinger equation itself. The nature and size of the system needs to be taken into account, as do the available computational resources and the experience and "patience" of the practitioner. Practical models usually share one common feature, in that they are not likely to be the "best possible" treatments which have been formulated. Compromise is almost always an essential component of model selection. Continued advances in both digital computers and computer software will continue to "raise the bar" higher and higher. There is much to be done before fully reliable models will be routinely applicable to all chemical systems of interest.

Molecular modeling, like most technical disciplines, has its own language ("jargon"). Interpreting this jargon is important to "experts" (they need to know the specifics of the model they are using), but not very important for the purpose of using models to teach and learn chemistry. This said, there is one point of nomenclature which needs clarification. 3-21G and 6-31G* following "Hartree-Fock/" or HF/ designate a so-called "basis set", that is, a set of atom-centered functions from which molecular-centered functions (molecular orbitals) are to be built. The numbers "3" and "6" to the left of the "-" in these basis sets indicate that 3 and 6 functions ("primitives") are used to describe each inner-shell atomic function. The numbers "21" and "31" to the right of the "-" indicate that two groups of 2 and 1 and 3 and 1 primitives are used to describe each valence-shell atomic function. "G" is used to specify that the primitives are Gaussian type functions, and "*" designates that additional valence functions are supplied.

The table below provides an overview of the performance of the molecular mechanics model and three quantum chemical models available in your edition of Spartan, for the calculation of equilibrium and transition-state geometries, conformation and thermochemistry. Three different "grades" have been assigned: G is good, C is good with cautious application and P is poor. NA signifies "not applicable".

task	molecular mechanics	PM3 semi-empirical	Hartree-Fock 3-21G	6-31G*
geometry (organic)	C	G	G	G
geometry (metals)	NA	G	P	P
transition-state geometry	NA	C	G	G
conformation	G	P	C	G
thermochemistry	NA	P	C	G
computation time	low ------------------------------> high			

In Terms of Task

i) All models provide a good account of equilibrium geometries for organic and main-group inorganic molecules and, where they are applicable, of transition-state geometries. (Transition-state geometries cannot be judged by comparison with experimental data but only with the results of very good quantum chemical calculations.) Molecular mechanics and semi-empirical models only rarely yield very poor geometries. HF/3-21G and HF/6-31G* models do not provide a reliable account of the geometries of compounds incorporating transition metals, but the PM3 semi-empirical model has been especially parameterized for this task and generally provides a reasonable account.

ii) The molecular mechanics model generally provides a good account of conformational energy differences in organic compounds. The PM3 semi-empirical model and the HF/3-21G model are suitable for identifying conformational minima, and for determining the geometries of these minima, but they are not suitable for providing accurate relative conformer energies. The HF/6-31G* model generally provides a good description of conformational energy differences in organic compounds.

iii) The HF/6-31G* model generally provides an acceptable account of the energetics of reactions which do not involve bond making or breaking. The HF/3-21G model is not as satisfactory. Neither Hartree-Fock model provides an acceptable account of the energetics of reactions which involve bond breaking.

Neither the HF/3-21G nor Hartree-Fock/6-31G* model provides an acceptable account of absolute activation energies, but both models generally provide an excellent description of relative activation energies.

The PM3 semi-empirical model is unsatisfactory in describing the energetics of all types of processes.

In Terms of Model

The molecular mechanics model is restricted to the description of equilibrium geometry and conformation. It performs reasonably well for both.

The PM3 semi-empirical model is particularly attractive for:

i) Equilibrium geometry determinations for large molecules, where the cost of Hartree-Fock models may be prohibitive.

ii) Transition-state geometry determinations, where the cost of Hartree-Fock models may be prohibitive.

iii) Equilibrium and transition-state geometry determinations involving transition metals, where Hartree-Fock models are known to produce poor results.

The PM3 semi-empirical model is unsuitable for:

i) Calculation of reaction energies.

ii) Calculation of conformational energy differences.

The HF/3-21G and HF/6-31G* models are particularly attractive for:

i) Equilibrium and transition-state structure determinations of organic and main-group inorganic molecules (except molecules with transition metals), where increased accuracy over that available from the semi-empirical model is required.

ii) Calculation of reaction energies (except reactions involving bond making or breaking), where the PM3 semi-empirical model yields unacceptable results.

The HF/3-21G and HF/6-31G* models are unsuitable for:

i) Calculation of reaction energies which involve bond making or breaking and calculation of absolute activation energies.

ii) Equilibrium and transition-state structure determinations for transition-metal inorganic and organometallic molecules.

Total Energies and Thermodynamic and Kinetic Data

In addition to molecular geometry, the most important quantity to come out of molecular modeling is the energy. Energy can be used to reveal which of several isomers is most stable, to determine whether a particular chemical reaction will have a thermodynamic driving force (an "*exothermic*" reaction) or be thermodynamically uphill (an "*endothermic*" reaction), and to ascertain how fast a reaction is likely to proceed. Other molecular properties, such as the dipole moment, are also important, but the energy plays a special role.

There is more than one way to express the energy of a molecule. Most common to chemists is as a heat of formation, ΔH_f. This is the heat of a hypothetical chemical reaction that creates a molecule from well defined but arbitrary "standard states" of each of its constituent elements. For example, ΔH_f for methane is the energy required to create the molecule from graphite and H_2, the "standard states" of carbon and hydrogen, respectively. The heat of formation cannot be directly measured, but it must be obtained indirectly. An alternative, total energy, is the heat of a hypothetical reaction that creates a molecule from a collection of separated nuclei and electrons. Like the heat of formation, total energy cannot be measured directly, and is used solely to provide a standard method for expressing and comparing energies. Total energies are always negative numbers and, in comparison with the energies of chemical bonds, are very large. By convention, they are expressed in "so-called" atomic units[*] or au, but may be converted to other units as desired:

---

[*]   The "exact" energy of hydrogen atom is -0.5 atomic units.

It makes no difference which "standard" (heats of formation or total energies) is used to calculate the thermochemistry of balanced chemical reactions (reactant 1 + reactant 2 + . . . → product 1 + product 2 + . . .):

$$\Delta E(\text{reaction}) = E_{\text{product 1}} + E_{\text{product 2}} + \cdots - E_{\text{reactant 1}} - E_{\text{reactant 2}} - \cdots$$

We will use total energies in the discussion which follows. A negative ΔE indicates an *exothermic* (thermodynamically favorable) reaction, while a positive ΔE an *endothermic* (thermodynamically unfavorable) reaction.

A special case involves differences in isomer stability. This is the energy of a chemical reaction in which the "reactant" is one isomer and the "product" is another isomer (isomer 1 → isomer 2):

$$\Delta E(\text{isomer}) = E_{\text{isomer 2}} + E_{\text{isomer 1}}$$

A negative ΔE means that isomer 2 is more stable than isomer 1.

Total energies may also be used to calculate activation energies, $\Delta E^{\ddagger}$:

$$\Delta E^{\ddagger} = E_{\text{transition state}} - E_{\text{reactant 1}} - E_{\text{reactant 2}} - \cdots$$

Here, $E_{\text{transition state}}$ is the total energy of the transition state. Activation energies will always be positive numbers[*], meaning that the transition state is less stable that reactants.

Reaction and activation energies are sufficient to know whether a reaction is *exothermic* or *endothermic* or whether it proceeds with small or large activation barrier. There are, however, other situations where energies need to be replaced by "Gibbs energies" in order to take proper account of the role of entropy. For example, a proper account of the equilibrium concentrations of reactants and products requires calculation of the equilibrium constant, K_{eq}, which according to the Boltzmann equation, is related to the Gibbs energy of reaction, ΔG_{rxn}:

$$K_{eq} = \exp(-\Delta G_{rxn}/RT)$$

---

[*] Note, however, that some reactants proceed with zero activation energy, meaning no transition state can be identified. Further discussion is provided later in this essay.

Here R is the gas constant and T is the temperature (in K). At room temperature (298K) and for ΔG_{rxn} in au, this is given by:

$$K_{eq} = \exp(-1060\, \Delta G_{rxn})$$

ΔG_{rxn} has two components, the enthalpy of reaction, ΔH_{rxn}, and the entropy of reaction, ΔS_{rxn}. These are defined as follows:

$$\Delta G_{rxn} = \Delta H_{rxn} - T\Delta S_{rxn}$$

$$\Delta H_{rxn} \approx \Delta E_{rxn} = E_{product\,1} + E_{product\,2} + \ldots - E_{reactant\,1} - E_{reactant\,2} - \ldots$$

$$\Delta S_{rxn} = S_{product\,1} + S_{product\,2} + \ldots - S_{reactant\,1} - S_{reactant\,2} - \ldots$$

Although ΔG_{rxn} depends on both enthalpy and entropy, there are many reactions for which the entropy contribution is small, and can be neglected. Further assuming that $\Delta H_{rxn} \approx \Delta E_{rxn}$, equilibrium constants can then be estimated according to the Boltzmann equation:

$$K_{eq} \approx \exp(-\Delta E_{rxn}/RT) \approx \exp(-1060\, \Delta E_{rxn})$$

This Boltzmann equation may also be used to establish the equilibrium composition of a mixture of isomers:

$$\text{Isomer 1} \rightleftharpoons \text{Isomer 2} \rightleftharpoons \text{Isomer 3} \rightleftharpoons \ldots$$

$$\%\ \text{Isomer } i = \frac{100 \exp(-1060\, E_{\text{Isomer } i})}{\sum_k \exp(-1060\, E_{\text{Isomer } k})}$$

Isomer energies, E_{isomer}, are given in atomic units relative to the energy of the lowest-energy isomer. An important special case is that involving an equilibrium between two isomers:

$$\text{Isomer 1} \rightleftharpoons \text{Isomer 2}$$

$$\frac{[\text{Isomer 1}]}{[\text{Isomer 2}]} = \exp[-1060\, (E_{isomer1} - E_{isomer2})]$$

Reaction rate constants, k_{rxn}, are also related to Gibbs energies. As before, if entropy contributions can be neglected, the rate constant can be obtained directly from the activation energy, $\Delta E^{\ddagger}$, according to the Arrhenius equation:

$$k_{rxn} \approx (k_B T/h)[\exp(-\Delta E^{\ddagger}/RT)]$$

Here k_B and h are the Boltzmann and Planck constants, respectively. At room temperature and for $\Delta E^{\ddagger}$ in au, k_{rxn} is given by:

$$k_{rxn} = 6.2 \times 10^{12} \exp(-1060 \, \Delta E^{\ddagger})$$

Another way to describe reaction rates is by half-life, $t_{1/2}$, the amount of time it takes for the reactant concentration to drop to one half of its original value. When the reaction follows a first-order rate law, rate = $-k_{rxn}$[reactant], $t_{1/2}$ is given by:

$$t_{1/2} = \ln 2/k_{rxn} = 0.69/k_{rxn}$$

It is useful to associate reaction energies and reaction rates with potential energy diagrams (see the essay *"Potential Energy Surfaces"*). The connections are actually quite simple.

The thermodynamics of reaction is given by the relative energies of the reactant and product on the potential surface.

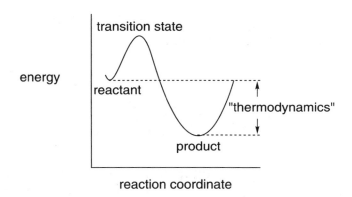

In the case of bond rotation in ethane (see discussion in the essay *"Potential Energy Surfaces"*), the reactant and product are the same and the reaction is said to be "thermoneutral". This is also the case for the overall ring-inversion motion in cyclohexane (see the essay *"Potential Energy Surfaces"*).

The most common case is, as depicted in the above diagram, where the energy of the products is lower than that of the reactants. This kind of reaction is said to be *exothermic*, and the difference in stabilities of reactant and product is simply the difference in their energies. For example, the "reaction" of *gauche n*-butane to *anti n*-

butane is *exothermic* (see the essay "***Potential Energy Surfaces***"), and the difference in stabilities of the two conformers is simply the difference in the energies (3.8 kJ/mol).

Chemical reactions can also be *endothermic*, which give rise to a reaction profile.

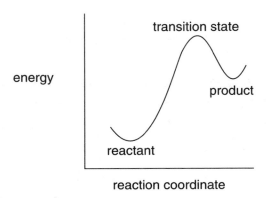

In this case, there would eventually be more reactant than product.

Where two or more different products may form in a reaction, thermodynamics tells us that if "we wait long enough", the product formed in greatest abundance will be that with the lowest energy irrespective of pathway.

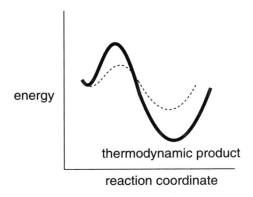

In this case, the product is referred to as the "thermodynamic product" and the reaction is said to be "thermodynamically controlled".

The energy of the transition state above the reactants (the activation energy) provides the connection with reaction rate (kinetics).

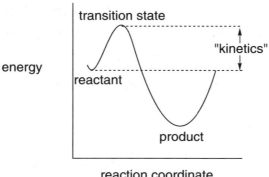

reaction coordinate

While absolute reaction rate also depends on the concentrations of the reactants and on such factors as the "likelihood" that encounters between molecules will actually lead to reaction, generally speaking, the lower the activation energy, the faster the reaction.

The product formed in greatest amount in a kinetically controlled reaction (the kinetic product) is that proceeding via the lowest energy transition state, irrespective of whatever or not this is lowest energy product (the thermodynamic product).

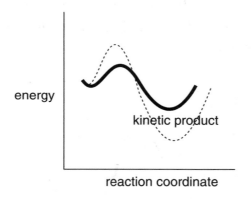

reaction coordinate

Kinetic product ratios show dependence with activation energy differences which are identical to thermodynamic product ratios with difference in reactant and product energies.

An example of a reaction where thermodynamic and kinetic products differ is found in the activity *"Thermodynamic vs. Kinetic Control of Chemical Reactions"*.

5

Finding and Verifying Equilibrium and Transition-State Geometries

The energy of a molecule depends on its geometry. Even small changes in structure can lead to quite large changes in total energy. Proper choice of molecular geometry is therefore quite important in carrying out modeling studies. Experimental geometries, where available, would certainly be suitable. Whereas "high-quality" structures are available for stable molecules[*], experimental data for reactive or otherwise short-lived molecules are scarce, and data for transition states are completely lacking. In the final analysis, there is no alternative to obtaining geometries from calculation. Fortunately, this is not difficult, although it may be demanding in terms of computer time.

Determination of geometry ("geometry optimization") is an iterative process. The energy and energy "gradient" (first derivatives of the energy with respect to all geometrical coordinates) are calculated for the guess geometry, and this information is then used to project a new geometry. This process continues until three criteria are satisfied. First, the gradient must closely approach zero. This insures that the optimization is terminating in a "flat region" of the potential surface (either the "bottom" in the case of equilibrium geometry or the "top" in the case of transition-state geometry). Second, successive iterations must not change any geometrical parameter by more than specified (small) value. Third, successive iterations must not charge the total energy by more than a specified (small) value.

---

[*] The vast majority of experimental structures derive from X-ray crystallography on crystalline solids and may be different from gas-phase geometries due to requirements of crystal packing.

Equilibrium Geometries

In order for a geometry to correspond to an energy minimum, the curvature of the energy surface must be positive, i.e., the structure must lie at the "bottom" of an energy well. The surface's curvature is defined by the "Hessian" (the matrix of second derivatives of the energy with respect to geometrical coordinates).

What is actually done is to find a set of geometrical coordinates ("normal coordinates") for which the Hessian will be diagonal, i.e., all off-diagonal elements will be zero. In this representation, all (diagonal) elements must be positive for the geometry to correspond to an energy minimum. "Normal coordinate analysis" as it is termed is required for the calculation of vibrational frequencies, which relate directly to the square root of the elements of the (diagonal) Hessian. Positive Hessian elements yield real frequencies; negative Hessian elements yield imaginary frequencies. Further discussion and an example are provided in the activity "*Transition States are Molecules Too*".

Geometry optimization does not guarantee that the final structure has a lower energy than any other structure of the same molecular formula. All that it guarantees is a "local minimum", that is, a geometry the energy of which is lower than that of any similar geometry, but which may still not be the lowest energy geometry possible for the molecule. Finding the absolute or "global minimum" requires repeated optimization starting with different initial geometries. Only when all local minima have been located is it possible to say with certainty that the lowest energy geometry has been identified.

In principle, geometry optimization carried out in the absence of symmetry, i.e., in C_1 symmetry, must result in a local minimum. On the other hand, imposition of symmetry may result in a geometry which is not a local minimum. For example, optimization of ammonia constrained to a planar trigonal geometry (D_{3h} symmetry) will result in a structure which corresponds to an energy maximum in the direction of motion toward a puckered trigonal geometry (C_{3v} symmetry). This is the transition state for inversion at nitrogen in ammonia. The most conservative tactic is always to optimize geometry

112

in the absence of symmetry. If this is not done, it is always possible to verify that the structure located indeed corresponds to a local minimum by performing a normal-coordinate analysis on the final (optimized) structure. This analysis should yield all real frequencies.

Transition-State Geometries

Chemists recognize a transition state as the structure that lies at the top of a potential energy surface connecting reactant and product (see the essay "*Potential Energy Surfaces*").

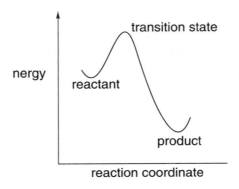

More precisely, a transition state is a point on the potential energy surface for which the gradient is zero (just as it is for an equilibrium geometry; see preceding discussion), but for which the diagonal representation of the Hessian has one and only one negative element, corresponding to the "reaction coordinate" (see diagram above). All the other elements are positive. In other words, a transition state is a structure that is an energy minimum in all dimensions except one, for which it is an energy maximum. Mathematically, such a structure is referred to as a first-order saddle point.

The geometries of transition states on the pathway between reactants and products are not as easily anticipated as the equilibrium geometries of the reactants and products themselves. This is not to say that they do not exhibit systematic properties as do "normal" molecules, but rather that there is not sufficient experience to identify what systematics do exist, and more importantly how to capitalize on structural similarities. It needs to be recognized that transition states cannot even be detected let alone characterized experimentally, at least not directly. While measured activation energies relate to the energies of transition states above reactants, and while activation entropies and activation volumes as well as kinetic isotope effects may be interpreted in terms of transition-state structure, no experiment can actually provide direct information about the detailed geometries and/or other physical properties of transition states. Quite simply, transition states do not exist in terms of a stable population of molecules on which experimental measurements may be made. Experimental activation parameters may act as a guide, although here too it needs to be pointed out that their interpretation is in terms of a theory ("transition state theory"), which assumes that all molecules proceed over a single transition state (the high point along the reaction coordinate) on their way to products. Even then, experiments tell little about what actually transpires in going from reactants to products.

Lack of experience about "what transition states look like" is one reason why their detailed geometries are more difficult to obtain than equilibrium geometries. Other reasons include:

i)   The mathematical problem of finding a transition state is probably (but not necessarily) more difficult than that of finding an equilibrium structure. What is certainly true, is that techniques for locating transition states are much less well developed than procedures for finding equilibrium structures. After all, minimization is an important task in many diverse fields of science and technology, whereas saddle point location has few if any important applications outside of chemistry.

ii)   It is likely that the potential energy surface in the vicinity of a transition state is more "flat" than the surface in the vicinity of a local minimum. (This is entirely reasonable; transition states represent a delicate balance of bond breaking and bond making, whereas overall bonding is maximized in equilibrium structures.) As a consequence, the potential energy surface in the vicinity of a transition state may be less well described in terms of a simple quadratic function (assumed in all common optimization procedures) than the surface in the vicinity of a local minimum.

114

iii) To the extent that transition states incorporate partially (or completely) broken bonds, it might be anticipated that very simple theoretical models will not be able to provide entirely satisfactory descriptions.

In time, all of these problems will be overcome, and finding transition states will be as routine as finding equilibrium geometries is today. Chemists can look forward to the day when reliable tools become available for the elucidation of reaction mechanisms.

The same iterative procedure previously described for optimization of equilibrium geometry applies as well to transition states. However, the number of "steps" required for satisfactory completion is likely to be much larger. This is due to the factors discussed above. What is important to emphasize is that the task of transition state determination may be completely automated and needs no more "human intervention" than that involved in locating equilibrium geometries.

Having found a transition-state geometry, two "tests" need to be performed in order to verify that it actually corresponds to a "proper" transition state, and further that it actually corresponds to the transition state for the process of interest, i.e., it smoothly connects energy minima corresponding to reactant and product:

i) Verify that the Hessian yields one and only one imaginary frequency. This requires that a normal mode analysis be carried out on the proposed transition-state geometry. The imaginary frequency will typically be in the range of 400-2000 cm^{-1}, quite similar to real vibrational frequencies. In the case of flexible rotors, e.g., methyl groups, or "floppy rings", the analysis may yield one or more additional imaginary frequencies with very small (<100 cm^{-1}) values. While these can usually be ignored, make certain to verify what motions these small imaginary frequencies actually correspond to (see below) before doing so. Be wary of structures that yield only very small imaginary frequencies. This suggests a very low energy transition state, which quite likely will not correspond to the particular reaction of interest.

ii) Verify that the normal coordinate corresponding to the imaginary frequency smoothly connects reactants and products. A simple way to do this is to "animate" the normal coordinate corresponding to the imaginary frequency, that is, to "walk along" this coordinate without any additional optimization. This does not require any additional calculations beyond the normal mode analysis already performed. "Incorrect" transition states located by calculation, that is, not linking the expected reactant to the expected product, may indicate new chemistry. Don't discard them so quickly!

Reactions Without Transition States

It may come as a surprise that not all chemical reactions have transition states, and that the rates of some reactions depend only on the speed with which reactants diffuse into one another (so-called diffusion controlled reactions). In fact, reactions without energy barriers are quite common. Two radicals will typically combine without activation, for example, two methyl radicals to form ethane.

$$H_3C^\bullet + {}^\bullet CH_3 \longrightarrow H_3C\text{---}CH_3$$

Radicals will often add to paired-electron species with no (or very small) activation, for example, methyl radical and ethylene forming 1-propyl radical.

$$H_3C^\bullet + H_2C{=}CH_2 \longrightarrow H_3C\text{--}CH_2\text{--}CH_2^\bullet$$

Exothermic ion-molecule reactions may require activation in solution, but probably not in the gas phase. Any "complex" of an ion and a neutral molecule is likely to be lower in energy than the separated species and the entire reaction coordinate for an ion-molecule reaction might lie below the energy of the separated reactants e.g., nucleophilic attack by OH^- on CH_3Cl to give CH_3OH and Cl^-.

Failure to find a transition state, and location instead of what appears to be a stable intermediate or even the final product, does not necessarily mean failure of the theoretical model (nor does it rule this out). It may simply mean that there is no transition state! Unfortunately it is very difficult to tell which is the true situation.

Calculations Using Approximate Geometries

Given that semi-empirical models and even molecular mechanics models often provide geometries that are quite close to those obtained from Hartree-Fock models, it is legitimate to ask whether or not structures from semi-empirical and molecular mechanics techniques may be used for energy and property calculations with Hartree-Fock models. It would be of great help were this the case as geometry optimization is a major "cost" in any modeling investigation. In fact, the answer depends on what "property" is being calculated and the level of confidence required. Experience suggests that, except for "unusual molecules", use of either semi-empirical or molecular mechanics geometries has very little effect on relative energetics. Errors in reaction energies of 4 - 10 kJ/mol, which may arise from the use of "approximate geometries", must be balanced against the large savings in computer time. Other properties such as dipole moments, may show greater sensitivity to choice of structure, and use of appropriate geometries may lead to unacceptable errors.

Semi-empirical techniques are not as successful in reproducing the results of Hartree-Fock models for transition-state geometries as they are for equilibrium geometries. However, the energy surface is typically very "flat" in the vicinity of the transition state, and any errors (in energy) incurred because of the use of approximate transition-state geometries may be manageable. (The magnitudes of errors for other quantities are not predictable.) Molecular mechanics techniques are not applicable to the description of transition states.

"Exact" geometries must be used for frequency (infrared spectra) calculations. The reason for this is that frequencies are related to the first finite term in a Taylor series expansion of the energy (as a function of geometry). This is (assumed to be) the second-derivative term, which will not be true if the first-derivative term (the gradient) is not precisely zero. Frequencies evaluated at non-equilibrium (or non-transition-state) geometries are meaningless.

6

Interpreting Conformational Preferences

Rotation about single bonds is periodic, retracing itself every 360°. Therefore, any function that seeks to describe the energy of internal rotation must also repeat itself every 360°. In fact, it is possible to write a general energy function, $E^{torsion}$, as a combination of simpler functions, V_n, each of which repeats n times in a 360° interval.

$$E^{torsion} (\omega) = V_1(\omega) + V_2(\omega) + V_3(\omega)$$

V_1, V_2, and V_3 are independent functions of the torsion angle ω that repeat every 360°, 180°, and 120°, respectively. These functions are referred to as one-fold, two-fold, and three-fold potentials.

The different n-fold potentials are useful because each can be associated with a particular chemical phenomenon. For example, a one-fold potential describes the different energies of *anti* and *syn* conformers of dimethylperoxide, while a two-fold potential describes the different energies of planar and perpendicular conformers of benzyl cation. Three-fold potentials, which are more familiar to chemists, describe the difference between staggered and eclipsed conformers in molecules like ethane.

one-fold   two-fold   three-fold

While rotation in a symmetric molecule might be described using only one potential or a combination of two potentials, less symmetric

119

molecules require more complex combinations of potentials. This is illustrated by fluoromethylamine.

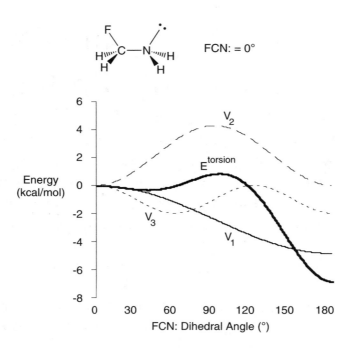

The heavy solid line in the figure describes $E^{torsion}$ for rotation about the CN bond., while the light solid line, the dashed line and the dotted line correspond to the one-fold, two-fold and three-fold components, respectively. There are two distinct minima.

The lower (global minimum) arises when the CF bond and the nitrogen lone pair are *anti*, while the higher and much more shallow minimum is almost, but not precisely, a *gauche* structure (FCN: dihedral angle ~45°). Also, note that one of the two energy maxima (FCN: dihedral angle ~115°) does not exactly correspond to an eclipsed structure.

The unusual behavior of $E^{torsion}$ becomes clearer when it is resolved into its components (in this case, the sum of these components provides a virtually perfect fit of $E^{torsion}$). The one-fold term reflects a clear and very strong preference for the CF bond and the nitrogen lone pair to be *anti* and not *syn*. This preference might be electrostatic since the *anti* structure arranges the dipoles associated with the CF bond and nitrogen lone pair in opposite directions.

FCN: = 180°
dipoles subtract

FCN: = 0°
dipoles add

The three-fold term is also easy to explain. It reflects the preference for staggered over eclipsed structures. This terms contributes much less to $E^{torsion}$ than either the one-fold or two-fold terms, consistent with the low steric demands of the CH_2F and NH_2 groups.

What is most interesting perhaps, and what might not have been anticipated without this type of analysis, is the large contribution made by the two-fold potential. This potential reflects a strong preference for a planar arrangement of FCN:, and can be attributed to a stabilizing interaction between the lone pair orbital on nitrogen and a low-energy unfilled molecular orbital associated with the CF bond. This interaction involves "donation" from the lone pair into the empty orbital, and is permissible only when the FCN: "unit" is planar, but not so when the unit is twisted into a perpendicular geometry, i.e.

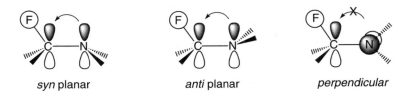

syn planar   anti planar   perpendicular

Most of the peculiar features of $E^{torsion}$ can now be attributed to either V_1 or V_2. V_1 accounts for the *anti* geometry being the global minimum. V_2, however, is responsible for the position of the maximum and the shift in the higher-energy minimum to smaller dihedral angles.

It is important to note that the terms that contribute to $E^{torsion}$ are completely independent of each other, and each may be treated as one part of a larger picture. Thus, the observation that electron donation from the nitrogen lone pair into the empty orbital associated with the CF bond is optimal when the two groups are planar is independent of the observation that the *cis* coplanar structure is destabilized, relative to the *anti* structure, by dipole-dipole interactions.

Such analyses, as provided above for fluoromethylamine, point out that conformational preferences, even for simple systems, may arise from a combination of factors, and that molecular modeling may help to unravel these factors.

7

Atomic and Molecular Orbitals

Chemists have developed a variety of methods for describing electrons in molecules. Lewis structures are the most familiar. These drawings assign pairs of electrons either to single atoms (lone pairs) or pairs of atoms (bonds)*. The quantum mechanical "equivalents" are atomic and molecular orbitals which arise from solution of (approximate) Schrödinger equations for atoms and molecules, respectively. Molecular orbitals are spread throughout the entire molecule, that is, they are "delocalized". Because of this, they are typically more difficult to interpret than Lewis structures.

Orbital Surfaces

Molecular orbitals provide important clues about chemical reactivity, but before we can use this information we first need to understand what molecular orbitals look like. The following figure shows two representations, a "hand" drawing and a Spartan-generated image of an unoccupied molecular orbital of hydrogen molecule, H_2.

unoccupied molecular orbital in hydrogen

Open *"hydrogen empty"*. Note that except for the colors (sign of the orbital) the two sides of the graphic are identical. The junction between "red" and "blue" regions is where the value of the orbital is zero. Close *"hydrogen empty"* when you are finished.

---

* Treatment here is limited to systems in which all electrons are paired. Spartan can also treat systems with one or more unpaired electrons ("radicals", triplet states, etc.).

The hand drawing shows the orbital as two circles and a dashed line. The circles identify regions where the orbital takes on a significant value, either positive (*shaded*) or negative (*unshaded*). The dashed line identifies locations where the orbital's value is exactly zero (a "node"). The drawing is useful, but it is also limited. We only obtain information about the orbital in two dimensions, and we only learn the location of "significant" regions and not how the orbital builds and decays inside and outside of these regions.

The Spartan-generated image depicts the same orbital as a "surface" of constant value. The surface is "accurate" in that it is derived from an authentic (but approximate) calculated solution to the quantum mechanical equations of electron motion. Equally important, the image is three-dimensional. It can be manipulated using Spartan, and can be looked at from a variety of different perspectives. Note that what we call an "orbital surface" actually consists of two distinct surfaces represented by different colors. The two surfaces have the same meaning as the two circles in the orbital drawing. They identify regions where the orbital takes on a significant value, either positive (blue) or negative (red). The orbital node is not shown, but we can guess that it lies midway between the two surfaces (this follows from the fact that the orbital's value can only change from positive to negative by passing through zero).

Atomic Orbitals

Atomic orbitals, "descriptions of atoms", are the fundamental building blocks from which molecular orbitals "descriptions of molecules" are assembled. The familiar atomic orbitals for the hydrogen atom are in fact exact solutions of the Schrödinger equation for this one electron system. They form an infinite collection (a "complete set"), the lowest-energy member representing the "best" location for the electron, and higher-energy members representing alternative locations. Orbitals for "real" many-electron atoms are normally assumed to be similar in form to those of hydrogen atom, the only difference being that, unlike hydrogen, more than the lowest-energy atomic orbital is utilized. In practical quantum chemical calculations, atomic orbitals for many-electron atoms are made up of sums and differences of a finite collection of hydrogen-like orbitals (see the essay "*Theoretical Models*").

It is common practice to divide the full set of atomic orbitals into core and valence orbitals, and further to "ignore" the former. Valence orbitals for an element in the first long row of the *Periodic Table* are 2s, $2p_x$, $2p_y$ and $2p_z$, and for the second long row are 3s, $3p_x$, $3p_y$ and $3p_z$. In the case of first-row elements, a single orbital, 1s, lies underneath (is a core orbital) while in the case of second-row elements, a set of five orbitals, 1s, 2s, $2p_x$, $2p_y$ and $2p_z$, lie underneath.

Open "*fluoride and chloride*". On the top row are the four valence orbitals of fluoride anion and on the bottom row the four valence orbitals of chloride anion. You can select among them by *clicking* (left mouse button) on each in turn. First note that the three 2p orbitals in fluoride are identical except for the direction in which they point. The same is true for the three 3p orbitals in chloride. Next, note that the valence orbitals in chloride are larger than those in fluoride. Atoms further down in the *Periodic Table* are generally larger than analogous atoms further up. Close "*fluoride and chloride*" when you are finished.

Orbitals and Chemical Bonds

Although molecular orbitals and Lewis structures are both used to describe electron distributions in molecules, they are used for different purposes. Lewis structures are used to count the number of bonding and non-bonding electrons around each atom. Molecular orbitals are not useful as counting tools, but orbitals and orbital energies are useful tools for describing chemical bonding and reactivity. This section describes a few common orbital shapes and illustrates their use.

Molecular orbital surfaces can extend over varying numbers of atoms. If the orbital surface (or surfaces) is confined to a single atom or to atoms which are not "close together", the orbital is regarded as non-bonding. If the orbital contains a surface that extends continuously over two neighboring atoms, the orbital is regarded as "bonding" with respect to these atoms. Adding electrons to such an orbital will strengthen the bond between these atoms and cause them to draw closer together, while removing electrons will have the opposite effect. Two different kinds of bonding orbitals are depicted below. The drawing and surface on the left correspond to a σ bond while the drawing and surface on the right correspond to a π bond.

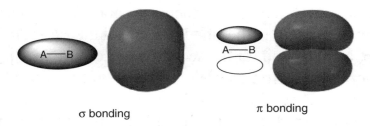

σ bonding   π bonding

Open "***nitrogen bonding***". The image on the left corresponds to the σ bonding orbital of N_2, while that on the right corresponds to one of two equivalent π bonding orbitals. Switch to a transparent or mesh model to see the underlying molecular skeleton. For Windows, *click* on the graphic and select the appropriate entry from the menu which appears at the bottom right of the screen. For Mac, position the cursor over the graphic, hold down either the left or right button and select from the menu which appears alongside. Note that the σ orbitals is drawn in a single color (insofar as NN bonding is concerned) while the π orbital is made up of "red" and "blue" parts. This indicates a "node" or a break in the latter, although not involving the NN bond. Close "***nitrogen bonding***" when you are finished.

It is also possible for an orbital to contain a node that divides the region between two neighboring atoms into separate "atomic" regions. Such an orbital is regarded as "antibonding" with respect to these atoms. Adding electrons to an antibonding orbital weakens the bond and "pushes" the atoms apart, while removing electrons from such an orbital has the opposite effect. The following pictures show drawings and orbital surfaces for two different kinds of antibonding orbitals. As above, the left and right-hand sides correspond to σ and π type arrangements, respectively.

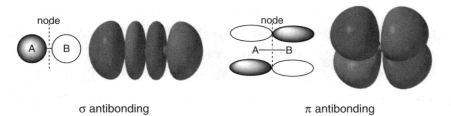

σ antibonding   π antibonding

126

Open "*nitrogen antibonding*". The image on the left corresponds to the σ antibonding (σ*) orbital of N_2 while that on the right corresponds to one of the two equivalent π antibonding (π*) orbitals. Switch to a mesh or transparent surface to see the underlying molecular skeleton. Note that the σ* orbital has a single node (change in color from "red" to "blue") in the middle of the NN bond, while the π* orbital has two nodes (one in the middle of the NN bond and to the other along the bond). Close "*nitrogen antibonding*" when you are finished.

Bonds can be strengthened in two different ways, by adding electrons to bonding orbitals, or by removing electrons from antibonding orbitals. The converse also holds. Bonds can be weakened either by removing electrons from bonding orbitals or by adding electrons to antibonding orbitals. An example of the consequences is provided in the activity "*Removing and Adding Electrons*".

Singlet Methylene

Molecular orbitals in molecules which contain many atoms are typically spread throughout the molecule (they are "delocalized"). Delocalized orbitals have complicated shapes and contain multiple interactions that may be bonding, non-bonding, antibonding, or any mixture of all three. Nevertheless, these shapes can still be broken down into two-atom interactions and analyzed using the principles outlined earlier. This process is illustrated for a triatomic molecule, "singlet" methylene, CH_2. ("Singlet" refers to the fact that the eight electrons in this highly reactive molecule are organized into four pairs, and that each pair of electrons occupies a different molecular orbital. The lowest-energy state of methylene is actually a triplet with three electron pairs and two unpaired electrons.)

The lowest energy molecular orbital of singlet methylene is not very interesting in that it looks like a 1s atomic orbital on carbon. The electrons occupying this orbital restrict their motion to the immediate region of the carbon nucleus and do not significantly affect bonding. Because of this restriction, and because the orbital's energy is very low, this orbital is referred to as a "core" orbital and its electrons are referred to as "core" electrons.

core orbital for methylene

The next orbital is much higher in energy. It consists of a single surface which is delocalized over all three atoms. This means that it is simultaneously (σ) bonding with respect to each CH atom pair.

CH bonding orbital for methylene

The next higher energy orbital is described by two surfaces, a positive (blue) surface that encloses one CH bonding region and a negative (red) surface that encloses the other CH bonding region*. Since each surface encloses a bonding region, this orbital is also (σ) bonding with respect to each CH atom pair. This reinforces the bonding character of the previous orbital. The node that separates the two surfaces passes through the carbon nucleus, but not through either of the CH bonding regions, so it does not affect bonding.

CH bonding orbital for methylene

Thus, the two CH bonds in the Lewis structure for singlet methylene are "replaced" by two "bonding" molecular orbitals.

The highest-occupied molecular orbital (the HOMO) is also described by two orbital surfaces. One surface extends into carbon's "non-bonding" region opposite the two hydrogens. The other surface encompasses the two CH bonding regions. Although it is hard to

---

*   Note that the absolute signs (colors) of a molecular orbital are arbitrary, but that the relative signs (colors) indicate bonding and antibonding character.

track the exact path of the orbital node in this picture, it happens to pass almost exactly through the carbon. This means that this particular orbital possesses only weak CH bonding character (it is H---H bonding). It turns out that the non-bonding character of the orbital is much more important than the bonding character, in that it leads to the fact that singlet methylene is able to behave as an electron-pair donor (a "nucleophile").

HOMO of methylene

The above analysis shows that while the occupied orbitals of singlet methylene are spread over all three atoms, they are comprehensible. The orbitals divide into two groups, a single low-energy "core" orbital and three higher-energy "valence" orbitals. The latter consist of two CH bonding orbitals and a non-bonding orbital on carbon. There is no one-to-one correspondence between these orbitals and the Lewis structure. The bonding orbitals are not associated with particular bonds, and the non-bonding orbital contains bonding interactions as well.

> Open "**methylene bonding**". Four images appear corresponding to the core and three valence orbitals of singlet methylene. Switch to a mesh or transparent surface to see the underlying molecular skeleton. Close "**methylene bonding**" when you are finished.

Singlet methylene also possesses unoccupied molecular orbitals. The unoccupied orbitals have higher (more positive) energies than the occupied orbitals, and these orbitals, because they are unoccupied, do not describe the electron distribution in singlet methylene.* Nevertheless, the shapes of unoccupied orbitals, in particular, the lowest-unoccupied orbital (LUMO), is worth considering because it provides valuable insight into the methylene's chemical reactivity.

---

* There is no direct analogy between unoccupied molecular orbitals and Lewis structures (which attempt to describe electron pair bonds and non-bonding electron pairs).

The LUMO in methylene has non-bonding character, and looks like a 2p atomic orbital on carbon. This suggests that singlet methylene should be able to behave as an electron-pair acceptor (an "electrophile"). Note, however, that were the molecule to accept electrons, these would go into non-bonding orbital; carbon would become more electron-rich, but the CH bonds would not be much affected.

LUMO of methylene

Open "*methylene LUMO*" and switch to a mesh or transparent surface to see the underlying skeleton. Close "*methylene LUMO*" when you are finished.

Frontier Orbitals and Chemical Reactivity

Chemical reactions typically involve movement of electrons from an "electron donor" (base, nucleophile, reducing agent) to an "electron acceptor" (acid, electrophile, oxidizing agent). This electron movement between molecules can also be thought of as electron movement between molecular orbitals, and the properties of these "electron donor" and "electron acceptor" orbitals provide considerable insight into chemical reactivity.

The first step in constructing a molecular orbital picture of a chemical reaction is to decide which orbitals are most likely to serve as the electron-donor and electron-acceptor orbitals. It is obvious that the electron-donor orbital must be drawn from the set of occupied orbitals, and the electron-acceptor orbital must be an unoccupied orbital, but there are many orbitals in each set to choose from.

Orbital energy is usually the deciding factor. The highest-energy occupied orbital (the HOMO) is most commonly the relevant electron-donor orbital and the lowest-energy unoccupied orbital (the LUMO) is most commonly the relevant electron-acceptor orbital. For example, the HOMO and LUMO of singlet methylene (σ and π non-bonding orbitals, respectively) would serve as the donor and acceptor orbitals. The HOMO and LUMO are collectively referred to as the "frontier orbitals", and most chemical reactions involve electron movement between them. In this way, the energy input required for electron movement is kept to a minimum.

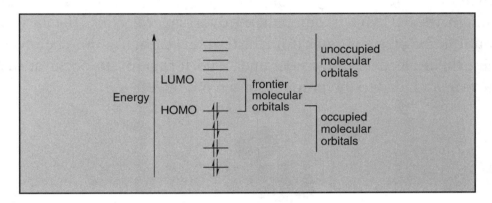

One very important question for chemists concerns chemical selectivity. Where more than one combination of reagents can react, which combination will react first? The answer can often be found by examining frontier orbital energies. Consider a set of electron-donor reagents, where chemical reaction requires electron donation from the donor's HOMO. It is reasonable to expect that the donor with the highest energy HOMO will give up its electrons most easily and be the most reactive. Electron-acceptor reagents should follow the opposite pattern. The reagent with the lowest energy LUMO should be able to accept electrons most easily and be the most reactive. For a mixture of several donor and acceptor reagents, the fastest chemical reaction would be expected to involve the reagent combination that yields the smallest HOMO-LUMO energy gap.

Another kind of selectivity question arises when a molecule has multiple reactive sites. In this case, then the orbital's energy is useless as a guide to "site selectivity", and only the shape of the relevant orbital is important. For example, the enolate of ethyl acetate shown below might react with an electrophile (E^+) at two different sites.

Because the anion acts as an electron donor, we can find clues to its reactivity preferences by examining the shape of its HOMO. Even though the HOMO is delocalized over several sites, the largest contribution clearly comes from the terminal carbon atom. Therefore, we expect electron movement and bond formation to occur at this carbon, and lead to the product shown on the left.

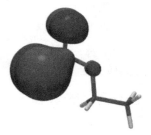

HOMO for enolate of ethyl acetate

> Open "*ethyl acetate enolate HOMO*", and switch to a mesh or transparent surface to see the underlying skeleton. Note that the orbital is most heavily concentrated on carbon, meaning that electrophilic attack will likely occur here. Close "*ethyl acetate enolate HOMO*" when you are finished.

The Woodward-Hoffmann Rules

In certain cases, multiple frontier orbital interactions must be considered. This is particularly true of so-called "cycloaddition reactions", such as the Diels-Alder reaction between 1,3-butadiene and ethylene.

The key feature of this reaction is that the reactants combine in a way that allows two bonds to form simultaneously. This implies two different sites of satisfactory frontier orbital interaction (the two new bonds that form are sufficiently far apart that they do not interact with each other during the reaction). If we focus exclusively on the interactions of the terminal carbons in each molecule, then three different frontier orbital combinations can be imagined.

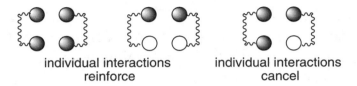

individual interactions reinforce   individual interactions cancel

In all combinations, the "upper" orbital components are the same sign, and their overlap is positive. In the two cases on the left, the lower orbital components also lead to positive overlap. Thus, the two interactions reinforce, and the total frontier orbital interaction is non zero. Electron movement (chemical reaction) can occur. The right-most case is different. Here the lower orbital components lead to negative overlap (the orbitals have opposite signs at the interacting sites), and the total overlap is zero. No electron movement and no chemical reaction can occur in this case.

As it happens, the frontier orbital interactions in the Diels-Alder cycloaddition shown above are like those found in the middle drawing, i.e., the upper and lower interactions reinforce and the reaction proceeds.

> Open "*1,3-butadiene+ethylene*". The image on top is the LUMO of ethylene while that on the bottom is the HOMO of 1,3-butadiene. They are properly "poised" to interact, but you can manipulate them independently. Close "*1,3-butadiene+ethylene*" when you are finished.

Cycloaddition of two ethylene molecules (shown below), however, involves a frontier orbital interaction like that found in the right drawing, so this reaction does not occur.

$$\| \ + \ \| \xrightarrow{\ \ x\ \ } \ \square$$

Open *"ethylene+ethylene"*. The image on top corresponds to the LUMO of one ethylene while that on the bottom corresponds to the HOMO of the other ethylene. You can manipulate them independently or in concert (hold down on the **Ctrl** key while you carry out rotation and translation). Note, that in this case, the two individual "atom-atom" interactions cancel. Close *"ethylene+ethylene"* when you are finished.

The importance of orbital overlap in determining why certain chemical reactions proceed easily while other "similar reactions" do not go at all was first advanced by Woodward and Hoffmann, and collectively their ideas are now known as the Woodward-Hoffmann rules.

Electron Densities:
Sizes and Shapes of Molecules

How "big" is an atom or a molecule? Atoms and molecules require a certain amount of space, but how much? A gas can be compressed into a smaller volume but only so far. Liquids and solids cannot be easily compressed. While the individual atoms or molecules in a gas are widely separated and can be pushed into a much smaller volume, the atoms or molecules in a liquid or a solid are already close together and cannot be "squeezed" much further.

Space-Filling Models

Chemists have long tried to answer the "size" question by using a special set of molecular models known as "space-filling" or "CPK" models. The space-filling model for an atom is simply a sphere of fixed radius. A different radius is used for each element, and this radius has been chosen to reproduce certain experimental observations, such as the compressibility of a gas, or the spacing between atoms in a crystal. Space-filling models for molecules consist of a set of interpenetrating atomic spheres. This reflects the idea that the chemical bonds that hold the molecule together cause the atoms to move very close together. "Interpenetration" can be used as a criterion for chemical bonding. If two atomic spheres in a space-filling model strongly interpenetrate then the atoms must be bonded.

space-filling models for ammonia (left), trimethylamine (center) and 1-azaadamantane (right)

Space-filling models for ammonia, trimethylamine and 1-azaadamantane show how "big" these molecules are, and also show that the nitrogen in ammonia is more "exposed" than the corresponding nitrogen atoms in trimethylamine and 1-azaadamantane.

> Open *"amines space filling"*. Space-filling models for ammonia, trimethylamine and 1-azaadamantane all appear on screen. Carbon atoms are colored dark grey, hydrogen atoms white and nitrogen blue. Note that the models clearly reveal the extent to which the nitrogen is "exposed". Close *"amines space filling"* when you are finished.

Electron Density Surfaces

An alternative technique for portraying molecular size and shape relies on the molecule's own electron cloud. Atoms and molecules are made up of positively-charged nuclei surrounded by a negatively-charged electron cloud, and it is the size and shape of the electron cloud that defines the size and shape of an atom or molecule. The size and shape of an electron cloud is described by the "electron density" (the number of electrons per unit volume). Consider a graph of electron density in the hydrogen atom as a function of distance from the nucleus.

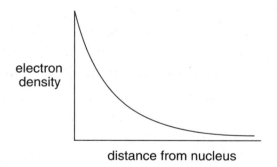

The graph brings up a problem for chemists seeking to define atomic and molecular size, in that the electron cloud lacks a clear boundary. While electron density decays rapidly with distance from the nucleus, nowhere does it fall to zero. Therefore, when atoms and molecules "rub up against each other", their electron clouds overlap and merge to a small extent.

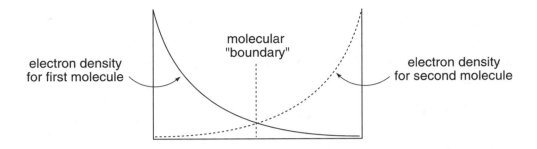

electron density
for first molecule

molecular
"boundary"

electron density
for second molecule

What this means is that it is really not possible to say how big a molecule is. The best that can be done is to pick a value of the electron density, and to connect together all the points which have this value. The criteria for selecting this value is the same as that for selecting atomic radii in space-filling models, the only difference being that only a single "parameter" (the value of the electron density) is involved. The result is an electron density surface which, just like a space-filling model, is intended to depict overall molecular size and shape.

electron density surfaces for ammonia (left), trimethylamine (center)
and 1-azaadamantane (right)

Open *"amines electron density"*. Electron density surfaces for ammonia, trimethylamine and 1-azaadamantane all appear on screen. Switch to a mesh or transparent surface in order to see the underlying skeletal model. On Windows, *click* on one of the surfaces, and select **Mesh** or **Transparent** from the menu which appears at the bottom right of the screen. On the Mac, position the cursor over the graphic, hold down either the left or right button and select from the menu which appears alongside. With "mesh" selected, change the model to **Space Filling** (**Model** menu). This allows you to see how similar the electron density representation is to that offered by a simple space-filling model. Close *"amines electron density"* when you are finished.

Both space-filling and electron density models yield similar molecular volumes, and both show differences in overall size among molecules. Because the electron density surfaces provide no discernible boundaries between atoms, the surfaces may appear to be less informative than space-filling models in helping to decide to what extent a particular atom is "exposed". This "weakness" raises an important point, however. Electrons are associated with a molecule as a whole and not with individual atoms. (As a consequence, it is actually not possible to define the charge on an atom; see the activity "***Charges on Atoms in Molecules***".) The space-filling representation of a molecule with its discernible atoms does not reflect reality.

Bond Density Surfaces

Another useful surface, termed the "bond density surface", is one that marks points corresponding to a much higher value of the electron density[*]. Since points of high electron density are located much closer to the atomic nuclei, bond density surfaces enclose relatively small volumes, and do not give a correct impression of molecular size. On the other hand, bond density surfaces identify regions corresponding to bonding electron density, and the volume of these surfaces may be roughly correlated with the number of electrons that participate in bonding. In this sense, bond density surfaces are analogous to conventional line drawings and skeletal models.

The bond density surface for hex-5-ene-1-yne clearly shows which atoms are connected, although it does not clearly distinguish single, double and triple carbon-carbon bonds.

bond density surface for hex-5-ene-1-yne

---

[*] An even higher value of the electron density leads to a surface in which only "spheres" of electrons around the non-hydrogen atoms are portrayed. This serves to locate the positions of these atoms and is the basis of the X-ray diffraction experiment.

Open *"hex-5-ene-1-yne bond density"*, and switch to a mesh or transparent surface to see the connection between the chemical bonds in a conventional model and the electron density. Close *"hex-5-ene-1-yne bond density"* when you are finished.

The usefulness of the bond density surface is more apparent in the following model of diborane. The surface clearly shows that there is relatively little electron density between the two borons. Apparently there is no boron-boron bond in this molecule. This is information extracted from the bond density surface model, and has been obtained without reference to any preconceived ideas about the bonding in diborane. (See the activity *"Too Few Electrons"*.)

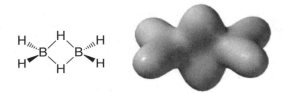

bond density surface for diborane

Open *"diborane bond density"*, and switch to a mesh or transparent surface to see how few electrons are actually collected in the region between the two borons. Close *"diborane bond density"* when you are finished.

Bond density surfaces can also be informative in describing changes in bonding in moving from reactants to products through a transition state in a chemical reaction. For example, heating ethyl formate causes the molecule to fragment into two new molecules, formic acid and ethylene. A line drawing can show which bonds are affected by the overall reaction, but it cannot tell us if these changes occur all at once, sequentially, or in some other fashion.

On the other hand, the bond density surface is able to provide quantitative information.

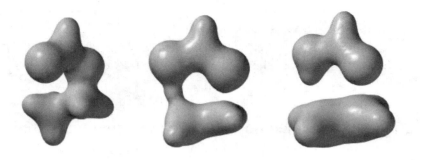

bond density surfaces for the reactant, ethyl formate (left), pyrolysis transition state (center) and for the products, formic acid and ethylene (right)

Compare the bond density surface in the pyrolysis transition state to those of the reactant and the products. The CO single bond of the reactant is clearly broken in the transition state. Also, the migrating hydrogen seems more tightly bound to oxygen (as in the product) than to carbon (as in the reactant). It can be concluded that the transition state more closely resembles the products than the reactants, and this provides an example of what chemists call a "late" or "product-like" transition state.

To see the smooth change in electron density throughout the course of the ethyl formate pyrolysis reaction, open *"pyrolysis bond density"*. *Click* on ▶ at the bottom left of the screen to animate the graphic (*click* on ▮▮ to stop the animation). Switch to a mesh or transparent surface to follow the change in bonding. Close *"pyrolysis bond density"* when you are finished.

Additional information about the ethyl formate pyrolysis reaction is found in the activity *"What Do Transition States Look Like?"*, and a closely related example is provided in the tutorial *"Ene Reaction"*.

9

Electrostatic Potential Maps: Charge Distributions

The charge distribution in a molecule can provide critical insight into its physical and chemical properties. For example, molecules that are charged, or highly polar, tend to be water-soluble, and polar molecules may "stick together" in specific geometries, such as the "double helix" in DNA. Chemical reactions are also associated with charged sites, and the most highly-charged molecule, or the most highly-charged site in a molecule, is often the most reactive. The "sign" of the charge is also important. Positively-charged sites in a molecule invite attack by bases and nucleophiles, while negatively-charged sites are usually targeted by acids and electrophiles.

One way to describe a molecule's charge distribution is to give a numerical "atomic charge" for each atom. A particularly simple and familiar recipe yields so-called "formal charges" directly from Lewis structures. (For more detail, see the activity *Charges on Atoms in Molecules*".) Unfortunately, formal charges are arbitrary. In fact, all methods for assigning charge are arbitrary and necessarily bias the calculated charges in one way or another. This includes methods based on quantum mechanics.

An attractive alternative for describing molecular charge distributions makes use of a quantity termed the "electrostatic potential". This is the energy of interaction of a point positive charge with the nuclei and electrons of a molecule. The value of the electrostatic potential depends on the location of the point positive charge. If the point charge is placed in a region of excess positive charge (an electron-poor region), the point charge-molecule interaction is repulsive and the electrostatic potential will be positive. Conversely, if the point charge is placed in a region of excess negative charge (an electron-rich

141

region), the interaction is attractive and the electrostatic potential will be negative. Thus, by moving the point charge around the molecule, the molecular charge distribution can be surveyed.

Electrostatic potentials can be depicted in various ways. For example, it is possible to make an electrostatic potential "surface" by finding all of the points in space where the electrostatic potential matches some particular value. A much more useful way to show molecular charge distribution is to construct an electrostatic potential "map". This is done first by constructing an electron density surface corresponding to a space-filling model (see the essay *"Electron Densities: Sizes and Shapes of Molecules"*). The electrostatic potential is then "mapped" onto this surface using different colors to represent the different values of the electrostatic potential. Mapping requires an arbitrary choice for a color scale. Spartan uses the "rainbow". Red, the low energy end of the spectrum, depicts regions of most negative (least positive) electrostatic potential, and blue depicts the regions of most positive (least negative) electrostatic potential. Intermediate colors represent intermediate values of the electrostatic potential, so that potential increases in the order: red < orange < yellow < green < blue.

The connection between a molecule's electron density surface, its electrostatic potential surface, and an electrostatic potential map is illustrated below for benzene. The electron density surface defines molecular shape and size. It performs the same function as a conventional space-filling model by indicating how close two benzenes can get in a liquid or in a crystal.

space-filling model for benzene

electron density surface for benzene

An electrostatic potential surface corresponding to points where the potential is negative shows two different surfaces, one above the face of the ring and the other below. Since the molecule's π electrons lie closest to these surfaces, we conclude that these electrons are responsible for the attraction of a point positive charge (or an electrophile) to the molecule. An electrostatic potential surface corresponding to points where the potential is positive has a completely different shape. It is disk-shaped and wrapped fairly tightly around the nuclei. The shape and location of this surface indicates that a point positive charge is repelled by this region, or that a point negative charge (a nucleophile) would be attracted here.

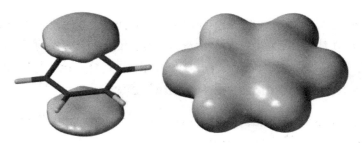

negative (left) and positive (right) electrostatic potential surfaces for benzene

Next, combine the electron density and electrostatic potential surfaces to produce a so-called electrostatic potential map. The map for benzene conveys both the molecule's size and shape as well as its charge distribution in a compact and easily interpretable manner. The size and shape of the map are, of course, identical to that of the electron density surface, and indicate what part of the molecule is easily accessible to other molecules (the "outside world"). The colors reveal the overall charge distribution. The faces of the ring, the π system, are "red" (electron rich), while the plane of the molecule and especially the hydrogens are "blue" (electron poor).

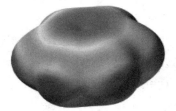

electrostatic potential map for benzene

Open "**benzene electrostatic potential map**". Manipulate the image to convince yourself that the "red" regions are on the π faces and the "blue" regions are around the edges. Close "**benzene electrostatic potential map**" when you are finished.

A comparison of electrostatic potential maps for benzene and pyridine is provided in the tutorial "**Electrophilic Reactivity of Benzene and Pyridine**". This clearly points out the value of the models in revealing differences in chemical properties and reactivity.

Electrostatic potential maps have now made their way into mainstream general and (especially) organic chemistry textbooks as a means of displaying charge distributions in molecules. In addition, they have found application as a "natural" step beyond "steric models" for interpreting and predicting the way in which molecules fit together. A good example of this follows from the electrostatic potential map for benzene, which recall is "negative" on the π faces and "positive" around the periphery. The benzene dimer would, therefore, be expected to exhibit a "perpendicular" geometry, to best accomodate

144

Coulombic interactions, instead of a parallel arrangement which might be expected to be favored on steric grounds.

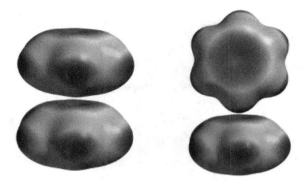

electrostatic potential maps for parallel (left) and perpendicular (right) benzene dimers

Open "***benzene dimer electrostatic potential map***". Note that the parallel arrangement forces the negative region of one benzene onto the negative region of the other, while the perpendicular structure associates the negative region of one benzene with a positive region of the other. Close "***benzene dimer electrostatic potential map***" when you are finished.

Of greater interest is the structure of benzene in solid state. "Intuition" suggests a parallel stack. Afterall, benzene is "flat" and flat things (plates, pancakes, hamburgers) make stacks. However, Coulombs law favors a perpendicular arrangement.

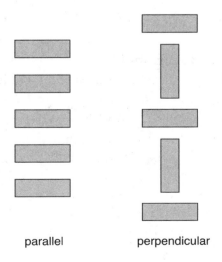

parallel   perpendicular

The experimental X-ray crystal structure shows a perpendicular arrangement, but in three dimensions. There are two "lessons" here. Intermolecular interactions go beyond steric interactions and sometimes our simple "one-dimensional" view of the world will lead us astray.

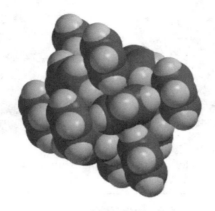

X-ray crystal structure of benzene

Open "*benzene crystal*". Manipulate in order to see the packing of benzene molecules. Close "*benzene crystal*" when you are finished.

Electrostatic potential maps may also be used to describe in great detail the "workings" of chemical reactions. For example, a map may be used to show the transfer of negative charge during the S_n2 reaction of cyanide with methyl iodide.

$$:N{\equiv}C:^- \quad CH_3{-}I \longrightarrow :N{\equiv}C{-}CH_3 + I^-$$

Open "*Sn2 cyanide+methyl iodide*". One "frame" of a sequence of electrostatic potential maps for the S_n2 reaction will appear. Animate by *clicking* on ▶ at the bottom left of the screen (stop the animation by *clicking* on ❚❚). Note that the negative charge (red color) flows smoothly from cyanide to iodide during the reaction. Note also, that cyanide (as the reactant) is "more red" than iodide (as the product). Iodide is better able to carry negative charge, i.e., it is the better leaving group. Switch to mesh or transparent map to "see" the making and breaking of "bonds". Close "*Sn2 cyanide+methyl iodide*" when you are finished.

10

Local Ionization Potential Maps and LUMO Maps: Electrophilic and Nucleophilic Reactivities

The Hammond Postulate states that the transition state in a ***one-step*** reaction will more closely resemble the side of the reaction that is higher in energy. Thus, the transition state of an *endothermic* reaction will more closely resemble the products. Conversely, the transition state of an *exothermic* reaction will resemble the reactants. One way to rationalize the Hammond postulate is to suggest that similarity in energy implies similarity in structure. That is, the transition state will resemble whichever reactants or products to which it is closer in energy. As seen in the reaction coordinate diagrams below this is the product in an *endothermic* reaction and the reactants in an *exothermic* reaction.

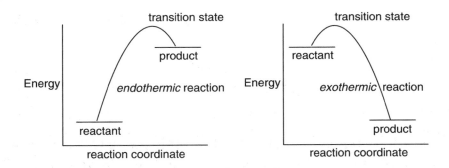

The Hammond Postulate provides a conceptual basis both for the Woodward-Hoffmann rules (see the essay "***Atomic and Molecular Orbitals***") and for the use of graphical models. Both consider the properties of reactants as an alternative to direct calculations of transition states and reaction pathways as a way to assess chemical reactivity and selectivity. In this context, two models stand out as being particularly useful: the local ionization potential map for electrophilic reactions and the LUMO map for nucleophilic reactions.

Local Ionization Potential Maps and Electrophilic Reactivity

The local ionization potential provides a measure of the relative ease of electron removal ("ionization") at any location around a molecule. For example, a surface of "low" local ionization potential for sulfur tetrafluoride demarks the areas which are most easily ionized, is clearly recognizable as a lone pair on sulfur.

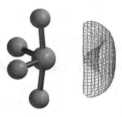

local ionization potential for sulfur tetrafluoride

The local ionization potential by itself is not generally a useful model. However, a map of the local ionization potential onto an electron density surface is a useful model, in that it reveals those regions from which electrons are most easily ionized.

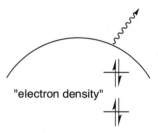

"electron density"

Local ionization potential maps may be employed to reveal sites which are susceptible to electrophilic attack. For example, they show both the positional selectivity in electrophilic aromatic substitution (NH_2 directs *ortho/para*, and NO_2 directs *meta*), and the fact that π-donor groups (NH_2) activate benzene while electron-withdrawing groups (NO_2) deactivate benzene.

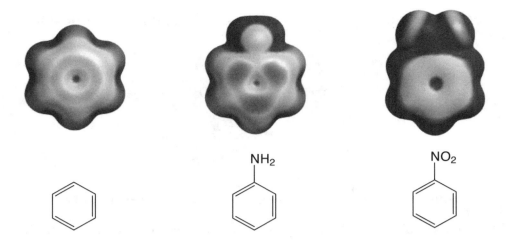

local ionization potential maps for benzene (left), aniline (center) and nitrobenzene (right)

Open "*benzene, aniline, nitrobenzene local ionization potential maps*". Here, the color red corresponds to regions of lowest ionization potential (most accessible to electrophiles). Note, that the π system in aniline is more accessible than the π system in benzene (the standard) and that the *ortho* and *para* positions are more accessible than *meta* positions. Note also, that the π system in nitrobenzene is less accesible than the π system in benzene and that here the *meta* positions are more accessible than the *ortho* and *para* positions, in accord with observation.

LUMO Maps and Nucleophilic Reactivity

As elaborated in an earlier essay ("*Atomic and Molecular Orbitals*"), the energies and shapes of the so-called frontier molecular orbitals often fortell the "chemistry" which a particular molecule might undergo. Maps of "key" molecular orbitals may also lead to informative models. The most common of these is the so-called "LUMO map", in which the (absolute value) of the lowest-unoccupied molecular orbital (the LUMO) is mapped onto an electron density surface. This fortells where an electron pair (a nucleophile) might attack.

LUMO ⎯⎯

electron pair

"electron density"

A good example is provided by the LUMO map for cyclohexenone.

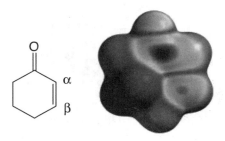

LUMO map for cyclohexenone showing positions for nucleophilic attack in blue

The LUMO shows which regions of a molecule are most electron deficient, and hence most subject to nucleophilic attack. In this case, one such region is over the carbonyl carbon, consistent with the observation that carbonyl compounds undergo nucleophilic addition at the carbonyl carbon. Another region is over the β carbon, again consistent with the known chemistry of α,β-unsaturated carbonyl compounds, in this case conjugate or Michael addition.

The buildup of positive charge on the β carbon leading to possibility of Michael addition could have been anticipated from resonance arguments, although the LUMO map, like an experiment, has the advantage of "showing" the result ("you don't have to ask").

Open *"cyclohexenone LUMO map"* and *click* on the resulting surface. Switch to a mesh or transparent surface in order to see the underlying skeletal model. On Windows, *click* on the graphic and select **Mesh** or **Transparent** from the menu which appears at the bottom right of the screen. On the Mac, position the cursor over the graphic, hold down on either the left or right button and select from the menu which appears alongside. Orient the molecule such that the two "blue regions" are positioned over the appropriate carbons and then switch back to a solid surface.

Section D

"Hands-On" Activities

This section comprises a selection of "hands-on" activities for individual or group study. These activities may be divided into five categories: general chemistry (1-13), organic chemistry (14-32), spectroscopy (33-35), inorganic/organometallic chemistry (36-39) and biochemistry (40,41), although many if not most of the activities carry over into two or more categories. Each activity is intended to illustrate how molecular modeling can contribute to a student's understanding of a particular topic. Wherever possible, the activities have been kept "open ended" to allow them to serve as "templates" for countless other activities which could be devised.

The activities are brief and "focused", and most can be completed in twenty minutes to one hour and require only a few minutes of computer time. Where appropriate, they contain "hints" on using Spartan, but a working knowledge of the basic operation of the program is assumed. Students should complete the tutorials provided in **Section B** before attempting this material.

Spartan files associated with the activities are grouped in the "activities" directory on the CD-ROM. File names relate to the names of the molecules used in the activities. Only the entries for activities 19, 20, 27 and 40 are required for completion of the activity, and the remainder have been provided only to show the "proper outcome".

1

How Big are Atoms and Molecules?

The "sizes" of atoms and molecules depend not on the nuclei but rather on the distribution of electrons. Molecules with more electrons will tend to be larger (require more space) than comparable molecules with fewer electrons. Molecules in which electrons are "loosely bound" will tend to be larger than molecules with the same number of "more tightly bound" electrons.

Electron distribution, or electron density as it is commonly referred to, is obtained as part of a quantum chemical calculation. The electron density is a "molecular property" which can actually be measured experimentally (using X-ray diffraction). However, X-ray diffraction is almost exclusively used only to locate the regions in a molecule of highest electron density, which in turn locates the nuclei. As detailed in the essay *Electron Densities: Sizes and Shapes of Molecules*, a surface of electron density with a value of 0.002 electrons/au^3 provides a measure of overall molecular size and in most cases closely resembles a conventional space-filling (CPK) model.

In this activity, you will explore relationships between number of electrons and atomic/molecular size and between the "looseness" of the electron distribution and size.

1. "Build" lithium cation, atom and anion, and put all into a single document. Specify calculation of a single-point energy using the HF/6-31G* model.

   Inside the inorganic model kit, select the appropriate element from the *Periodic Table* and one coordinate from the available hybrids, and *click* on screen. Then select **Delete** from the **Build** menu and *click* on the free valence. To group the atoms, select **New Molecule**

> instead of **New** after you have built the first. Set **Total Charge** inside the **Calculations** dialog to **Cation** (+1) for lithium cation and to **Anion** (-1) for lithium anion, and **Multiplicity** to **Doublet** for lithium atom. Also, remove the checkmark beside **Global Calculations** (**Apply Globally** for the Mac) at the bottom of the dialog.

Finally, specify calculation of a density surface for all three species. When the calculations have completed, place all three density surfaces side-by-side on screen.

> Bring up the spreadsheet (**Spreadsheet** from the **Display** menu). For Windows, *check* the box to the right of "Label" (first column) for all three atoms. For Mac, *click* on ▣ at the bottom left of the screen and *check* the box to the left of the atom name (in the spreadsheet) for all three atoms. Also, select (*uncheck*) **Coupled** from the **Model** menu (to turn it "off"), so that the three atoms can be moved independently.

Compare the three surfaces. Which is smallest? Which is largest? How does "size" relate to the number of electrons? Which surface most closely resembles a conventional space-filling model? What does this tell you about the kinds of molecules which were used to establish the space-filling radius of lithium?

2. Build methyl anion, CH_3^-, ammonia, NH_3, and hydronium cation, H_3O^+, and put all three molecules into a single document.

> To build hydronium cation, start from ammonia, move to the inorganic model kit, select oxygen from the *Periodic Table* and *double click* on nitrogen.

Specify calculation of equilibrium geometry using the HF/6-31G* model. Adjust the total charge for methyl anion and hydronium cation. Finally, request calculation of a density surface for all three molecules. When the calculations have completed, place all three density surfaces side-by-side on screen. Which is smallest? Which is largest? How does size relate to the total number of electrons? How does it relate to the total nuclear charge?

2

The Changing Nature
of Hydrogen

What is the charge on hydrogen in a molecule? We tend to think of hydrogen as "neutral" or nearly so in hydrocarbons, while we give it a partial positive charge in a molecule like hydrogen fluoride and a partial negative charge in a molecule like sodium hydride. This is conveyed in our chemical nomenclature "sodium *hydride*", meaning like H⁻.

Is hydrogen unique among the elements in that it is able (and willing) to change its "personality" to reflect its chemical environment? Are the changes as large as the nomenclature suggests "protic to hydridic" or are they much more subtle? Can we detect and "measure" any changes with the tools available to us? These are questions which you will explore in this activity.

1. One after the other, build hydrogen molecule and the one-heavy-atom hydrides of first-row elements: LiH, BeH_2 (linear), BH_3 (trigonal planar), CH_4 (tetrahedral), NH_3 (trigonal pyramidal), H_2O (bent) and HF. Put them into a single document, and obtain equilibrium geometries using the HF/6-31G* model.

> You need to use the inorganic model kit to construct LiH, BeH_2 and BH_3.

Is there a correlation between the calculated charges on hydrogen in the first-row hydrides and the difference in electronegativity between hydrogen and the first-row element? Use the electronegativities tabulated below.

H	2.2	B	2.0	O	3.4
Li	1.0	C	2.6	F	4.0
Be	1.6	N	3.0		

2. Request an electron density surface for each of the molecules. This reflects the overall "size" of the molecule as well as the size of hydrogen inside the molecule. Display the surfaces side-by-side on screen to allow visual comparison. Do you see a trend in the size of hydrogen as you move from lithium hydride to hydrogen fluoride? If so, for which molecule is hydrogen the smallest? For which is it the largest? Are your results consistent with the previous characterization of hydrogen as taking on "protic" or "hydridic" identity depending on the environment? Elaborate.

While you cannot calculate the electron density for proton (there are no electrons), you can for the hydride anion, H⁻. "Build" H⁻, calculate its energy using the HF/6-31G* model as well as surface of electron density. How does the size of hydride anion compare with the "largest hydrogen" in your compounds? What does this say regarding the extent to which the bond in this compound has dissociated into ions?

3. Request an electrostatic potential map for each of the molecules. This reflects the distribution of charge, the color red meaning excess negative charge and the color blue meaning excess positive charge. Display the maps side-by-side on screen to allow visual comparison. "Measure" the maximum (or minimum) value of the electrostatic potential at hydrogen in each of the compounds.

> Bring up the **Surface Properties** dialog by selecting **Properties** from the **Display** menu and *clicking* on a surface. Remove the checkmark from **Global Surfaces** (**Apply Globally** on the Mac) and *click* on the **Reset** button. The property range given in the dialog will now apply to the selected molecule. Repeat for all molecules.

Is there a correlation between maximum (minimum) potential at hydrogen and difference in electronegativity between the two atoms which make up the bond?

3

Too Few Electrons

At first glance, the structure of diborane, B_2H_6, would seem unusual. Why shouldn't the molecule assume the same geometry as ethane, C_2H_6, which after all has the same number of heavy atoms and the same number of hydrogens?

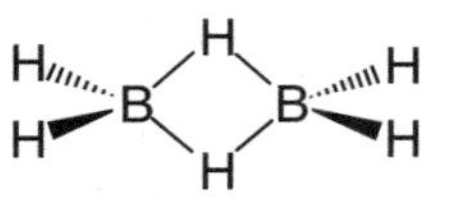

diborane 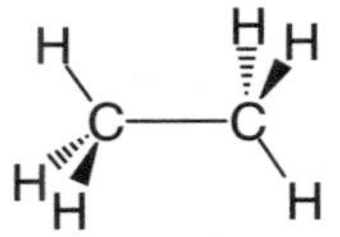   ethane

The important difference between the two molecules is that diborane has two fewer electrons than ethane and is not able to make the same number of bonds. In fact, it is ethylene which shares the same number of electrons to which diborane is structurally related.

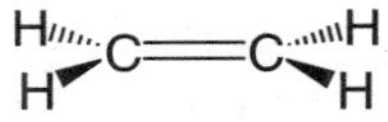

ethylene

This activity explores isoelectronic (equal electron) relationships, and shows how they can be employed to anticipate the structures of molecules which have too few electrons to make the "required" bonds. We will begin with the relationship between ethylene and diborane (both of which structures are well known) and then try to predict the geometry of the (unknown) borane analogue of acetylene.

1. Build ethylene and diborane, and put them into the same document.

Construct diborane using the inorganic model kit. Select boron from the *Periodic Table* and the five coordinate trigonal-bipyramid structure from the list of atomic hybrids. Notice that an *icon* of fragment is displayed at the top of the model kit. Identify the *axial* and *equatorial* positions in this fragment,

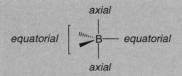

axial

equatorial B *equatorial*

axial

and *click* on one of the *equatorial* positions. In response a yellow circle will move to this position. Next *click* anywhere on screen, and orient the fragment such that you can clearly identify *axial* and equatorial positions. *Click* on an *equatorial* position to make a two-boron fragment.

B—B

Next select hydrogen from the *Periodic Table* and two coordinate linear from the list of hybrids. *Click* on the upper *axial* free valence on one boron and then on the lower *axial* free valence on the other boron. You are left with the structure.

H
B—B
H

Select **Make Bond** from the **Build** menu, and *click* on the free valence of the upper hydrogen and then on the *axial* free valence on the adjacent boron. Repeat for the lower hydrogen.

H
B—B
H

Select **Minimize** from the **Build** menu to produce a "reasonable" geometry for diborane.

2. Obtain equilibrium geometries for ethylene and diborane using the HF/3-21G model. Also request that all six valence molecular orbitals for the two molecules be drawn. After the calculations have completed, sketch the two sets of orbitals. As best you can, associate each valence orbital in ethylene with its counterpart in diborane. Focus on similarities in the structure of the orbitals and not on their "position" in the lists of orbitals. To what orbital in

diborane does the π orbital in ethylene (the HOMO) best relate? How would you describe this orbital in diborane? Is it BB bonding, BH bonding or both?

3. Build acetylene, C_2H_2, and optimize its geometry using the HF/3-21G model. Request all valence molecular orbitals be drawn. On the basis of the orbital shapes (for acetylene) and on your experience with diborane, suggest at least two "plausible" geometries for the hypothetical molecule B_2H_4. Build each, (use techniques similar to those you used to build diborane) calculate its equilibrium geometry using the HF/3-21G model and request all valence molecular orbitals. Also request calculation of the infrared spectrum.

Of the possible geometries you suggested, which is favored energetically? Is this structure actually a minimum on the energy surface? To tell, examine the infrared spectrum for the existence of imaginary frequencies (see the essay *"Potential Energy Surfaces"*). Are any or all of your other selections also energy minima? Sketch the molecular orbitals of your preferred B_2H_4 geometry alongside those of acetylene and, as best you can, pair them up. Pay particular attention to the orbitals relating to the two π bonds in acetylene.

4

Too Many Electrons

What happens to electron pairs which are "left over" after all bonds have been formed? Is each electron pair primarily associated with a single atom and directed tetrahedrally from this atom as implied by Lewis structures, or is it "spread out"? Are these extra pairs ("lone pairs") just "hangers on", or do they contribute to (or even dominate) the "chemistry".

In this activity you will examine molecules with "too many electrons" (the exact opposite you did in the previous activity "*Too Few Electrons*"). You will use electrostatic potential surfaces to probe where these extra (non-bonded) electrons reside and try to associate what you find with conventional (Lewis) structures.

1. Build ammonia, water and hydrogen fluoride, and put them in the same document. Request equilibrium geometries using the HF/6-31G* model. Before you submit for calculation, also request calculation of electrostatic potential surfaces for the three molecules. The requested isosurfaces correspond to an electrostatic potential isovalue of -80 kJ/mol. These will demark the highly electron-rich regions for the three molecules.

    After the calculations have completed, display all three potential surfaces side-by-side on screen.

> Bring up the spreadsheet. For Windows, *check* the box to the right of the first ("Label") column for each molecule. For Mac, *click* on ⊙ at the bottom left of the screen and *check* the box to the left of the molecule name (in the spreadsheet) for each molecule. You also need to select (*uncheck*) **Coupled** from the **Model** menu in order to "uncouple" the motions of the three molecules so that you can move them independently.

Describe the three surfaces and relate them to the conventional Lewis structures.

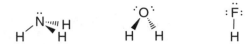

In this context, rationalize the unusual shape of the potential for water. Also, elaborate and rationalize the difference in the shapes of the ammonia and hydrogen fluoride potentials (which at first glance appear to be nearly identical).

2. Revisit the isoelectronic series, methyl anion, ammonia and hydronium cation (see the activity *"How Big are Atoms and Molecules?"*).

> If you have performed this earlier activity, you don't need to build and optimize these molecules a second time, but only compute electrostatic potential surfaces.

Display the three potential surfaces side-by-side on screen. For which does the potential extend furthest away from the nuclei? For which is the extension the least? Does this correlate with the sizes of the electron densities (see previous activity)? What do the relative sizes (extensions) of the potential tell you about the relative "likelihood" of these three molecules to act as electron sources ("nucleophiles")?

3. Hydrazine, N_2H_4, is a very "high-energy" molecule and is used as a "rocket fuel". Like ethane, it should prefer a staggered arrangement of hydrogens (see the essay *"Potential Energy Surfaces"*). The difference is that two of the CH bonds in ethane have been replaced by electron pairs in hydrazine. A consequence of this is that there are two staggered arrangements, one with the electron pairs *anti* and the other with the electron pairs *gauche*.

anti hydrazine   *gauche* hydrazine

162

On the basis of the same arguments made in VSEPR theory ("electron pairs take up more space than bonds") you might expect that *anti* hydrazine would be the preferred structure. Here, you will use quantum chemical calculations to test your "intuition".

Build both *anti* and *gauche* hydrazine and put into the same document. Request equilibrium geometries using the HF/6-31G* model. Also request calculation of electrostatic potential surfaces.

> With hydrazine on screen (in the builder), you can rotate about the NN bond by first *clicking* on it (a red arrow will ring the bond; if the ring disappears, *click* again), and then moving the mouse "up and down" with both the **Alt** key (**space bar** for the Mac) and left button depressed. Rotate into the proper (*anti* or *gauche*) structure and then select **Minimize** from the **Build** menu to give a better geometry. The *anti* structure will have C_{2h} symmetry and the *gauche* structure will have C_2 symmetry.

After the calculations have completed, examine the energies for the two molecules. Which is favored? By how much? Is this result in accord with what you would expect from VSEPR theory?

> The energy will be given in atomic units (au). To convert to kJ/mol, multiply by 2625. The HOMO energy (in eV) which will be needed below is also available in this dialog. To convert from eV (electron volts) to kJ/mol, multiply by 96.49.

Examine the two potential surfaces side-by-side on screen. Is there a noticeable difference in the extent to which the two electron pairs interact ("delocalize") between the two conformers? If so, is the "more delocalized" conformer lower or higher in energy than the "less delocalized" conformer?

You can rationalize your result by recognizing that when electron pairs interact they form combinations, one of which is stabilized (relative to the original electron pairs) and one of which is destabilized. Destabilization is greater than stabilization, meaning that overall interaction of two electron pairs is unfavorable energetically.

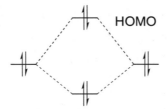

destabilized combination

HOMO

stabilized combination

In terms of molecular orbital theory, the higher-energy (destabilized) combination of electron pairs is the HOMO. You can judge the extent to which the electron pairs interact (and the overall destabilization) by measuring the energy of the HOMO. Which hydrazine conformer has the higher HOMO energy? Is this the higher-energy conformer? If so, is the difference in HOMO energies similar to the energy difference between conformers?

5

Removing and Adding Electrons

Molecular orbital theory leads to a description of a molecule in which electrons are assigned (in pairs) to functions called molecular orbitals, which in turn are made up of combinations of atom-centered functions called atomic orbitals (see the essay "*Atomic and Molecular Orbitals*"). Except where "core" electrons are involved, molecular orbitals are typically delocalized throughout the molecule and show distinct bonding or antibonding character. Loss of an electron from a specific molecular orbital (from excitation by light or by ionization) would, therefore, be expected to lead to distinct changes in bonding and changes in molecular geometry.

Not all molecular orbitals are occupied. This is because there are more than enough atomic orbitals to make the number of molecular orbitals needed to hold all the electrons. "Left-over combinations" or unoccupied molecular orbitals are also delocalized and also show distinct bonding or antibonding character. Normally, this is of no consequence. However, were these orbitals to become occupied (from excitation or from capture of an electron), then changes in molecular geometry would also be expected.

In this activity, you will examine the highest-occupied molecular orbital (the HOMO) and the lowest-unoccupied molecular orbital (the LUMO) for a number of simple molecules and try to "guess" what changes in geometry would occur from electron removal from the former and electron addition to the latter. You will then obtain geometries for the radical cation (electron removal) and radical anion (electron addition) for each of the molecules to see how successful your guesses were. Finally, you will attempt to rationalize the observed geometry of the first excited state of a simple molecule.

1. Build ethylene, $H_2C=CH_2$, formaldimine, $H_2C=NH$, and formaldehyde, $H_2C=O$, and put all in a single document. Obtain equilibrium geometries using the HF/ 6-31G* model and following this request HOMO and LUMO surfaces.

2. Examine the HOMO for each of the three molecules, with particular focus on bonding or antibonding character among the atoms involved. "Guess" what would happen to the geometry around carbon (remain planar vs. pyramidalize), to the C=X bond length and (for formaldimine) to the C=NH bond angle were an electron to be removed from this orbital. Choose from the possibilities listed below.

		remove electron from HOMO	add electron to LUMO
$H_2C=CH_2$	geometry around carbon	remain planar pyramidalize	remain planar pyramidalize
	C=C	lengthen shorten remain the same	lengthen shorten remain the same
$H_2C=NH$	geometry around carbon	remain planar pyramidalize	remain planar pyramidalize
	C=N	lengthen shorten remain the same	lengthen shorten remain the same
	<CNH	increase decrease remain the same	increase decrease remain the same
$H_2C=O$	geometry around carbon	remain planar pyramidalize	remain planar pyramidalize
	C=O	lengthen shorten remain the same	lengthen shorten remain the same

On the basis of your "guesses", build radical cations for ethylene, formaldimine and formaldehyde, and then obtain their actual equilibrium geometries using the HF/6-31G* model.

Are the calculated structures in line with what you expect? Elaborate.

3. Examine the LUMO for each of the three molecules. Guess what would happen to the geometry around carbon, C=X bond length and (for formaldimine) the C=NH bond angle were an electron to be added to this orbital. Choose from the possibilities listed on the previous page.

On the basis of your "guesses", build radical anions for ethylene, formaldimine and formaldehyde, and then obtain their actual equilibrium geometries using the HF/6-31G* model.

Are the calculated structures in line with what you expect? Elaborate.

4. The first excited state of formaldehyde (the so-called n→π* state) can be thought of as arising from the "promotion" of one electron from the HOMO (in the ground-state of formaldehyde) to the LUMO. The experimental equilibrium geometry of the molecule shows lengthening of the CO bond and a pyramidal carbon geometry (ground-state values in parentheses).

Rationalize this experimental result on the basis of what you know about the HOMO and LUMO in formaldehyde and your experience with calculations on the radical cation and radical anion of formaldehyde.

6

Water

Water is unusual (unique) in that it incorporates an equal number (two) of electron pairs (electron-donor sites) and "acidic hydrogens" (electron-acceptor sites) in such a "small package".

two electron pairs $\ddot{O}\overset{\text{\tiny{H}}}{\underset{\text{H}}{\swarrow}}$ two acidic hydrogens

Water molecules use these two "complementary resources" fully by forming a network of electron-donor/electron-acceptor interactions (hydrogen bonds), with each water molecule participating in up to four hydrogen bonds. Other "similar" molecules like ammonia and hydrogen fluoride, are no match, simply because they incorporate an unequal number of electron-donor and electron-acceptor sites

one electron pair $:N\overset{\text{\tiny{H}}}{\underset{\text{H}}{\swarrow}}_{\text{H}}$ three acidic hydrogens

three electron pairs $:\ddot{F}{-}H$ one acidic hydrogen

The ability of water to establish a network of hydrogen bonds accounts for its unusually high boiling point (other molecules of similar molecular weight are gases at temperatures where water is a liquid).

This activity lets you "see" the network of hydrogen bonds in a tiny sample of water (a so-called water cluster) and then lets you see the effect of introducing different molecules.

1. Build a cluster of water molecules, and display hydrogen bonds.

> Select sp³ oxygen in the organic model kit, hold down the **Insert** key (**option** key for the Mac) and *click* repeatedly at different locations on the screen. Turn the cluster every few molecules to obtain a three-dimensional structure. Continue until your cluster has at least 30-40

> water molecules in it. Select **Minimize** from the **Build** menu. When complete, select **Hydrogen Bonds** from the **Model** menu.

Focus your attention on one or a few water molecules in "the middle" of your cluster. Are these involved in the "maximum" number of hydrogen bonds? Elaborate. Measure the lengths of the hydrogen bonds in your cluster. Do they all fit into a narrow range (± 0.05Å) as would be the case for normal (covalent) bonds, or do they show more widely ranging behavior? Is what you observe consistent with the fact that hydrogen bonds are much weaker than covalent bonds? Elaborate.

Display your water cluster as a space-filling model. This provides an alternative view of hydrogen bonding (spheres representing hydrogens "interpreting" into spheres representing oxygens). It also gives an "impression" of how much "space" is left in a sample of liquid water. Describe what you see (with regard to these two issues).

2. Add a molecule of ammonia into (the center of) your cluster and minimize the energy. How many hydrogen bonds are there to the ammonia molecule which you added? On average, how many hydrogen bonds are there to the water molecules immediately surrounding the ammonia molecule? Does the situation appear to be similar or different from that for the "pure" water cluster? Has your cluster noticeably expanded or contracted in the vicinity of ammonia? (Look at a space-filling model.) Would you expect water to dissolve ammonia? Elaborate.

3. Replace ammonia by methane and minimize the energy.

> Select sp³ carbon from the organic model kit and *double click* on the nitrogen of ammonia in your cluster.

Has the cluster noticeably expanded or contracted in the vicinity of methane? Rationalize your result in terms of changes in hydrogen bonding (relative to the "pure" water cluster). Would you expect water to dissolve methane?

7

Beyond VSEPR Theory

Valence State Electron Pair Repulsion (VSEPR) theory allows chemists to anticipate the geometry about an atom in a molecule using two simple rules.

1. Start with a coordination geometry which depends only on the number of electron pairs associated with an atom (a bond contributes one electron pair).

number of electron pairs	coordination
2	linear
3	trigonal planar
4	tetrahedral
5	trigonal bipyramidal
6	octahedral

2. Given this coordination geometry, position the bonds such that bond angles between lone pairs are as large as possible and, following this, that bond angles involving lone pairs and bonds are as large as possible.

In effect, VSEPR theory tells us to keep lone pairs as far apart from each other as possible, and then as far away from bonds as possible, and finally to keep bonds as far away from other bonds as possible.

VSEPR theory will generally provide a "unique" structure, but will not tell whether other structures are "possible" and, if they are, how they relate in stability to that of the "best" structure. Quantum chemical models are able to do this. This activity explores their utility as a viable alternative to VSEPR theory.

1. The sulfur atom in sulfur tetrafluoride is "surrounded" by five pairs of electrons. According to VSEPR theory what is the geometry of SF_4? Build this structure. Perform a HF/3-21G

calculation to obtain an equilibrium geometry and energy for the molecule, and request an infrared spectrum.

While you are waiting for the calculation to complete, propose an additional structure for SF_4 which satisfies the "first rule" (good coordination geometry), but which does not fully satisfy the "second rule". Note that the alternative structure dealt with in the tutorial *"Sulfur Tetrafluoride: Building an Inorganic Molecule"* does not even satisfy the first rule. Build your alternative structure and obtain its geometry, energy and infrared spectrum using the HF/3-21G model.

Examine the energies of both your preferred and alternative SF_4 structures. Is the geometry of SF_4 preferred by VSEPR theory that with the lower (more negative) total energy according to the calculations? If not, what is the HF/3-21G structure of sulfur tetrafluoride? If VSEPR and HF/3-21G models are in agreement with regard to the "best" structure for SF_4, is the higher-energy alternative structure actually an energy minimum? Elaborate. Hint: look at the calculated infrared spectrum for imaginary frequencies (see the essay *"Potential Energy Surfaces"* for a discussion). If the second structure is an energy minimum, what would be the composition of an equilibrium mixture of the two forms at room temperature? Use a special case of the Boltzmann equation for only two molecules "in equilibrium" (see the essay *"Total Energies and Thermodynamic and Kinetic Data"* for a discussion).

$$A \rightleftharpoons B$$

$$[A]/[B] = e^{-1060(E_A - E_B)}$$

where [A]/[B] is the ratio of molecules A and B in equilibrium and E_A and E_B are their energies in atomic units.

2. The chlorine atom in chlorine trifluoride, like the sulfur in sulfur tetrafluoride, is "surrounded" by five pairs of electrons. Repeat the analysis you performed on SF_4 for this molecule. Start with the structure that VSEPR theory suggests and look for stable alternatives. Do the VSEPR and quantum chemical models reach

the same conclusion with regard to preferred structure? Does a stable alternative structure exist?

3. The xenon atom in xenon tetrafluoride is surrounded by six pairs of electrons. Repeat the analysis you performed on SF_4 for this molecule. Start with the structure that VSEPR theory suggests and look for a stable alternative. Do the two models reach the same conclusion with regard to preferred structure? Is there a stable alternative structure?

4. According to VSEPR theory, xenon hexafluoride, XeF_6, is not octahedral. Why not? How many pairs of electrons are associated with xenon in XeF_6? Does VSEPR theory tell you what the structure should actually be? "Ask" the quantum chemical calculations by starting out with a six-coordinate structure which has been distorted from octahedral.

> Build octahedral XeF_6 using the inorganic model kit. Set several of the FXeF bond angles to "non 90°" values. For each, select **Measure Angle** from the **Geometry** menu, select a FXeF bond angle, replace the 90° value which appears at the bottom of the screen by a different value and *press* the **Enter** key (**return** key for the Mac). Do not minimize in the builder or your structure will revert back to octahedral symmetry.

Obtain an equilibrium geometry using the HF/3-21G model. This will require several tens of minutes as your "guess" is likely not very close to the real equilibrium structure. Is the resulting XeF_6 geometry distorted from octahedral in accord with the prediction of VSEPR theory?

To get an estimate of the energy gained by distorting XeF_6, build octahedral XeF_6 and obtain its equilibrium geometry using the HF/3-21G model. Also request an infrared spectrum. This calculation will also require several tens of minutes. When completed, compare the energy of this structure with that of the non-octahedral form above. How much stabilization has been gained as a result of distortion? How does this energy difference compare with those you obtained earlier in examining different structures of SF_4, ClF_3 and XeF_4?

Examine the infrared spectrum of octahedral XeF_6. Does it show any imaginary frequencies? What does this tell you about whether octahedral XeF_6 is an energy minimum on the overall energy surface? If there are imaginary frequencies, animate their motions. Is the direction of the vibrational motion (away from an octahedral geometry) consistent with the non-octahedral structure you located?

8

Bond Angles in Main-Group Hydrides

The HNH bond angles in ammonia are 106.7°, somewhat less than the tetrahedral values (109.5°). So too is the HOH bond angle in water (104.5°). These data are usually rationalized by suggesting that the lone pair on nitrogen and the two lone pairs on oxygen "take up more space" than NH and OH bonds, respectively (see the activity "*Too Many Electrons*"). As seen from the experimental data in the table below, HXH bond angles in second-row and heavier main-group analogies of ammonia and water deviate even more from "ideal" tetrahedral values.

NH_3	106.7	AsH_3	92.1	H_2O	104.5
PH_3	93.3	SbH_3	91.6	H_2S	92.1
H_2Se	90.6	H_2Te	90.3		

Is this further reduction in bond angle due to increased size of lone pairs on the heavy elements or are other factors involved? You will explore the question in this activity.

1. Build the eight hydrides listed above and obtain the equilibrium geometry of each using the HF/3-21G model. Put them all in one document. Do the calculations show the same trend in bond angles as seen in the experimental data? Point out any significant exceptions.

2. Calculate and display electrostatic potential surfaces for all the hydrides. Set the isovalue to -10. What is the ordering of sizes of lone pairs (as indicated by the electrostatic potential surfaces) in the series NH_3, PH_3, AsH_3, SbH_3? In the series H_2O, H_2S, H_2Se, H_2Te?

You will have noticed that the sizes of the lone pairs appear to decrease, not increase, in going to the heavier analogues of ammonia and water. Other factors must be at work. You will examine two possibilities, electrostatics and orbital hybridization.

Coulomb's law states that "like charges repel" and will seek to move as far apart as possible. Do charges on hydrogen increase in moving down the *Periodic Table*?

3. Examine hydrogen charges in ammonia and its analogues. Do they increase (hydrogen becoming more positive), decrease or remain about the same in moving to heavier analogues? Rationalize your result in terms of what you know about the electronegativities of nitrogen and its heavier analogues (relative to the electronegativity of hydrogen). Given Coulomb's law and ignoring any other factors, predict the trend in HXH bond angles in the series NH_3, PH_3, AsH_3, SbH_3.

Repeat your analysis for water and its analogues.

Both the bonds and lone pair(s) in ammonia, water and their heavier analogues are commonly viewed as made up of sp^3 hybrids. It is reasonable to expect that "p contribution" to the bonds (which are lower in energy than the lone pair(s), will increase as the energy of the (atomic) p orbitals move closer to the energy of the s orbital.

4. In order to get a measure of relative valence s and p orbitals (2s, 2p for first-row elements, 3s, 3p for second-row elements, etc.) perform calculations on the Noble gas atoms from each row (Ne, Ar, Kr and Xe).

> Use the inorganic model kit and delete any free valences. *Check* **Orbitals** inside the **Calculations** dialog. The orbital energies will be written to the text output (**Output** under the **Display** menu).

Do valence s and p orbitals move closer, move further apart or don't significantly alter their relative positions in going from Ne to Xe? If they do change their relative positions, how would you expect the HXH bond angles to change in moving from NH_3 to SbH_3 and from H_2O to H_2Te? Elaborate.

9

Bond Lengths and Hybridization

Each of the carbons in ethane is surrounded by four atoms in a roughly tetrahedral geometry, while each carbon in ethylene is surrounded by three atoms in a trigonal-planar geometry and each carbon in acetylene by two atoms in a linear geometry. These structures can be rationalized by suggesting that the valence 2s and 2p orbitals of carbon are able to "combine" either to produce four equivalent "sp^3 hybrids" directed toward the four corners of a tetrahedron, or three equivalent "sp^2 hybrids" directed toward the corners of an equilateral triangle, or two equivalent "sp hybrids" directed along a line.

| four sp^3 hybrids | three sp^2 hybrids | two sp hybrids |

In the first instance, no atomic orbitals remain, while in the second instance, a 2p atomic orbital, directed perpendicular to the plane made by the three sp^2 hybrids, remains and in the third instance, a pair of 2p atomic orbitals, directed perpendicular to the line of the two sp hybrids and perpendicular to each other, remain. Thus, the "bonding" in ethane is described by four sp^3 hybrids, that in ethylene by three sp^2 hybrids and a p orbital and that in acetylene by two sp hybrids and two p orbitals.

2p atomic orbitals are higher in energy and extend further from carbon than the 2s orbital. The higher the "fraction of 2p" in the hybrid, the more it will extend. Therefore, sp^3 hybrids will extend further than sp^2 hybrids, which in turn will extend further than sp hybrids. As a consequence, bonds made with sp^3 hybrids should be longer than those made with sp^2 hybrids, which should in turn be longer than bonds made with sp hybrids. In this activity, you will first test such an hypothesis and explore its generality. Finally, you will search for a molecule with a very short carbon-carbon single bond.

1. Build ethane, ethylene, and acetylene and put into a single document. Obtain HF/3-21G equilibrium geometries for all three molecules. Is the ordering in CH bond lengths what you expect on the basis of the hybridization arguments presented above? Using the CH bond length in ethane as a standard, what is the % reduction in CH bond lengths in ethylene? In acetylene? Is there a rough correlation between % reduction in bond length and % of 2p in the hybrid?

2. Obtain the HF/3-21G equilibrium geometry for cyclopropane and measure the CH bond length. Based on your experience in the previous part, would you say that the carbons are sp^3 hybridized? Elaborate.

3. Choose one or more of the following sets of molecules: propane, propene and propyne or fluoroethane, fluoroethylene and fluoroacetylene or chloroethane, chloroethylene and chloroacetylene. Build all molecules in the set and again obtain HF/3-21G equilibrium geometries. When completed, measure the C–C (C–F or C–Cl) bond lengths.

   Is the ordering of bond lengths the same as that observed for the CH bond lengths in ethane, ethylene and acetylene? Are the % reductions in bond lengths from the appropriate standards (propane, fluorethane and chloroethane) similar (±10%) to those seen for ethylene and acetylene (relative to ethane)?

4. How short can a carbon-carbon single bond be? Propose one or more "shortest bond" candidates and perform HF/3-21G calculations. (You might find several of your "candidates" in the database of HF/3-21G calculations supplied with Spartan. Look for the molecule name at the bottom of the screen.) Is your shortest carbon-carbon single bond shorter or longer than the typical carbon-carbon double bond?

10

Dipole Moments

The dipole moment provides a measure of the extent to which charge is non uniformly distributed in a molecule. In a molecule like H_2, where both "sides" are the same and the charge on both atoms is necessarily equal, the dipole moment is zero. Increasing the difference in charge increases the dipole moment. The magnitude of the dipole moment also depends on the extent to which charge is separated. The larger the separation of charge, the larger the dipole moment. The overall situation is particularly simple for a diatomic molecule where the dipole moment is proportional to the product of the absolute difference in charge between the two atoms, $|q_A - q_B|$, and the bond length, r_{AB}. The greater the difference in charge and the greater the bond length, the greater the dipole moment.

$$\text{dipole moment } \alpha \ \left| q_A - q_B \right| \ r_{AB}$$

In this activity you will explore this relationship. You will also examine to what extent the difference in atomic electronegativities between the atoms in a diatomic molecule anticipate the difference in atomic charge, and so can be used to estimate dipole moments.

1. Build hydrogen molecule, hydrogen fluoride, hydrogen chloride, hydrogen bromide, and hydrogen iodide. Put all into a single document. Obtain HF/3-21G equilibrium geometries for all five molecules. Is there a "reasonable" correlation between calculated dipole moments and the product of bond lengths and electronegativity differences? Use the electronegativities tabulated below.

H	2.2		F	4.0
Li	1.0		Cl	3.2
Na	0.9		Br	3.0
			I	2.7

If so, does the correlation properly reproduce the fact that the dipole moment in hydrogen is zero?

2. Repeat your analyses for the series: lithium hydride, lithium fluoride, lithium chloride, lithium bromide and lithium iodide and for the series: sodium hydride, sodium fluoride, sodium chloride, sodium bromide and sodium iodide.

> You will need to use the inorganic model kit to build these molecules.

11

Charges on Atoms in Molecules

What is the charge on an individual atom in a molecule? Surprisingly, this is not a simple question. While the total charge on a molecule is well defined, being given as the sum of the nuclear charges (atomic numbers) minus the total number of electrons, defining charges on individual atoms requires accounting both for the nuclear charge and for the charge of any electrons uniquely "associated" with the particular atom. It is certainly reasonable to expect that the nuclear contribution to the total charge on an atom is simply the atomic number, but it is not at all obvious how to partition the total electron distribution by atoms. Consider, for example, the electron distribution for a simple diatomic molecule like hydrogen fluoride.

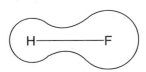

Here, the surrounding "line" is a particular "isodensity surface" (see the essay ***Electron Densities: Sizes and Shapes of Molecules***", say that corresponding to a van der Waals surface and enclosing a large fraction of the total electron density. In this picture, the surface has been drawn to suggest that more electrons are associated with fluorine than with hydrogen. This is entirely reasonable, given the known polarity of the molecule, i.e., $^{\delta+}$H-F$^{\delta-}$, as evidenced experimentally by the direction of its dipole moment.

It is, however, not at all apparent how to divide this surface between the two nuclei. Are any of the divisions shown below better than the rest?

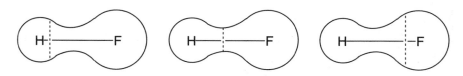

Clearly not! In fact, there is no "best" division. It is possible to calculate (and measure) the number of electrons in a particular volume of space, but it is not possible to say how many electrons belong to each atom.

Despite their ambiguity, charges are part of the everyday vocabulary of chemists. Most common are so-called "formal charges" which follow from a "back of the envelope" recipe:

$$\begin{matrix} \text{formal} \\ \text{charge} \end{matrix} = \begin{matrix} \text{number of} \\ \text{valence electrons} \end{matrix} - \begin{matrix} \text{number of} \\ \text{lone-pair electrons} \end{matrix} - \begin{matrix} \text{number of bonds} \\ \text{(single bond equivalents)} \end{matrix}$$

In general, it will be possible to write a Lewis structure (for an uncharged molecule) which will lead to formal charges for all atoms of zero. There is no guarantee, however, that this Lewis structure will properly account for the actual geometry and/or chemical behavior of the molecule. Also, formal charges are not able to reveal subtle differences among atoms in the same or in different molecules. They are really nothing more than a "bookkeeping" device.

Several different approaches are available for assigning atomic charges based on quantum chemical calculations. The approach implemented in your edition of Spartan fits the energy which a point charge "feels" as it approaches a molecule (the so-called "electrostatic potential"; see the essay "**Electrostatic Potential Maps: Charge Distributions**"), by a model in which the nuclei and electron distribution are replaced by "atomic charges". Such an approach would be expected to lead to charges which are much more "realistic" than formal charges and which vary with subtle changes in environment.

The purpose of this activity is both to point out differences between quantum chemical charges and formal charges, and to show the utility of the former in rationalizing molecular structure and properties.

1. Sulfur difluoride is bent, sulfur tetrafluoride is a trigonal bipyramid missing one (*equatorial*) "arm" and sulfur hexafluoride is

octahedral. Draw "proper" Lewis structures for each and assign formal charges at sulfur and at fluorine. Does the (formal) charge on sulfur change from one molecule to another?

Build all three molecules and put into a single document. Obtain equilibrium geometries using the HF/3-21G model. Also request electrostatic potential maps. When completed, measure the charge at sulfur in each of the three compounds.

> The charges (in units of electrons) are available under the **Atom Properties** dialog (**Properties** under the **Display** menu and *click* on an atom).

Does the calculated charge on sulfur change from one molecule to another? If so, for which molecule is sulfur the least charged? The most charged? Also compare the three electrostatic potential maps recalling that colors near "red" depict excess negative charge and that colors near "blue" depict excess positive charge. On the basis of the calculated charges and electrostatic potential maps, draw alternative (to those you provided above) Lewis structures (or sets of Lewis structures) for the three molecules.

2. Draw a Lewis structure for cyanide anion (CN^-), and assign formal charges. Does your structure incorporate a double bond like formaldimine ($H_2C=NH$) or a triple bond like hydrogen cyanide ($HC\equiv N$)? On which atom does the negative charge reside?

To see if your Lewis structure presents a "realistic" picture, obtain equilibrium geometries for cyanide anion, formaldimine and hydrogen cyanide using the HF/6-31G* model. According to your calculations, is the CN bond in cyanide anion closer to double or triple (compare it to bond lengths in formaldimine and hydrogen cyanide)? Which atom bears the negative charge, or is it distributed over both carbon and nitrogen?

Further discussion of cyanide anion is provided in the activity "*S$_N$2 Reaction of Cyanide and Methyl Iodide*".

3. Draw two different "reasonable" geometries for ozone, O_3, provide Lewis structures for each and assign formal charges to the oxygen atoms in each. Build both (put into the same document) and obtain their equilibrium geometry using the HF/6-31G* model. Which of your structures is lower in energy? Is it in accord with the experimentally known equilibrium geometry? (Because ozone is so important in the production of "smog", it is well studied and its structure has been determined.) If the preferred structure has two (or three) distinct oxygen atoms, which is most positively charged? Most negatively charged? Is your result consistent with formal charges?

12

What Makes A Strong Acid?

HF is a much stronger acid than H_2O, which in turn is a stronger acid than NH_3. This parallels a decrease in the electronegativity of the atom bonded to hydrogen (F > O > N) and presumably to a decrease in bond polarity. In other words, the hydrogen in HF is more positive than the hydrogens in H_2O, which are in turn more positive than the hydrogens in NH_3. It might be expected, therefore, that acid strength would decrease in moving from HF to HI, paralleling the decrease in electronegativity of the halogen.

F	>	Cl	>	Br	>	I
4.0		3.2		3.0		2.7

In fact the opposite is true, and HI is the strongest acid in the series and HF is the weakest. Clearly, factors other than differences in bond polarity caused by differences in electronegativity are at work.

The key is recognizing that acid strength directly relates to the energy of bond fracture into separated positive and negative ions, the so-called heterocyclic bond dissociation energy.

$$HX \rightarrow H^+ + X^-$$

The present activity relates only to acidity in the gas phase. Gas phase heterolytic bond dissociation energies are much larger than the corresponding energies in a solvent such as water. This is because the solvent acts to stabilize the charged dissociation products much more than it does the uncharged reactants. See the next activity *"Is a Strong Base Always a Strong Base?"* for a discussion of solvent effects on acid/base properties.

In this activity, you will first compute heterolytic bond dissociation energies for HF, HCl, HBr and HI to establish whether or not these reflect the observed ordering of acidities.

1. Build HI, HCl, HBr and HI and calculate their equilibrium geometries using the HF/3-21G model. Also "build" F⁻, Cl⁻, Br⁻ and I⁻ and perform single-point energy calculations on each. Put these in a single document.

> To build an atom, first build the associated hydride and delete the free valence. Make certain that you set **Total Charge** to **Anion** in the **Calculations** dialog.

Compute heterolytic bond dissociation energies for the four molecules. (The energy of the proton is 0).

Is the ordering of calculated bond dissociation energies the same as the ordering of acidities observed for these compounds?

Heterolytic bond dissociation in these compounds leads to separated ions, one of which, H^+, is common to all. Is it reasonable to expect that bond dissociation energy will follow the ability of the anion to stabilize the negative charge. One measure is provided by an electrostatic potential map.

2. Calculate electrostatic potential maps for the four anions and display side-by-side on screen in the same color scale.

Which ion, F⁻, Cl⁻, Br⁻ or I⁻, best accommodates the negative charge? Which most poorly accommodates the charge? Elaborate. Is there a correlation between the "size" of the ion and its ability to accommodate charge? Elaborate. Overall, is the ability to accommodate charge in the atomic anion reflect the heterolytic bond dissociation energy of the corresponding hydride?

13

Is a Strong Base
Always a Strong Base?

What makes a strong base? In the absence of solvent, the most important factor is stabilizing (delocalizing) the positive charge. In general, "bigger" groups should be more effective "delocalizers" than smaller groups. For example, it is to be expected that a methyl group is superior to hydrogen, meaning that methylamine is a stronger base than ammonia, dimethylamine stronger than methylamine and trimethylamine stronger than dimethylamine.

$$NH_3 < MeNH_2 < Me_2NH < Me_3N$$
$$\xrightarrow{\text{increasing base strength}}$$

This situation is less obvious where a solvent is present. Here, the solvent might be expected to stabilize a localized positive charge more than it would a delocalized charge. In the case of the methylamines, solvent stabilization of (protonated) ammonia should be greater than that of (protonated) methylamine, which in turn should be greater than stabilization of (protonated) dimethylamine, and so forth.

In this activity, you will first apply the HF/6-31G* model to investigate the relative "gas phase" basicities of the methylamines. You will then "correct" your data for the effects of aqueous solvent using an approximate quantum chemical model. While the latter cannot realistically be expected to provide a quantitative account of relative aqueous-phase basicities, it should be sufficient to allow you to "see" the effects that solvent has in altering gas-phase basicities.

1. Build ammonia, methylamine, dimethylamine and trimethylamine and obtain equilibrium geometries using the HF/6-31G* model. Next, build protonated forms for the four amines and obtain equilibrium geometries using the HF/6-31G* model.

To build the protonated amines, build the analogous hydrocarbons (methane, ethane, propane and isobutane), bring up the inorganic model kit, select **N** from the *Periodic Table* and *double click* on the appropriate carbon.

Work out the energies of the following reactions:

$$MeNH_2 + NH_4^+ \longrightarrow MeNH_3^+ + NH_3$$

$$Me_2NH + NH_4^+ \longrightarrow Me_2NH_2^+ + NH_3$$

$$Me_3N + NH_4^+ \longrightarrow Me_3NH^+ + NH_3$$

What is the ordering of methylamine basicities in the gas phase? Is the effect of methyl substitution in altering basicity consistent throughout the series?

2. Repeat your analysis for the "aqueous calculations".

"Aqueous phase" energies (**Eaq**) and relative aqueous phase energies (**RelEaq**) are available from the spreadsheet.

What is the ordering of basicities in water? Is the range of basicity smaller, greater or about the same as the range you observed in the gas phase? Rationalize your result. Compare the changes in aqueous basicity in moving from ammonia to trimethylamine with the analogous changes in gas-phase basicity.

3. Experimental gas and aqueous-phase basicities (in kJ/mol) for the methylamines (relative to ammonia) are tabulated below.

	ΔH_{gas}	ΔH_{aq}
ammonia	0	0
methylamine	38	8
dimethylamine	67	8
trimethylamine	79	3

How well do these compare with your results both insofar as absolute numbers and with regard to "trends"?

14

Which Lewis Structure is Correct?

Some molecules cannot be adequately represented in terms of a single Lewis structure, but require a series of Lewis structures, which taken as a whole, provide an adequate representation. Such a picture is unambiguous where the individual Lewis structures are all "the same" (different but equivalent arrangements of bonds) and are, therefore, equally important. For example, taken together the two (equivalent) Lewis structures for benzene lead to the experimental result that the six carbon-carbon bonds are identical and midway in length between "normal" single and double bonds.

The situation is less clear where the Lewis structures are not all equivalent. For example, two of the three Lewis structures which can be written for naphthalene are equivalent, but the third is different.

In this case, any conclusions regarding molecular geometry depend on the relative importance ("weight") given to the individual Lewis structures. Choosing all three Lewis structures to have equal weight leads to the result that four of the bonds in naphthalene (which are double bonds in two of the three Lewis structures) should be shorter than the remaining ring bonds, (which are double bonds in only one of the three Lewis structures). This is exactly what is observed experimentally.

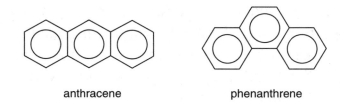

1.42Å 1.43Å

1.42Å

1.38Å

In the first part of this activity, you will attempt to guess the trends in bond lengths in anthracene and in phenanthrene by assuming that all Lewis structures are equally important (as done for naphthalene above), and compare your guesses with actual geometries obtained from HF/3-21G calculations.

1. Draw the complete set of Lewis structures for anthracene and phenanthrene.

anthracene   phenanthrene

Assuming that each Lewis structure contributes equally, assign which if any of the carbon-carbon bonds should be especially short or especially long. Next, obtain equilibrium geometries for the two molecules using the HF/3-21G model.

Are your assignments consistent with the results of the calculations? If not, suggest which Lewis structures need to be weighed more heavily (or which need to be weighed less heavily) in order to bring the two sets of data into accord.

Pyridine and pyridazine are each represented by a pair of Lewis structures.

pyridine   pyridazine

While the two structures are the same for pyridine, they are markedly different for pyridazine. In this part of the activity, you will compare calculated bond distances in pyridazine (using those in pyridine as a "reference") to decide whether or not the two Lewis structures should be given equal weight and if not, which is the more important.

2. Obtain equilibrium geometries for pyridine and pyridazine using the Hartree-Fock 3-21G model.

> To build pyridine, start with benzene, select aromatic nitrogen and *double click* on one carbon. To build pyrazine, start with benzene, select aromatic nitrogen and *double click* on two adjacent carbons.

Using the calculated geometry of pyridine as a reference, would you conclude that the two Lewis structures for pyridazine are equally important? If not, which should be given more weight?

Finally, perform the same analyses of a pair of more complex heterocyclic compounds.

3. Draw all Lewis structures for quinoline and for isoquinoline.

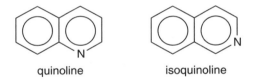

quinoline   isoquinoline

Given what you know about the geometry of pyridine (see previous part) and assuming that each of the Lewis structures contributes equally, assign which if any of the carbon-carbon bonds in the two molecules should be especially short or especially long. Obtain HF/3-21G geometries for quinoline and isoquinoline to support or refute your conclusions.

15

Is Azulene Aromatic?

Aromatic molecules are (thermodynamically) more stable than might have been anticipated. The famous case is benzene. Here, the first step in its complete hydrogenation (to cyclohexane) is *endothermic*, while both of the remaining steps are *exothermic*.

The difference in the hydrogenation energy between the first step and either the second or third steps (134 kJ/mol and 142 kJ/mol, respectively) provides a measure of the aromatic stabilization.

Aromatic molecules may also be distinguished in that they incorporate bonds intermediate in length between normal (single and double) linkages. For example, all carbon-carbon bond lengths in benzene are 1.39Å, which is longer than a double bond (1.30 to 1.34Å) but shorter than a single bond (1.48 to 1.55Å).

Is azulene, known for its intense blue color and the basis of numerous dyes, aromatic as is its isomer naphthalene? Both molecules incorporate 10 π electrons in a planar fused-ring skeleton.

azulene   naphthalene

In this activity, you will compare energies, geometries and electrostatic potential maps for azulene and naphthalene in an effort to decide.

1. Build azulene and naphthalene and obtain their equilibrium geometries using the HF/3-21G model. Is azulene more stable (lower in energy), less stable or about as stable as naphthalene? If

it is less stable, is the energy difference between the two isomers much less, much greater or about the same as the "aromatic stabilization" of benzene? On the basis of energy, would you conclude that azulene is or is not aromatic?

Calculate an "average" carbon-carbon bond length in azulene. Is this average similar to the carbon-carbon bond length in benzene? Next, calculate the mean absolute deviation from the average to provide a measure of the uniformity of bond lengths. Is this deviation similar to the corresponding quantity for naphthalene? On the basis of uniformity in bond lengths alone, would you conclude that azulene is or is not aromatic?

It is common to suggest that azulene is made up of the "fusion" of two aromatic ions, both with 6 π electrons, cycloheptatrienyl (tropylium) cation and cyclopentadienyl anion.

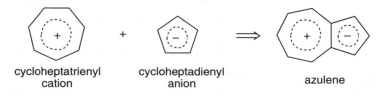

cycloheptatrienyl
cation

cycloheptadienyl
anion

azulene

This being the case, the "cycloheptatrienyl side" of azulene should be "positively charged" (relative to naphthalene) while the "cyclopentadienyl side" should be "negatively charged".

2. Request electrostatic potential maps for naphthalene and azulene, and display them in the same scale and side-by-side on screen.

> Set the "color scale" for both molecules to be the same and centered at "0". For each molecule, select **Properties** from the **Display** menu and *click* on the electrostatic potential map. Inside the **Surface Properties** dialog which results, change the property range to be the same for both molecules (-30 to 30 is a good range).

Do you see evidence of charge separation in azulene? Is it in the expected direction? What effect would you expect charge separation to have on the energy of azulene? Elaborate.

16

Why is Pyrrole a Weak Base?

Pyrrole and indole are known to be very weak bases, in striking contrast to the strong basicity exhibited by "related" aromatic amines such as pyridine, quinoline and isoquinoline.

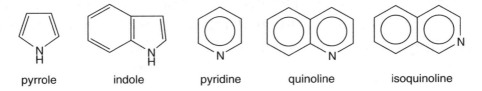

pyrrole   indole   pyridine   quinoline   isoquinoline

Assuming that protonation occurs on nitrogen in all compounds, the reason for the difference in basicity is clear. The nitrogen in pyridine (quinoline, isoquinoline) incorporates a non-bonded pair of electrons in the plane of the ring. Protonation does not directly affect the π system and the aromaticity of the ring. On the other hand, the "available" electrons on nitrogen in pyrrole (indole) are part of the ring's π system. Protonation "removes" electrons (or at least localizes them in NH bonds) leading to loss of aromaticity.

In this activity, you will first employ electrostatic potential maps to establish that the nitrogen in pyrrole (indole) is indeed less susceptible to protonation than the nitrogen in pyridine (quinoline, isoquinoline). You will then perform calculations on "isomers" of protonated pyrrole (indole) to establish where protonation is actually likely to occur.

1. Build pyrrole and pyridine. (Optionally, build indole, quinoline and/or isoquinoline.) Obtain equilibrium geometries and electrostatic potential maps for all molecules using the HF/3-21G model. Display the maps side-by-side on screen.

   Are there significant differences in the electrostatic potential at nitrogen in pyridine (quinoline, isoquinoline) and in pyrrole (indole), both in terms of magnitude and direction of maximum potential (most negative)? Are any differences consistent with the observed difference in basicities of pyridine and pyrrole and with the qualitative rationale used to explain these differences? Elaborate. On the basis of its electrostatic potential map, would you expect the nitrogen in pyridine (quinoline, isoquinoline) to be the most basic site? If not, where is the most basic site? Is the nitrogen in pyrrole (indole) the most basic site? If not, where is that site?

2. Build nitrogen-protonated pyrrole and obtain its equilibrium geometry using the HF/3-21G model. Also obtain equilibrium geometries for the two alternative (carbon-protonated) forms. (If you also examine protonated indole, consider only isomers resulting from protonation of the five-membered ring.)

nitrogen protonated   carbon protonated

Which of the three "isomers" is lowest in energy? Is your result consistent with what you expected based on examination of electrostatic potential maps? Elaborate.

3. Obtain and compare proton affinities of pyridine (quinoline, isoquinoline) and pyrrole (indole). This is simply the difference in energy between the neutral molecule and protonated form (the energy of the proton is zero). You already have all the data for pyrrole, but you will need to calculate the geometry of protonated pyridine using the HF/3-21G model. Which is the stronger base (larger proton affinity), pyridine or pyrrole? Is your result consistent with experiment?

17

Not the Sum of the Parts

N,N-dimethylaniline is more basic than pyridine, which leads to the expectation that the "aniline nitrogen" in 4-(dimethylamino)pyridine will be more basic than the "pyridine nitrogen".

N,N-dimethylaniline   pyridine   4-(dimethylamino)pyridine

While the site of protonation (the more basic site) in 4-(dimethylamino) pyridine is unknown, there is evidence to suggest that the reverse is true and that the "pyridine nitrogen" is actually the more basic of the two. Specifically, addition of methyl iodide to 4-(dimethylamino) pyridine leads exclusively to the "pyridine adduct".

In this activity, you will first confirm (or refute) that the preferred site of protonation in 4-(dimethylamino)pyridine is the pyridine nitrogen. If it is, then you will examine the interaction of the dimethylamino substituent with pyridine in both neutral and protonated 4-(dimethylamino)pyridine for clues to its behavior.

1. Build both forms of protonated 4-(dimethylamino)pyridine and obtain the geometry of each using the HF/3-21G model. Which protonated form is the more stable? Is your result consistent with

the product observed upon addition of methyl iodide? Is the energy of the other protonated form close enough so that one might expect to see both methyl cation adducts? Elaborate.

Assuming that you find 4-(dimethylamino)pyridine to favor protonation on the pyridine nitrogen, the next step is to establish what has caused the reversal from that noted in the "parent compounds" (N,N-dimethyl-aniline and pyridine). Either this is due to stabilization of protonated pyridine by the dimethylamino substituent or to destabilization of protonated dimethylaniline by the change in the aromatic ring from benzene to pyridine, or both. To tell, you will examine reactions 1 and 2 which separate the two protonated forms into their respective components.

2. Build all the molecules required for reactions 1 and 2 and obtain equilibrium geometries using the HF/3-21G model. (You already have data for the two protonated forms of 4-(dimethylamino) pyridine. Does the dimethylamino substituent stabilize or destabilize protonated pyridine? Does the change from carbon to nitrogen in the aromatic ring stabilize or destabilize protonated N,N-dimethylaniline? Which, if either, is the dominant factor behind the preference for protonation in 4-(dimethylamino) pyridine?

18

Stereoisomers vs. Conformers. A Matter of Degree

Stereoisomers are molecules with the same molecular formula in which the constituent atoms are connected to each other (bonded) in the same way but differ in their three-dimensional arrangement. For example, *cis* and *trans*-2-butene are stereoisomers but 2-methyl propene and *cis* (or *trans*) 2-butene are not.

cis-2-butene   trans-2-butene   2-methylpropene   anti-n-butane   gauche-n-butane

anti and *gauche-n*-butane like *cis* and *trans*-2-butene have the same molecular formula, the same arrangement of bonds but different three-dimensional geometry, but are not considered to be stereoisomers. Rather, they are referred to as conformers (see the tutorial "**Internal Rotation in n-Butane**").

The difference is one of degree. Interconversion of *cis* and *trans*-2-butene is "difficult" because it requires fracture of a π bond, whereas interconversion of *anti* and *gauche n*-butane is "easy" as it only involves rotation about a carbon-carbon single bond. In more quantitative terms, *cis*-2-butene needs to surmount an activation barrier of roughly 210 kJ/mol in order to isomerize to *trans*-2-butene, while *gauche n*-butane needs only to climb a 10 kJ/mol "hill" in order to yield the *anti* conformer. Isomerization of *cis*-2-butene to *trans*-2-butene will be very slow, while rotation of *gauche-n*-butane to *anti-n*-butane will be fast.

This activity explores a situation where it is not clear whether the term "isomer" and "conformer" is the more appropriate.

While amides, such as formamide, may be represented in terms of a single "uncharged" Lewis structure, both spectroscopic and chemical evidence suggests that such a picture is inappropriate, and that the CN bond may exhibit characteristics of a double bond. This suggests a significant contribution of the "charged" Lewis structure to the overall description.

$$\begin{matrix} H & & O \\ & \diagdown & \diagup\diagup \\ & N{-}C & \\ & \diagup & \diagdown \\ H & & H \end{matrix} \quad \rightleftharpoons \quad \begin{matrix} H & & O^- \\ & \diagdown & \diagup \\ & N{=}C & \\ & \diagup & \diagdown \\ H & & H \end{matrix}$$

1. Build formamide, H_2NCHO. Obtain an equilibrium geometry using the HF/3-21G model. For comparison, obtain equilibrium geometries for both methylamine, CH_3NH_2 and for methyleneimine, $H_2C=NH$. Is the CN bond length in formamide shorter than that in methylamine? Is it closer in length to the double bond in methyleneimine or to the single bond in methylamine?

2. Next, build a guess at the "transition state" for rotation about the CN bond in formamide. Start with formamide and twist the CN bond such that the NH_2 and CHO groups are approximately perpendicular. Specify calculation of a transition-state geometry using the HF/3-21G model and also request an infrared spectrum. When the calculations have completed, verify that your structure corresponds to a transition state, and that the motion associated with the imaginary frequency is consistent with rotation about the CN bond.

   Compare the energy of the transition state to that of formamide. Is it in the range of a "normal" single-bond rotation or closer to that *cis-trans* isomerization of a double bond? Compare the CN bond in the transition state to that in formamide. Is it shorter, longer or about the same length? Is this result consistent with the energetics of the process?

19

Enantiomers.
The Same and Not the Same

Enantiomers are non-superimposible mirror images. While they necessarily have identical physical properties, "under the right conditions" they may exhibit entirely different chemical behavior. The usual analogy is the human hand. Left and right hands are non-superimposible mirror images (they are enantiomers) and are identical in all respects. However, a right hand "shaking" another right hand provides an entirely different "experience" than the same right hand shaking a left hand.

1. One of the enantiomers of carvone occurs naturally in caraway while the other is found in spearmint oil. These enantiomers are responsible for the characteristic odors of these materials. Ibuprofen is an analgesic sold under various names, including Advil, Motrin, and Nuprin. The material is sold as a mixture, but only one enantiomer acts as an analgesic. The other enantiomer is inactive. This means that 800 mg of ibuprofen contains only 400 mg of analgesic. The two enantiomers of limonene have completely different tastes. One has the taste of lemon (as the name implies) and the other tastes of orange.

carvone   ibuprofen   limonene

Each of these molecules incorporates a single chiral center. Identify it, and draw R and S forms of each compound.

2. Select one (or more) molecule and bring it onto the screen.

> Select *carvone*, *ibuprofen* and/or *limonene* from the files in the "activities" directory. Both R and S forms will be placed in a single document.

Add R/S labels to your model to confirm that your assignments in the previous step are correct.

> **Configure...** from the **Model** menu and *check* R/S in the dialog which results.

3. Compare total energies and dipole moments for the two enantiomers of the compound you selected. Are the energies and dipole moments for the two enantiomers of carvone (ibuprofen and limonene) the same or are they different?

> You could have performed this activity by building and calculating the enantiomers of carvone (ibuprofen or limonene) instead of retrieving them from the "activities" directory. In this case, you would need to examine the different possible conformers available for each, which would entail performing a series of different equilibrium geometry calculations and, following that, selecting the lowest-energy conformer.

20

Diastereomers and Meso Compounds

We have seen in the previous activity that molecules with a single chiral center exist as a pair of enantiomers, the properties of which are identical. The situation is different where there are two chiral centers. In the case where the two chiral centers are different, as for example in 2-chloro-3-fluorobutane, there are four different chirality assignments; RR, RS, SR and SS, leading to four distinct molecules. However, there are two distinct kinds of relationships between the four molecules, enantiomeric relationships (as in the previous activity) and diasteriomeric relationships.

1. Draw all four forms of 2-chloro-3-fluorobutane and assign R/S chirality for each center.

2. Bring 2-chloro-3-fluorobutane onto the screen.

> Select *2-chloro-3-fluorobutane* from the files in the "activities" directory. All four forms will be placed in a single document.

Attach R/S labels to your models to confirm that your assignments in the previous step are correct.

> **Configure...** from the **Model** menu and *check* R/S in the dialog which results.

3. Compare total energies and dipole moments among the four molecules. How many different sets of energies and dipole moments are there? Are molecules with the same energy and dipole moment enantiomers (non-superimposible mirror images) or do they bear a different relationship to each other? Try to superimpose

to find out what is the relationship between molecules with different charges and dipole moments.

In the case where the two chiral centers are the same, as for example in 2,3-difluorobutane, there are also four different chirality assignments: RR, RS, SR and SS. Two of these lead to molecules which are enantiomers. The other two are the same (a meso compound) but are different from the first two.

4. Draw all four forms of 2,3-difluorobutane and assign R/S chirality to each center.

5. Bring 2,3-difluorobutane onto the screen (all four forms will be placed in a single group).

> Select **2,3-difluorobutane** from the files in the "activities directory.

Attach R/S label to your models to confirm that your assignments in the previous step are correct.

6. Compare total energies and dipole moments among the four molecules. How many different sets of energies and dipole moments are there? Are molecules with the same energy and dipole moment enatiomers or do they bear a different relationship. Try to superimpose to find out. What is the relationship between molecules with different energies and dipole moments?

> You could have performed this activity by building and calculating the different stereoisomers of 2-chloro-3-fluorobutane and of 2,3-difluorobutane instead of retrieving them from the "activities" directory. In this case, you would need to examine the different possible conformers available for each, which would entail performing a series of different equilibrium geometry calculations and, following that, selecting the lowest-energy conformer.

21

Are Reactive Intermediates "Normal" Molecules?

Bromine, Br_2, adds to alkenes stereospecifically in a stepwise fashion. The first step involves formation of a "cyclic" bromonium ion intermediate that then undergoes backside attack by Br^- (or another nucleophile) to give only *trans* products.

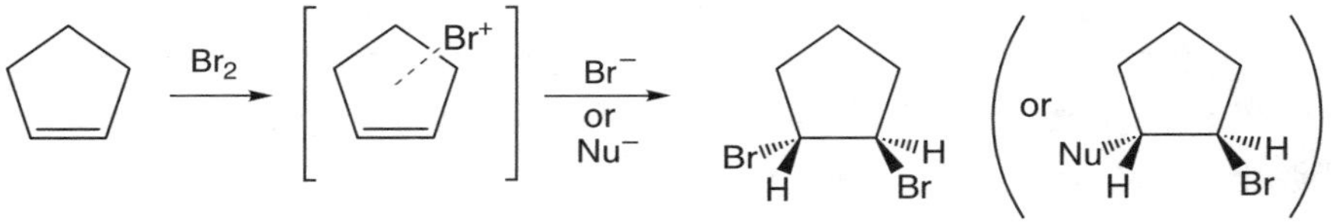

What is the structure of the reactive intermediate, a so-called bromonium ion? Does it take the form of a "saturated" three-membered ring (like cyclopropane or oxirane) as drawn above, or is it better represented in terms of a weak complex between the cation of bromine atom and an olefin, or is bromine only bonded to one carbon leaving the positive charge on the other carbon?

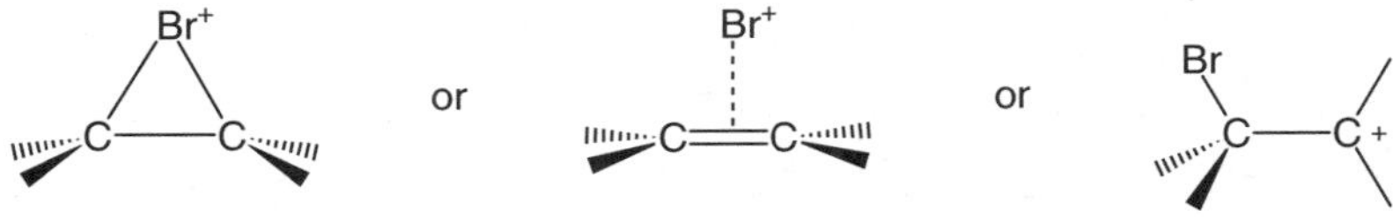

The geometries of the three alternatives should be sufficiently different to allow you to tell. In particular, the ring structure should exhibit a CC length typical of a single bond (1.48 - 1.55 Å) while the CC bond in a complex should resemble that in a free olefin (1.30 - 1.34Å). In both of these the bromine will be equidistant from the two carbons, in contrast to the situation for the open structure.

In this activity, you will calculate the geometry of "cyclic" bromonium ion to see which description (three-membered ring or complex) is a better fit. You will also obtain a structure for the open form of bromonium ion to see whether it is more or less stable than the cyclic form. You will then obtain a LUMO map for your best structure to see where a nucleophile would most likely attack. Finally, you will examine "ring" and "open" structures for analogous reactive intermediates in which bromine cation "attaches" to benzene rather than to the alkene.

1. Build ethylene bromonium ion, both as a cyclic structure and as two different "open" forms, and put all three in the same document.

> To build cyclic ethylene bromonium ion, start with oxirane, H_2C—CH_2 with O, bring up the inorganic model kit, select **Br** from the *Periodic Table* and *double click* on oxygen. To build the open structures, start with methyl bromide, bring up the inorganic model kit, select **C** from the *Periodic Table* and planar trigonal from the list of hybrids and *click* on a free valence. Use **Measure Dihedral** from the **Geometry** menu to set the dihedral angle in one conformer to 90° and in the other conformer to 0°.

Obtain equilibrium geometries for all three structures using the HF/3-21G model. Do all three forms appear to be energy minima or do one or more "collapse" to another? Elaborate. Which structure is the lowest in energy? Is the cyclic structure better represented as a three-membered ring or as a complex? Elaborate.

2. Obtain a LUMO map for your lowest-energy structure (only).

> A LUMO map, which indicates the extent to which the lowest-unoccupied molecular orbital (LUMO) "can be seen" at the "accessible surface" of a molecule, results from displaying the (absolute) value of the LUMO, indicating the "most likely" regions for electrons to be added, i.e., for nucleophilic attack to occur, on top of a surface of electron density, delineating the space taken up by a molecule. See the essay "*Local Ionization Potential Maps and LUMO Maps: Electrophilic and Nucleophilic Reactivity*".

Where is the LUMO most concentrated? Given that nucleophilic attack should occur here, is this consistent with the observed stereochemistry of Br_2 addition? Elaborate.

Bromine also reacts with arenes but leads to substitution rather than addition. The overall process is believed to involve an ionic intermediate analogous to ethylene bromonium ion.

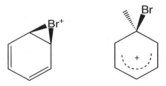

As with ethylene bromonium ion, both cyclic and open structures for the intermediate are plausible.

3. Obtain HF/3-21G equilibrium geometries for both cyclic and open intermediates.

> To build the cyclic structure, start with cyclic bromonium ion and to add four sp^2 carbons to make the ring. Use the inorganic model kit to build the open intermediate. Form a six-carbon ring from five trigonal planar and one tetrahedral hybrid and change four of the bonds involving two trigonal planar carbons from —— (single) to ----- (partial double).

Which structure is lower in energy? Is this the "same" structure predicted for ethylene bromonium ion?

22

Molecular Shapes I.
To Stagger or Not to Stagger

One of the first "rules" dictating molecular shape that organic chemistry students learn is that "single bonds stagger". Ethane is discussed and a plot presented showing that the staggered form is an energy minimum while the eclipsed form is an energy maximum.

staggered   eclipsed

The next example, is inevitably *n*-butane where more than one staggered form (and more than one eclipsed form) are possible. As with ethane, the staggered forms (so-called *anti* and *gauche* conformers) are energy minima while the eclipsed forms (*syn* and *skew*) are energy maxima.

anti   gauche   syn   skew

Does the "staggered rule" extend to bonds involving sp^2 hybridized elements, most important, sp^2 hybridized carbon? In this activity, you will examine the shapes of molecules incorporating bonds between sp^2 and sp^3 carbons to see if it does.

1. Build 1-butene and set and "lock" the C=CCC dihedral angle to be 0°. Next, define a range of values for this dihedral angle starting from 0° and going to 180° in 20° steps.

After you have built 1-butene, select **Measure Dihedral**, *click* on the four carbons in order, type 0.0 into the box to the right of **Dihedral (C1, C2, C3, C4)** at the bottom right of the screen and *press* the **Enter** key (**return** key on the Mac). For Windows, select **Constrain Dihedral** (🔒), *click* on the same four atoms and *click* on the 🔒 icon at the bottom right of the screen. The icon will change to 🔒 (locked). For the Mac, *click* on the 🔒 icon at the bottom right of the screen. The icon will change to 🔒. Next, select **Properties** from the **Display** menu. *Click* on the magenta colored constraint marker on your model to bring up the **Constraint Properties** dialog. For Windows, *check* **Dynamic** inside the dialog and type "180" into the second text box to the right of **Value** and *press* the **Enter** key. For Mac, type "180" in the **To** box and "10" in the **Steps** box.

Obtain the energy of 1-butene as a function of the CCCC dihedral angle. Use the HF/3-21G model. Plot the energy of 1-butene as a function of the C=CCC dihedral angle. How many energy minima are there? How many energy minima would there be if you had varied the dihedral angle from 0° to 360° instead of from 0° to 180°? Elaborate. Characterize the structures of the energy minima as "staggered" or "eclipsed" relative to the CC double bond. Characterize the structures of the energy maxima. Formulate a "rule" covering what you observe.

Next, consider the conformational preference in *cis*-2-butene, a molecule where "eclipsing" should result in strong unfavorable steric interactions.

2. Build *cis*-2-butene. Lock both HCC=C dihedral angles to 0° (eclipsed). Next, define a range of values for *only one* of these dihedral angles from 0° to 180° in 20° steps. As with 1-butene, obtain the energy of *cis*-2-butene as a function of this dihedral angle using the HF/3-21G model, and construct a plot. Characterize the structure of the energy minima as "staggered" or "eclipsed" relative to the CC double bond. Do you see any evidence that other structural parameters, that is, bond lengths and/or bond angles, have significantly altered in order to accommodate your result? Elaborate.

23

Molecular Shapes II.
cis 1,3-Dienes

In order for 1,3-butadiene to undergo Diels-Alder cycloaddition, it needs to be in a *cis* (or nearly *cis*) conformation.

Is this a minimum energy shape for the diene? Certainly it benefits from having the two double bonds coplanar. However, it also places the pair of "inside" hydrogens in close proximity presumably resulting in unfavorable steric repulsion.

In this activity, you will first examine the energy profile for rotation around the central carbon-carbon (single) bond in 1,3-butadiene to see if the *syn* form is an energy minimum and if not what the "closest" minimum-energy form actually is.

1. Build 1,3-butadiene and "lock" the C=CC=C dihedral angle to be 0°. Next, define a range of values for this dihedral angle starting from 0° and going to 180° in 20° steps. Obtain and plot the energy of 1,3-butadiene as a function of the C=CC=C dihedral angle using the HF/3-21G model.

211

Describe the lowest energy minima. Are the double bonds coplanar? Is it suitable for Diels-Alder cycloaddition? If not, is there a second energy minima? Are the double bonds coplanar in this structure? If not, what is the difference in energy between this structure and the "closest" structure in which the double bonds are coplanar?

2. Suggest one or more 1,3-dienes which have C=CC=C dihedral angles close to 0°. Test your suggestions by structures obtained from the HF/3-21G model.

24

Molecular Shapes III.
When is Axial Better?

Substituents on cyclohexane, or "cyclohexane-like" rings, may either be *equatorial* or *axial*, for example, methylcyclohexane.

equatorial

axial

The *equatorial* arrangement is favored in the majority of situations, but the difference in energy between the two is often small enough (4 - 12 kJ/mol) for the *axial* arrangement to be detected.

There is one very important exception to the "*equatorial* rule", not for cyclohexane itself but for derivatives of tetrahydropyran, a closely related molecule.

tetrahydropyran

Here, electronegative substituents on the carbon adjacent to oxygen typically prefer an *axial* arrangement. The so-called ***anomeric effect*** is particularly important in carbohydrate chemistry. An example is provided in the activity "***Molecular Shapes V. Which Conformer Leads to Product?***".

The usual explanation for the *equatorial* cyclohexanes is that a substituent in the *axial* position will "run into" the pair of *axial* hydrogens.

This is a "steric" (crowding) argument. May non-steric considerations also play a role? In this activity, you will look for substituted cyclohexanes that prefer to be *axial*. Specifically, you will draw on Coulomb's Law "charge separation requires energy" as a means to override (or at least reduce) unfavorable sterics. Dipole moment will be employed as a measure of charge separation. A reasonable starting point is fluorocyclohexane. The carbon fluorine bond is highly polar (C^+–F^-), giving rise to the possibility of a large Coulombic contribution, while fluorine is normally viewed as a "small" substituent, thereby minimizing steric factors.

1. Build both *equatorial* and *axial* fluorocyclohexane and obtain equilibrium geometries using the HF/3-21G model. As a reference, also perform HF/3-21G calculations on *equatorial* and *axial* methylcyclohexane.

   Which arrangement, *equatorial* or *axial* is predicted to be lower in energy? How does this result compare with that found for methylcyclohexane? Is the favored fluorocyclohexane structure also the one with the lower dipole moment? If so, what is the difference in dipole moments between the two structures? How does this difference compare with the difference in dipole moments between the two methylcyclohexane structures? Given what you observe, for which system, fluorocyclohexane or methylcyclohexane, would you expect "charge separation effects" to be more significant?

2. *trans*-1,2-difluorocyclohexane can exist as either a *diaxial* or a *diequatorial* structure. Build both and examine the relative orientation of the two CF bonds. For which would you expect the dipole moment to be smaller? Elaborate. Given your prediction about the relative magnitudes of the dipole moments in the two structures and your results from the first part of this activity, would you expect *trans*-1,2-difluorocyclohexane to be *diaxial* or *diequatorial*?

25

Molecular Shapes IV. The "Other" Cyclohexane

Cyclohexane plays a central role in organic chemistry. Not only is it incorporated into a wide variety of important compounds, but it also serves as one of the pillars on which the rules of organic stereochemistry have been built. Cyclohexane is drawn as a "chair-like" structure in which all bonds are staggered (see the activity "*Molecular Shapes I. To Stagger or Not to Stagger*") As discussed in the previous exercise "*Molecular Shapes III. When Axial is Better*", this leads to two sets of hydrogens, so-called *equatorial* and *axial* hydrogens, and to the possibility that a substituted cyclohexane will exist in two different shapes.

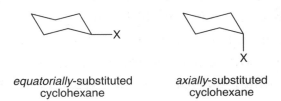

equatorially-substituted
cyclohexane

axially-substituted
cyclohexane

There is an additional shape available to cyclohexane (and substituted cyclohexanes) which also satisfies the "staggered rule". It is generally described as a "twist-boat" or "skew-boat" structure, the boat designation, meaning that opposite methylene groups in the ring point toward each other rather than away from each other as in the chair structure. (See also the essay "*Potential Energy Surfaces*".)

toward   away

H   H   H   H

H   H   H   H

                                H

twist-boat   chair

In this activity, you will locate the twist-boat form of cyclohexane and then attempt to rationalize why it is seldom given notice.

1. Build a form of cyclohexane which "looks like" a twisted boat. The easiest way to do this is start with a chain of six sp^3 carbons and to rotate around individual carbon-carbon bonds. Make certain that minimization in the builder does not lead either to the chair structure or to a "non-twisted" boat structure.* When you are satisfied, obtain an equilibrium geometry using the HF/3-21G model. Also perform a HF/3-21G geometry optimization on "normal" (chair) cyclohexane. Examine your alternative cyclohexane structure. Does it appear to satisfy the requirement that single bonds stagger each other? Examine the energy of the alternative relative to that of chair cyclohexane. Is it about the same (within 1-2 kJ/mol) or significantly higher? What would you expect the relative equilibrium populations of the two forms to be at room temperature (use the Boltzmann equation)?

2. Identify that site in your alternative cyclohexane structure which you believe to be the least "crowded". One after the other, substitute this site with methyl, fluoro and cyano groups and calculate the equilibrium geometry of each. Also obtain equilibrium geometries for the corresponding *equatorially-*substituted chair cyclohexanes. Are any of the alternative substituted cyclohexanes close enough in energy to the "normal" chair structures to be detectable in an equilibrium mixture at room temperature (> 1%)?

---

* Even though the non-twisted boat is an energy maximum, if you start with a C_{2v} symmetry structure, it will be maintained in the optimization procedure. A futher example of this is given in the activity "***Transition States are Molecules Too***".

26

Molecular Shapes V. Which Conformer Leads to Product?

Successful application of molecular modeling to the description of reactivity and product selectivity assumes knowledge of the structure of the reactant. As many, indeed most, molecules will have more than one conformation, this means knowledge of the "best" (lowest energy) conformation. A simple example is provided by reaction of sodium borohydride with the spiroketal **1** which proceeds with high stereospecificity.[*]

1		13	:	1

In order to model the process (which "face" of the carbonyl reacts fastest) it is necessary to know which of the four possible confomers of **1**, which differ in whether the oxygen in each ring is *equatorially* or *axially* disposed relative to the other ring, is most abundant.

In this activity, you will use HF/3-21G calculations to determine which of the four different conformers of **1** is lowest in energy and then model the selectivity of borohydride addition to this conformer using a LUMO map.

1. One after the other, build all four conformers of **1** and obtain an equilibrium geometry for each using the HF/3-21G model. Which conformer is the lowest in energy? Are any other conformers close enough in energy to contribute significantly (>1%) to an equilibrium mixture at room temperature? Can you offer any precedents to your assignment of favored conformer? Can you offer an explanation?

---

[*] De Shong *et al.* J. Org. Chem. 1991, 56, 3207.

2. Obtain a LUMO map for the lowest-energy conformer (only).

> A LUMO map, which indicates the extent to which the lowest-unoccupied molecular orbital (LUMO) "can be seen" at the "accessible surface" of a molecule, results from displaying the (absolute) value of the LUMO, indicating the "most likely" regions for electrons to be added, i.e., for nucleophilic attack to occur, on top of a surface of electron density, delineating the space taken up by a molecule. See the essay *"Local Ionization Potential Maps and LUMO Maps: Electrophilic and Nucleophilic Reactivity"* for additional insight.

3. When the calculation has completed, display the LUMO map. In this particular case, the LUMO will be localized on the carbonyl carbon, and the question of interest will be at which "face" of the carbonyl group is the LUMO more visible, that is at which face nucleophilic attack is likely to occur. At which face of the carbonyl carbon is the LUMO more visible? Is this result consistent with the experimental stereochemistry for nucleophilic addition? Elaborate.

4. Obtain LUMO maps for the remaining three conformers of **1**. Which (if any) give the same preference for nucleophilic addition as the lowest-energy conformer? Which (if any) give the opposite preference?

27

S$_N$2 Reaction of Cyanide and Methyl Iodide

S$_N$2 is usually the first reaction encountered by a beginning student of organic chemistry. The reaction of cyanide with methyl iodide, leading to acetonitrile and iodide is typical.

$$N\equiv C^- + CH_3I \longrightarrow CH_3CN + I^-$$

It proceeds via an "inversion" mechanism in which the nucleophile (cyanide) approaches the substrate (methyl iodide) "under the umbrella" made by carbon and its three hydrogens. In response, the umbrella opens (flattens out), leading to a five-coordinate carbon center (the transition state) with partially-formed bonds involving both the nucleophile (cyanide) and the leaving group (iodide).

Inversion continues and finally leads back to a four-coordinate tetrahedral carbon in which the cyanide has replaced iodide. (For an "animation" of this reaction showing migration of charge, see the essay "***Electrostatic Potential Maps: Charge Distributions***".) The importance of the S$_N$2 reaction, aside from the fact that it substitutes one group on carbon for another, is that the inversion of chiral carbon center leads to change of chirality at this center.

A great deal of effort is expended "talking about" S$_N$2 as it relates to the inversion of carbon. While this is, for the most part, warranted (synthesis of chiral molecules is a challenging enterprise), there are other important questions which could be . . . and should be . . . asked in order to truly understand what is "going on" in a simple S$_N$2 reaction. Two questions form the basis of this activity.

Why does cyanide react at carbon and not at nitrogen?

Doesn't the fact that nitrogen is more electronegative than carbon (3.0 vs. 2.6) imply that the "extra electrons" (the negative charge) should reside primarily on nitrogen and not carbon, and that nitrogen should be the source of the "attacking" electron pair? The key here is asking the right question. It isn't so much an issue of where the extra electrons are, but rather where the electrons which are most "available" and hence most likely to react are. According to molecular orbital theory, the most available electrons reside in the molecular orbital with the highest energy, the so-called highest-occupied molecular orbital or HOMO.

1. Build cyanide anion. Obtain its equilibrium geometry using the HF/3-21G model and request calculation of the HOMO. Display the HOMO. Is it bonding, antibonding or non-bonding? Does it have significant concentration on both carbon and nitrogen? Is it more concentrated on carbon or on nitrogen? How do your observations relate to cyanide serving as a "carbon nucleophile", a "nitrogen nucleophile" or both? Elaborate.

Why does iodide leave following nucleophilic attack onto carbon?

The real question here is whether or not we can "explain" what actually takes place (loss of iodide). The key is asking what happens to the electrons when they are put into methyl iodide. The obvious answer is that they go into a molecular orbital which is both empty and is as low an energy as is available. This is the so-called lowest-unoccupied molecular orbital or LUMO.

2. Build methyl iodide. Obtain its equilibrium geometry using the HF/3-21G model and request calculation of the LUMO. Display the LUMO. Is it bonding, antibonding or non-bonding? If it is bonding or antibonding, which bond(s) is (are) likely to be affected by the addition of electrons (from the nucleophile)? What changes in bond length(s) would you expect? How does your observation relate to what actually happens in the S_N2 reaction?

28

Transition States are Molecules Too

How can you tell a transition state from a stable molecule? The "reaction coordinate diagram" discussed in the essay "*Potential Energy Surfaces*" gives you the answer: "a transition state is an energy maximum along the reaction coordinate while a stable molecule is an energy minimum", but how exactly are you to put this information to use in classifying a particular molecule? The key is detailed knowledge of the way molecules vibrate as a result of their absorbing low-energy (infrared) light.

A diatomic molecule exhibits a single vibrational motion corresponding to expansion and contraction of the bond away from its equilibrium position. The frequency (energy) of vibration is proportional to the square root of the ratio of the "force constant" and the "reduced mass" (see also the tutorial "*Infrared Spectrum of Acetone*").

$$\text{frequency} \quad \alpha \quad \sqrt{\frac{\text{force constant}}{\text{reduced mass}}}$$

The force constant corresponds to the curvature of the energy surface in the vicinity of the minimum (it is the second derivative of the energy with respect to change in distance away from the equilibrium value). In effect, the magnitude of the force constant tells us whether the motion is "easy" (shallow energy surface meaning a low force constant) or "difficult" (steep energy surface meaning a high force constant).

Analysis of vibrational motions and energies (frequencies) in polyatomic molecules is more complicated, but follows from the same general principles. The main difference is that the vibrational motions in polyatomic molecules seldom correspond to changes in individual bond lengths, bond angles, etc., but rather to combinations of these motions. These combinations are called "vibrational modes" or "normal modes". A particularly simple example of this has already been provided for water molecule in the tutorial "***Basic Operations***".

This activity is intended to help you draw connections between the "formalism" and the motions which polyatomic molecules actually undergo when they vibrate. It is also intended to show you how knowledge of a molecule's vibrational frequencies will allow you to say with confidence that a molecule is or is not a minimum energy species, and (if it is not) to say whether it could or could not be a transition state.

1. Build ammonia, NH_3, and specify calculation of equilibrium geometry and infrared spectrum using the HF/6-31G* model. Display the vibrational frequencies and one after the other, animate the vibrational motions. Describe the motion associated with each frequency, and characterize each as being primarily bond stretching, angle bending or a combination of the two. Is bond stretching or angle bending "easier"? Do the stretching motions each involve a single NH bond or do they involve combinations of all three bonds?

All but a few elements occur naturally as a mixture of isotopes, which share the same number of protons and electrons but differ in the number of neutrons and so differ in overall mass. You are no doubt familiar with the isotopes of uranium. The common "stable" isotope, ^{238}U, has 92 protons and 92 electrons in addition to 146 neutrons, while the "radioactive" isotope ^{235}U has the same number of protons and electrons but only 143 neutrons.

Aside from their difference in mass, isotopes have virtually identical physical and chemical properties. Except for the lightest elements they are very difficult to distinguish and very difficult to separate. In addition, the electronic Schrödinger equation which the quantum chemical models in Spartan are based does not contain nuclear mass, meaning that potential energy surfaces for molecules with different isotopes are identical. However, nuclear mass does figure into a variety of physical properties, most important among them being vibrational frequencies (see equation at the beginning of this activity and also the essay *"Potential Energy Surfaces"*), and thermodynamic quantities such as entropy which depend on the vibrational frequencies.

2. Replace the three hydrogens in ammonia by three deuteriums, the isotope of hydrogen which contains one neutron (the "normal" isotope of hydrogen has no neutrons).

> Select **Properties** from the **Display** menu and *click* on a hydrogen. Change **Mass Number** in the **Atom Properties** dialog which appears from "1" to "2 (deuterium)". Repeat for the other hydrogens.

Repeat the calculations and compare the resulting vibrational frequencies (for ND_3) with those obtained above for NH_3. Rationalize any differences in terms of the expression provided earlier for the vibrational frequency of a diatomic molecule.

3. Next, build ammonia as a planar molecule (as opposed to a "pyramidal") molecule.

> Use trigonal planar nitrogen instead of tetrahedral nitrogen in the organic model kit

Calculate its equilibrium geometry and infrared spectrum using the HF/6-31G* model just as you did for pyramidal ammonia.

The first frequency listed is preceded by an "i". This indicates that it is an "imaginary" (as opposed to a "real") number. Given what you know from diatomic molecules, and given that reduced mass is necessarily a positive quantity, what does this tell you the sign of the force constant for this particular vibrational motion? What does this tell you about the position of planar ammonia on the potential energy surface? Describe the motion. Identify the analogous motion in pyramidal ammonia. Is it a low or high frequency (energy) motion?

A transition state, like a "stable molecule", is a well-defined point on the overall potential energy surface. It differs from a stable molecule in that not all of its "coordinates" are at minimum energy positions on the surface. Rather, one and only one coordinate is at an energy maximum on the surface. Liken the situation to a mountain pass, which is both a minimum (look to the left and right to see the mountain peaks towering above) and a maximum (look forward and backward to see the valleys below).

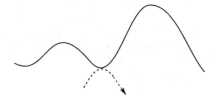

It is the "easiest way" to cross over a mountain range, just like a transition state in a chemical reaction is the easiest (lowest-energy) way to go between reactants and products.

Not all transition states are as simple as planar ammonia, connecting the two equivalent forms of pyramidal ammonia, but all are characterized by a single imaginary vibrational frequency.

4. Bring the boat form of cyclohexane onto the screen. This corresponds to a possible transition state connecting the chair and twist boat forms of cyclohexane (see the essay "*Potential Energy Surfaces*" as well as the activity "*Molecular Shapes IV. The "Other" Cyclohexane*").

> Select "*boat cyclohexane*" from the files in the "activities" directory.

Locate the imaginary frequency and describe the motion of atoms as best as you can.

29

What Do Transition States Look Like?

There is an enormous body of experimental knowledge about molecular geometry. The structures of upwards of 400,000 crystalline solids have been determined, primarily through X-ray crystallography. The diversity is enormous, ranging from small inorganic and organic molecules to proteins, polymers and materials. In addition, the geometries of more than 3000 small molecules have been determined, either in the gas phase or in solution. While not as diverse a collection, included are structures for a variety of highly-reactive species. Taken all together, this information has given chemists a clear picture of what is "normal" and what is not, and enabled them to accurately "guess" the geometries of molecules that are not yet known.

What is completely missing from this picture is experimental information about transition states. The reason is simple. A transition state is not a minimum on a potential energy surface and therefore cannot serve as a "trap" (see the previous activity "***Transition States are Molecules Too***" as well as the essay "***Potential Energy Surfaces***"). In other words, transition states "do not exist" in the sense of being able to put a collection of them "into a bottle". This is not a problem for quantum chemical calculations. Any molecule, real or imaginary, in fact, any collection of nuclei and electrons, may be "calculated", and the results of the calculations be used to show that the molecule could "exist" or could be a "transition state".

The purpose of this activity is to show you how to calculate transition states for simple chemical reactions, and to have you relate their structures to those of "normal" (stable molecules). You will first examine the rearrangement of methyl isocyanide, CH_3NC, to acetonitrile, CH_3CN. This is an example of a "unimolecular" process

225

in which a molecule remains "intact", but reorganizes to give rise to a lower-energy geometry. You will confirm that the process is energetically "downhill", and then to identify and characterize the transition state. Following this, you will then look at a somewhat more complicated "bimolecular" reaction involving the splitting of ethyl formate into formic acid and ethylene.

1. Build both acetonitrile, $CH_3C{\equiv}N$ and methyl isocyanide, $CH_3N{\equiv}C$.

> To construct methyl isocyanide, first build propyne, $CH_3C{\equiv}CH$ and delete the alkyne hydrogen (**Delete** from the **Build** menu). Next, bring up the inorganic model kit (*click* on the **Inorganic** tab at the top of the organic model kit), select N from the *Periodic Table* and *double click* on the central carbon.

Obtain HF/3-21G equilibrium geometries for both molecules. Which molecule, methyl isocyanide or acetonitrile is more stable (lower in energy) according to your calculations? How does the calculated energy difference between the two compare with the experimental enthalpy difference of 86 kJ/mol in favor of acetonitrile?

2. Build a guess at the transition state for geometrical rearrangement.

> Start with acetonitrile. Select **Transition States** from the **Search** menu (⌒), *click* on the CC bond and, while holding down the **Shift** key, *click* on the methyl carbon and on the nitrogen. Finally, *click* on ⌾ at the bottom of the screen (R P on the Mac) to produce a guess at the transition state.

Specify calculation of transition-state geometry using the HF/3-21G model and also request an infrared spectrum. The calculations will require several minutes.

When complete, first examine the vibrational (infrared) frequencies. Is there one imaginary frequency? If so, animate the vibrational motion associated with this frequency to convince yourself that it corresponds to a "reasonable" reaction coordinate (connecting methyl isocyanide and acetonitrile).

Examine the geometry of the transition state. Does it incorporate a "full" triple bond (as does both reactant and product)? Is the migrating methyl group midway between reactant and product or is it "closer" to either the reactant or product? Elaborate. Given the thermodynamics of the reaction, is this result consistent with the "Hammond Postulate"?

> The Hammond Postulate states that the transition state for an *exothermic* reaction will more closely resemble reactants than products.

A somewhat more complicated reaction is that involving "splitting' of ethyl formate into formic acid and ethylene in response to heat (a so-called "pyrolysis" reaction). This reaction is quite similar to the "ene" reaction of 1-pentene (leading to propene and ethylene) already discussed in the tutorial "***Ene Reaction***". Both reactions involve single bond cleavage and transfer of a hydrogen.

ethyl formate   ethylene   formic acid

3. Build ethyl formate, ethylene and formic acid. Obtain equilibrium geometries for all three molecules using the HF/3-21G model. Is the reaction as written above *exothermic* or *endothermic* (see the essay "***Total Energies and Thermodynamic and Kinetic Data***")? Based on this and on the Hammond Postulate, would you expect the transition state to more closely resemble reactants or products?

4. Build a guess at the pyrolysis transition state.

Start with ethyl formate in a conformation in which one of the CH_3 hydrogens is close to the (carbonyl) oxygen (as in the figure above). *Click* on [∿]. *Click* on bond "a" in the figure below and then click on bond "b".

A curved arrow from bond "a" to bond "b" will be drawn (as shown above). Next, *click* on bond "c" and then on bond "d". A second curved arrow from bonds "c" to "d" will be drawn. Finally, *click* on bond "e" and, while holding down the **Shift** key, *click* on the (methyl) hydrogen to be transferred and on the (carbonyl) oxygen to receive this hydrogen. A third curved arrow from bond "e" into the "space" between the hydrogen and oxygen will be drawn. If you make a mistake, you can remove one or more "arrows" using **Delete** from the **Build** menu. With all three arrows in place, *click* on [↺] ([R P] on the Mac) at the bottom right of the screen. Your initial structure will be replaced by a guess at the pyrolysis transition state.

Specify calculation of transition-state geometry using the HF/3-21G model and also request an infrared spectrum. The calculations will require several minutes to complete. When complete, first examine the vibrational (infrared) frequencies. Is there one imaginary frequency? If so, convince yourself that this corresponds to the reaction of interest.

5. Compare the geometry of the transition state with both ethyl formate (the reactant) and formic acid and ethylene (the products). Is the CC bond at the transition state less or more than "halfway" between a single and double bond? Are the two CO bonds in the transition state less or more than halfway to their lengths in the product? Overall, does the transition state appear to be more "reactant like" or more "product like"? Given the energetics of the reaction, is your result consistent with the Hammond postulate?

30

Reactions that "Twist and Turn"

Carbenes are reactive intermediates in which one carbon atom is surrounded by only six valence electrons instead of the normal complement of eight. Triplet carbenes, for example, methylene (CH_2), have two half-filled molecular orbitals, one in the plane of the molecule and the other perpendicular to the plane.

methylene

Their chemistry closely resembles that of radicals. Singlet carbenes, for example, difluorocarbene (CF_2) have two electrons in an in-plane molecular orbital, leaving the out-of-plane molecular orbital vacant.[*]

difluorocarbene

This suggests that singlet carbenes should, in principle, either be able to act as nucleophiles by "donating" their electron pair, or as electrophiles, by "accepting" an electron pair.

In the first part of this activity, you will compare the HOMO and LUMO of difluorocarbene with the qualitative descriptions provided above.

---

[*] The molecular orbitals of singlet methylene have previously been described in the essay *"Atomic and Molecular Orbitals"*.

1. Build difluorocarbene.

Obtain its equilibrium geometry using the HF/3-21G model and request HOMO and LUMO surfaces.

One after the other, display the HOMO and LUMO for difluorocarbene, and point out any "significant" difference with the qualitative descriptions provided above.

Among the "textbook reactions" of singlet carbenes is their addition to alkenes to yield cyclopropanes, e.g.

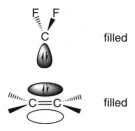

Here, a π bond is destroyed but two new σ bonds are formed (net gain of one bond). This reaction presents an interesting dilemma, in that the "obvious" approach of the two molecules; that is, the approach leading directly to a cyclopropane with the "correct" geometry, has the in-plane orbital on the carbene pointing directly at the π orbital on the alkene.

Both orbitals are filled and the resulting interaction is repulsive. A better approach is for the carbene to twist 90°. In this case, the empty out-of-plane molecular orbital on the carbene points toward the π orbital leading to stabilizing interaction.

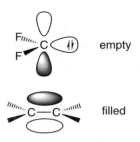

empty

filled

However, the cyclopropane product is now in the "wrong" geometry!

In the second part of this activity, you will again use the HF/3-21G model to obtain the transition state for addition of difluorocarbene to ethylene. You will examine the motion which the reagents take in order to avoid unfavorable interaction between their filled molecular orbitals yet still land up with the proper geometry.

2. Build a guess at the transition state for difluorocarbene adding to ethylene.

> Start by building ethylene. Select sp³ carbon, *click* on the **Insert** key (**option** key on the Mac) at the bottom of the model kit and *click* on screen. Add fluorines to two of the free valences on the sp³ carbon and delete the remaining two free valences. You are left with two fragments, ethylene and difluorocarbene. Orient the two as to be poised for reaction.
>
>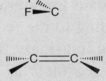
>
> Translations and rotations normally refer to the complete set of fragments, but that they can be made to refer to an individual fragment. For Windows, *click* on a fragment to identify it, and then hold down the **Ctrl** key while manipulations are being carried out. For Mac, *click* on one of the fragments to select it (the other fragments will be "dimmed") and move it around using the mouse. *Click* on the background to move both fragments as a unit.

Click on ⟳. *Click* on the carbon on the CF_2 fragment and then, while holding down the **Shift** key, *click* first on the CF_2 carbon and then on one of the carbons on the ethylene fragment. A curved arrow will be drawn.

Next, *click* on the CC double bond and then, while holding down the **Shift** key, *click* on the other ethylene carbon and then on the CF_2 carbon. A second arrow is added to the structure.

With both arrows in place, *click* on ⟳ (R P on the Mac) at the bottom right of the screen.

Obtain a transition-state geometry using the HF/3-21G model and request an infrared spectrum. The calculations will require several minutes.

Does the transition state more reflect the need to minimize unfavorable interaction between the electron pairs on difluorocarbene and ethylene, or does it more reflect the geometry of the product? Animate the vibrational mode (in the infrared spectrum) corresponding to the reaction coordinate, that is, the mode described by an imaginary frequency. This allows you to "see" the motion of reactants as the approach and leave the transition state. Account for this motion on the basis of the two requirements noted above.

31

Thermodynamic vs. Kinetic Control of Chemical Reactions

Organic chemists will easily recognize that cyclohexyl radical is more stable than cyclopentylmethyl radical, because they know that "6-membered rings are more stable than 5-membered rings", and (more importantly) that "2° radicals are more stable than 1° radicals". It may come as a surprise then that loss of bromine from 6-bromohexene leading initially to hex-5-enyl radical, results primarily in product from cyclopentylmethyl radical, rather than from the (presumably) more stable cyclohexyl radical.

There are two reasonable interpretations for this result: (i) that the reaction is thermochemically controlled but our understanding of radical stability is "wrong", and (ii) that the reaction is kinetically controlled.

Obtain relative energies for cyclohexyl and cyclopentylmethyl radicals to determine the thermodynamic product.

1. Build cyclohexyl and cyclopentylmethyl radicals and obtain their equilibrium geometries using the HF/3-21G model. Which is more stable? Is the energy difference large enough such that only one is likely to be observed? (Recall that, according to the Boltzmann equation, at room temperature an energy difference of 12 kJ/mol corresponds to a product ratio of >99:1.) Do you conclude that ring closure is under thermodynamic control?

Establish the kinetic product, i.e., which ring closure, to cyclohexyl radical or to cyclopentylmethyl radical, is "easier".

2. Build guesses for transition states for closure of hex-5-enyl radical into cyclohexyl radical and into methylcyclopentyl radical.

Build hex-5-enyl radical, *click* on [↷], and draw reaction arrows as follows for closure to cyclohexyl radical: from C_1 to a new bond between C_1 and C_6; from the C_5C_6 bond to C_5, and for closure to cyclopentylmethyl radical: from C_1 to a new bond between C_1 and C_5; from the C_5C_6 bond to C_6. *Click* on [↻] ([R P] on the Mac).

Which radical, cyclohexyl or cyclopentylmethyl, is more easily formed? Given the relationship between transition-state energy difference, $\Delta E^{\ddagger}$, and the ratio of major to minor (kinetic) products,

$\Delta E^{\ddagger}$ (kJ/mol)	major: minor (at room temperature)
4	90:10
8	95:5
12	99:1

what is the approximate ratio of products suggested by the calculations? How does this compare with what is observed? Do you conclude that ring closure is under kinetic control?

32

Anticipating Rates of Chemical Reactions

The rate of Diels-Alder reactions generally increases with π-donor ability of the electron-donor group (EDG) on the diene, and with π-acceptor ability of the electron-withdrawing group (EWG) on the dienophile.

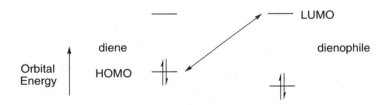

EDG = R, OR

EWG = CN, CHO, CO_2H

The usual interpretation is that donors will "push up" the energy of the HOMO on the diene and acceptors will "push down" the energy of the LUMO on the dienophile. Any decrease in "HOMO-LUMO gap" should lead to stronger interaction between diene and dienophile and to a decrease in barrier.

In this activity, you will first test such a hypothesis using the following rate data for Diels-Alder cycloadditions involving cyclopentadiene as a diene and cyano-substituted alkenes as dienophiles (expressed in log units relative to the rate of cyclopentadiene and acrylonitrile).

acrylonitrile	0	1,1-dicyanoethylene	4.64
trans-1,2-dicyanoethylene	1.89	tricyanoethylene	5.66
cis-1,2-dicyanoethylene	1.94	tetracyanoethylene	7.61

You will then obtain transition states for reactions of cyclopentadiene and both acrylonitrile and tetracyanoethylene.

1. Build acrylonitrile, 1,1-dicyanoethylene, *cis* and *trans*-1,2-dicyanoethylene, tricyanoethylene and tetracyanoethylene and obtain their equilibrium geometries using the HF/3-21G model. Plot LUMO energy vs. the log of the relative rate. Which dienophile has the smallest LUMO energy (smallest HOMO-LUMO gap)? Is this the dienophile which reacts most rapidly with cyclopentadiene? Which has the largest LUMO energy? Is this the compound which reacts most slowly? Does the HOMO-LUMO gap correlate with relative reaction rate?

2. Build guesses for transition states for Diels-Alder cycloaddition of cyclopentadiene and both acrylonitrile and tetracyanoethylene.

To build a guess at the transition state for cycloaddition of cyclopentadiene and acrylonitrile, first build cyclopentadiene, then *press* the **Insert** key (**option** key on the Mac) and build acrylonitrile on the same screen. Orient the two molecules into an *endo* geometry.

Click on ⌃. Draw reaction arrows from the C_1C_2 bond in acrylonitrile to a new bond between C_1 on acrylonitrile and C_1 on cyclopentadiene; from the C_1C_2 to the C_2C_3 bonds in cyclopentadiene; from the C_3C_4 bond in cyclopentadiene to a new bond between C_4 on cyclopentadiene and C_2 on acrylonitrile. *Click* on ↻ (R P on the Mac).

Obtain transition states for the two reactions using the HF/3-21G model. Also, build cyclopentadiene and obtain its geometry using the HF/3-21G model. Calculate activation energies for the two Diels-Alder reactions, and then use the Arrhenius equation (see the essay *"Total Energies and Thermodynamic and Kinetic Data"*) to calculate the difference in rates for the two reactions. How does the calculated difference compare with the experimental difference?

236

33

Identifying Greenhouse Gases

The earth and all the other planets can be thought of as blackbodies which radiate into the universe. This provides a means to dissipate the energy which falls on the planets due to the sun. Because of their low ambient temperatures, so-called blackbody radiation occurs primarily in the infrared.

The earth is actually warmer than such a picture would predict, due to the fact that some of the blackbody radiation is absorbed by its gaseous atmosphere. This is known as the "greenhouse effect". The magnitude of the effect, "greenhouse warming", is obviously due to both the extent and chemical makeup of the atmosphere.

To be an effective "greenhouse gas", a molecule must absorb in the infrared. Neither nitrogen nor oxygen, which together make up 99% of the earth's atmosphere, satisfy this requirement. However, several "minor" atmospheric components, carbon dioxide, water and ozone most important among them, absorb in the infrared and contribute directly to greenhouse warming. These "subtract" from the earth's blackbody radiation leaving actual radiation profile (in the range of 500 to 1500 cm^{-1}) that is given below.

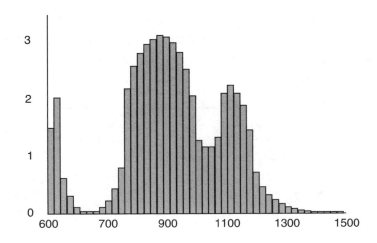

This leads to a further requirement for an effective greenhouse gas, mainly that it absorbs in a frequency region where blackbody radiation is intense.

In this activity, you will calculate infrared spectra for molecules which are already present in the atmosphere, or might be introduced through human involvement. By matching any "strong" bands with the blackbody radiation profile given on the previous page, you should be able to tell whether they are reasonable candidates for effective greenhouse gases.

> This is an oversimplification. A more realistic model needs to account not only for intense infrared bands in the "proper place", but also needs to establish the quantity of material likely to get into the atmosphere and a reasonable lifetime for this material in the atmosphere. These factors are addressed in a beautiful paper proposing an experimental investigation suitable for an undergraduate laboratory. (M.J. Elrod, J. Chem. Ed., **76**, 1702, 1999). The present activity is based on this paper.

Start by comparing calculated and experimental infrared spectra for carbon dioxide. This will allow you to establish a "scaling factor" bringing calculated and measured frequencies into agreement.

1. Build carbon dioxide and calculate its equilibrium geometry and infrared spectrum using the HF/6-31G* model.

   How do the calculated infrared frequencies compare with the experimental values given below? How do the calculated infrared intensities compare with the (qualitative) experimental designations? Can you see evidence in the "experimental" blackbody profile for the presence of carbon dioxide in the atmosphere? Elaborate.

	description of mode	frequency cm^{-1}	intensity
carbon dioxide	bend	667	strong
	symmetric stretch	1333	inactive
	asymmetric stretch	2349	very strong

Propose a single multiplicative factor which, when applied to the calculated frequencies, will bring them into best agreement with the experimental values.

Methane and nitrous oxide (N_2O) are both introduced into the atmosphere from agriculture. Methane is also released as a result of oil recovery and fuel production. 1,1,1,2-tetrafluoroethane is now widely used in automobile air conditioners and is likely also introduced into the atmosphere in significant quantities.

2. Build methane, nitrous oxide and 1,1,1,2-tetrafluoroethane, and calculate the equilibrium geometry and infrared spectrum of each.

> Nitrous oxide is linear. To build it, start with **Allene** from the **Groups** menu and delete all four free valences. Then, bring up the inorganic model kit, select **N** from the *Periodic Table* and *double click* on two adjacent carbons. Finally, select **O** from the *Periodic Table* and *double click* on the remaining carbon.

One after the other, display the infrared spectrum for each of the three molecules. Using as a selection criterion the presence of a (modestly) strong infrared absorption in the range of 500 - 1500 cm^{-1} (use scaled frequencies), comment as to whether each might be an effective greenhouse gas.

34

"Unseen" Vibrations

The infrared spectrum of *trans*-1,2-dichloroethylene in the region of 500 to 3500 cm^{-1} comprises only four lines, while nine lines can be seen in the spectrum of the corresponding *cis* isomer.

trans-dichloroethylene   *cis*-dichloroethylene

Both molecules have six atoms and both will undergo twelve (3 times number of atoms -6) different vibrational motions. It might, therefore, be expected that the infrared spectra of both would contain twelve lines. While a few of the "missing lines" are below the 500 cm^{-1} measurement range, the primary reason for the discrepancy is that some vibrational motions may give rise to absorptions which are too weak to be observed or be "infrared inactive", meaning that they will not appear at all in the infrared spectrum.

While discussion of the theory underlying infrared spectroscopy is beyond the present focus, it can be stated that in order for a particular vibrational motion to be "infrared active" (and hence "seen" in the infrared spectrum), it needs to lead the change in the overall polarity of the molecule as reflected in a change in dipole moment. In fact, the intensity of absorption is proportional to the change in dipole moment, meaning that vibrational motions which lead only to small changes in dipole moment, while "infrared active", may be "too weak" to actually be observed in the infrared spectrum.

In this activity, you will calculate the vibrational spectra of *cis* and *trans* isomers of 1,2-dichloroethylene. Unlike the experimental (infrared) spectra, the calculations reveal all twelve vibrations for each isomer as well as the expected intensity (including zero intensity).

A comparison with the experimental spectra will allow you to see which lines are unobserved because they are outside the measurement range and which are unobserved because they are weak or inactive.

1. Build both *trans* and *cis*-dichloroethylene. Calculate the equilibrium geometry for each along with the infrared spectrum using the HF/3-21G model.

   Examine the infrared spectrum for *cis*-dichloroethylene. (It is better to look at the table of frequencies and intensities rather than the actual spectrum.) Associate each vibration falling between 500 and 3500 cm^{-1} and having an intensity 1% or greater of the maximum intensity with the experimental data provided below. Use the (experimentally assigned) "description of vibration" as well as the labels describing the "symmetry of vibration" to assist you.

description of vibration	symmetry of vibration	frequency
CCCl deformation	b_1	571
CH bend	b_2	697
CCl stretch	a_1	711
CCl stretch	b_1	857
CH bend	a_1	1179
CH bend	b_1	1303
CC stretch	a_1	1587
CH stretch	b_1	3072
CH stretch	a_1	3077

   Repeat your analysis with *trans*-1,2-dichloroethylene.

description of vibration	symmetry of vibration	frequency
CCl stretch	b_u	828
CH bend	a_u	900
CH bend	b_u	1200
CH stretch	b_u	3090

   Do the calculations provide a quantitatively correct description of the observed infrared spectra for *cis* and *trans*-dichloroethylene, that is, properly assign those lines which are intense enough to actually be observed?

2. Identify the most intense line in the calculated infrared spectrum of *trans*-dichloroethylene. Make a list of structures corresponding to distortion of the molecule away from its equilibrium geometry along this vibration. Calculate the dipole moment for each distorted structure (using the HF/3-21G model) and plot them (vs. motion away from the equilibrium geometry).

> *Click* on the appropriate frequency inside the **Spectra** dialog. Next, change the value inside the box to the right of **Steps** at the right of the dialog to "5" and *click* on **Make List**. A list of five structures "walking along" the vibrational coordinate will result. Enter the **Calculations** dialog and request a **Single Point Energy** calculation using the HF/3-21G model. Submit. When completed, enter the dipole moment into the spreadsheet. For Windows, *click* on the header cell for an empty column, then *click* on the **Add** button at the bottom of the spreadsheet, select **dipole** from the menu and finally *click* on **OK**. For Mac, *click* on **Add** button at the bottom of the spreadsheet and *drag* **dipole** from the menu into the spreadsheet. (Alternatively, bring up the **Molecule Properties** dialog, *click* on **Dipole** at the bottom and *drag* it into the spreadsheet.) Bring up the **Plots** dialog and select **Molecule** (the number in the list) under **X Axis** and **Dipole** under **Y Axes**.

What is the dipole moment of *trans*-dichloroethylene in its equilibrium geometry? What, if anything, happens to the dipole moment as the molecule is distorted along the selected vibrational coordinate?

3. Locate the vibrational frequency in the calculated infrared spectrum corresponding to the stretching of the CC bond. It should have an intensity of zero. Perform the same dipole moment calculations as above using this frequency. How is this situation different from that in the previous step? How does your result here together with that from the previous step fit in with the fact that intensity depends on change in dipole moment?

35

Benzyne

Benzyne has long been implicated as an intermediate in nucleophilic aromatic substitution, e.g.

While the geometry of benzyne has yet to be conclusively established, the results of a ^{13}C labeling experiment leave little doubt that two (adjacent) positions on the ring are equivalent.

The infrared spectrum of a species purported to be benzyne has been recorded and a line in the spectrum at 2085 cm^{-1} assigned to the C≡C stretch.

In this activity, you will obtain an equilibrium geometry for benzyne using the HF/3-21G model and, following this, obtain an infrared spectrum for the molecule. Comparison with the experimental spectrum (specifically the line at 2085 cm^{-1} attributed to the C≡C stretch) should allow you to comment one way or another about its reported "sighting".

1. Build benzyne.

> Start with benzene and delete two adjacent free valences (**Delete** from the **Build** menu).

Also build 2-butyne and benzene. The structures of those molecules will help you to judge the bonding in benzyne. Additionally, the calculated $C \equiv C$ stretching frequency for 2-butyne, which is known experimentally, will serve to calibrate the calculations for benzyne. Obtain equilibrium geometries for all three molecules using the HF/3-21G model and following that, calculate infrared spectra for benzyne and 2-butyne only.

2. After the calculations have completed, examine the geometry of benzyne, and compare it to the structures for 2-butyne and benzene. Does it incorporate a "real" triple bond (as does 2-butyne) or is the length closer to that in benzene? Based on a comparison of structures among the three molecules, draw what you feel is an appropriate Lewis structure (or set of Lewis structures) for benzyne.

3. Display the infrared spectrum for 2-butyne. Locate the line in the spectrum corresponding to the $C \equiv C$ stretch and record its frequency. You will use the ratio of the experimental $C \equiv C$ stretching frequency ($2240 \ cm^{-1}$) and the calculated value to scale the calculated vibrational frequencies for benzyne.

4. Display the infrared spectrum for benzyne. Is benzyne an energy minimum? How do you know? Locate the line in the spectrum corresponding to the "$C \equiv C$" stretch. Is it "weak" or "intense" relative to the other lines in the spectrum? Would you expect that this line would be easy or hard to observe? Scale the calculated frequency by the factor you obtained (for 2-butyne) in the previous step. Is your (scaled) stretching frequency in reasonable accord with the reported experimental value of $2085 \ cm^{-1}$?

36

Why are Silicon-Carbon Double Bonds so Rare?

With the exception of so-called "phosphorous ylides", compounds incorporating a double bond between carbon and a second-row element are quite rare. Most curious perhaps is the dearth of stable compounds incorporating a carbon-silicon double bond, in stark contrast to the common occurrence of the carbon-carbon double bond in organic compounds.

In this activity, you will first examine the three-dimensional structures of one or more of the silaolefins, **1-4**, which have been synthesized for "hints" why such compounds have proven to be so elusive.

You will then employ two different graphical models to compare both electrophilic and nucleophilic reactivities of a simpler silaolefin, $Me_2Si=CMe_2$, with that of the analogous olefin, $Me_2C=CMe_2$.

1. Build one or more of the compounds, **1 - 4**. Display the molecule as a space-filling model. Given that the "chemistry" of olefins (and presumably of silaolefins as well) is associated with the π bond, do you anticipate any "problems" that the molecule might have reacting? Elaborate.

2. Build tetramethylsilaethylene, $Me_2Si=CMe_2$, as well as its carbon analog 2,3-dimethyl-2-butene, $Me_2C=CMe_2$. Optimize the geometries of both molecules using the HF/3-21G model and following this, obtain both a local ionization potential map and a LUMO map. A local ionization potential map indicates the relative ease of electron removal ("ionization") at the "accessible surface" of a molecule. This would be expected to correlate with the relative ease of addition of an electrophile. A LUMO map indicates the extent to which the lowest-unoccupied molecular orbital (the LUMO) can be "seen" at the "accessible surface" of a molecule. This indicates the "most likely" regions for electrons to be added, and would be expected to correlate with the likelihood of nucleophilic attack. (Both types of maps are described and illustrated in the essay *Local Ionization Potential Maps and LUMO Maps: Electrophilic and Nucleophilic Reactivities*".) Place both molecules side-by-side on screen, and one after the other display the local ionization potential and LUMO maps.

> First, bring up the spreadsheet. For Windows, *check* the boxes to the right of the first ("Labels") column for each molecule. For Mac, *click* on ⊡ at the bottom left of the screen and then *check* the box to the left of the molecule name (in the spreadsheet) for each molecule. "Uncouple" the molecules so that they can be manipulated independently. Select (*uncheck*) **Coupled** from the **Model** menu.

On the basis of comparison of local ionization potential maps, would you conclude that the silaolefin is likely to be more or less reactive than the olefin toward electrophiles? Elaborate. On the basis of comparison of the LUMO maps, would you conclude that the silaolefin is likely to be more or less reactive than the olefin toward nucleophiles? Elaborate. How do your conclusions fit with the known silaolefins? Elaborate.

37

Carbon Monoxide and Metal-Ligand Bonding

Carbon monoxide is probably the single most common molecule to appear in organometallic compounds. Where a single metal is involved (or where two or more metals are involved but are widely separated), CO inevitably bonds "end on" from carbon, and contributes two electrons to the valence shell of the metal. Where two metals are "close", carbon monoxide can alternatively bond to both, again from carbon (it can bridge). In this case, it contributes one electron to the valence shell of each metal.

At first glance, both bonding modes use only the lone pair on carbon and neither should have much effect on the structure and properties of free CO. There is, however, evidence to suggest the contrary. Specifically, the infrared sketching frequency of CO complexed end-on to a metal is typically in the range of 1850 to 2100 cm^{-1}, which is smaller than the frequency in free carbon monoxide (2143 cm^{-1}). Changes are even greater in molecules where CO is a bridging group, typically falling in the range of 1700 - 1850 cm^{-1}. It would appear that the simple bonding models above involving only the lone pair need to be modified. This is the subject of the present activity.

1. Build CO and optimize its geometry using the semi-empirical (PM3) model. Request the HOMO and LUMO. Display the HOMO. This corresponds to the molecular orbital in which the highest-energy pair of electrons are held. Is it consistent with the usual Lewis structure for CO? Is the HOMO bonding, antibonding or essentially non-bonding between carbon and oxygen? What, if anything, would you expect to happen to the CO bond strength as

electrons are donated from the HOMO to the metal? Elaborate. Is this consistent with the changes seen in the infrared stretching frequency of carbon monoxide?

> Reduction in bond strength will generally be accompanied by increase in bond length and decrease in stretching frequency.

Display the LUMO. This corresponds to the molecular orbital in which the next (pair of) electrons will go.

> The LUMO in CO is one of a set of two equivalent "degenerate" orbitals. You can base any arguments either on the LUMO or the next orbital (LUMO+1).

Is the LUMO bonding, antibonding or essentially non-bonding between carbon and oxygen? What if anything would you expect to happen to the CO bond strength were electrons to be donated (from the metal) into this orbital? Elaborate. Is this consistent with the changes seen in the infrared stretching frequency of carbon monoxide?

To see if the metal center incorporates a high energy filled molecular orbital properly disposed to donate electrons into the LUMO of CO, you need to perform calculations on a simple organometallic from which a carbon monoxide ligand has been removed. You will use $FeCO_4$, arising from loss of CO from $FeCO_5$.

2. Build $FeCO_5$ and obtain its equilibrium geometry (a trigonal bipyramid) using the semi-empirical (PM3) model. When completed, delete one of the *equatorial* CO ligands to make iron tetracarbonyl and perform a single-point energy calculation. Request the HOMO.

   Does the HOMO have significant amplitude in the location where the next carbon monoxide ligand (the one you removed) will attach? If so, are signs (colors) of the orbital components consistent with the signs of the components for the LUMO in CO? Would you expect electron donation to occur?

38

Ethylene and Metal-Ligand Bonding

Two "limiting" structures can be drawn to represent ethylene "bonded" to a metal center. The first may be thought of as a "weak complex" in that it maintains the CC double bond, while the second completely destroys the double bond in order to form two new metal-carbon σ bonds, leading to a three-membered ring (a so-called "metallacycle").

The difference between the two representations is one of degree and "real" metal-alkene complexes are expected to span the full range of possible structures. (A similar situation has already been described in the activity *Are Reactive Intermediates "Normal" Molecules?*.)

In this activity, you will first examine the HOMO and LUMO of ethylene to see where electrons may be drawn from and where they may be put back, and to understand the consequences which these "electron movements" will have on its geometry.

1. Obtain an equilibrium geometry for ethylene using the semi-empirical PM3 model and request the HOMO and LUMO. Display the HOMO. Is it bonding, antibonding or essentially non-bonding between the two carbons? What if anything should happen to the CC bond as electrons are donated from the HOMO to the metal? Specifically, do you expect the carbon-carbon bond length to decrease, increase or remain about the same? Elaborate. Display the LUMO of ethylene. This corresponds to the molecular orbital where the next (pair of) electrons will go. Is this orbital bonding,

antibonding or essentially non-bonding between the two carbons? What, if anything, should happen to the CC bond as electrons are donated (from the metal) into the LUMO? Elaborate. Is the expected change in the CC bond due to this interaction in the same direction or in the opposite direction as any change due to interaction of the HOMO with the metal? Elaborate.

To see if the metal center incorporates appropriate unfilled and filled molecular orbitals to interact with the HOMO and LUMO of ethylene, respectively, perform calculations on $FeCO_4$, arising from loss of ethylene from ethylene iron tetracarbonyl, $CO_4FeC_2H_4$.

2. Build ethylene iron tetracarbonyl and obtain its equilibrium geometry (a trigonal bipyramid with ethylene occupying an *equatorial* position with the CC bond in the *equatorial* plane) using the semi-empirical (PM3) model. When completed, delete the ethylene ligand and perform a single-point energy calculation. Request both HOMO and LUMO.

   Does the LUMO in $FeCO_4$ have significant amplitude in the *equatorial* region where ethylene will fit to accept electrons from the (ethylene) HOMO? If so, are the signs (colors) of the LUMO orbital components consistent with the signs of the components of the ethylene HOMO? Would you expect electron donation from ethylene to be metal to occur? Does the HOMO in $FeCO_4$ have significant amplitude in the *equatorial* region where ethylene will fit? If so, are the signs of its components consistent with the signs of the components of the ethylene LUMO? Would you expect electron donation from the metal to ethylene to occur?

39

The Chromium Tricarbonyl "Substituent"

Benzene and other aromatics ("arenes") devoid of strong electron withdrawing groups such as cyano or nitro, are normally immune to nucleophilic aromatic substitution, e.g., anisole is non-reactive, while 4-cyanoanisole is reactive.

On the other hand, the analogous arene chromium tricarbonyl complexes are typically highly reactive, giving rise primarily to *meta* substitution products.

Does this imply that chromium tricarbonyl acts as an electron acceptor, having the same net effect on the arene ring as a directly bonded substituent such as cyano? This activity uses electrostatic potential maps to test such a hypothesis and further to see to what extent metal complexation is as effective as "conventional" ring substitution in enhancing and directing reactivity.

1. Build anisole, 4-cyanoanisole and anisole chromium tricarbonyl, and obtain PM3 (semi-empirical) equilibrium geometries for all three molecules and following this, electrostatic potential maps.

> To build anisole chromium tricarbonyl, bring up the inorganic model kit, select **Cr** from the *Periodic Table* and four-coordinate tetrahedral from the list of hybrids and *click* on screen. Add **Carbon Monoxide (Ligands** menu) to three of the free valences on chromium and **Benzene (Ligands** menu not **Rings** menu) to the remaining free valence. Bring up the organic model kit and introduce a methoxy group onto the (benzene) ring.

When the calculations have completed, put the molecules side-by-side on screen, and turn on the electrostatic potential maps.

> Bring up the spreadsheet. For Windows, *check* the box to the right of "Label" (first column) for all three molecules. For Mac, first *click* on ▣ at the bottom left of the screen and then *check* the box to the left of the molecule name (in the spreadsheet) for each molecule. Also, select (*uncheck*) **Coupled** from the **Model** menu, so that the three molecules can be moved independently.

The "blue" regions in the maps demark regions which are most electron deficient. Relative to anisole, is the (accessible) ring face in anisole chromium tricarbonyl more or less electron deficient? What does this suggest to you about the relative likelihood that the two molecules will undergo nucleophilic aromatic substitution? Is the complexed chromium tricarbonyl group more effective, less effective or about as effective as a *para* cyano group in increasing the electron deficiency of the benzene ring? Is there any evidence in the electrostatic potential map for anisole chromium tricarbonyl that nucleophilic attack will occur *meta* to the methoxy substituent? Elaborate. Is there any evidence for this in calculated carbon charges? Elaborate.

> To display the charge on an atom, select **Properties** from the **Display** menu and *click* on the atom. To "attach" charges to the model, select **Configure...** from the **Model** menu and *check* **Charge**.

40

Vitamin E

Molecules with unpaired electrons ("radicals") can cause biochemical damage through their reaction with the unsaturated fatty acids found in cellular membranes. Vitamin E may play an active role in defending cells from attack by reacting quickly with radicals to give stable products that can then be safely excreted. Such compounds are refered to as "antioxidants".

vitamin E

In order to be effective as a cellular antioxidant, vitamin E must be able to transfer a hydrogen atom to the offending radical, leading to a stable vitamin E radical, i.e.

$$R^{\bullet} + \text{vitamin E} \longrightarrow RH + \text{vitamin E}^{\bullet}$$

Of course, vitamin E must also be soluble in the cellular membrane which presumably is "hydrocarbon-like" as opposed to "water-like". The fact that vitamin E is an effective antioxidant implies that it does form a stable radical and that it is soluble in the membrane.

In this activity, you will first examine the electrostatic potential map for vitamin E for evidence that it should be soluble in a cellular membrane. You will then look at the radical formed by hydrogen abstraction from vitamin E for evidence that it should be "stable". Here, a map of spin density will be employed, revealing the extent to which the radical site remains localized or is delocalized. You will then examine an alternative to vitamin E and try to judge whether it too might be an effective antioxidant.

1. Bring vitamin E onto the screen.

> Select "*vitamin E*" from the files in the "activities" directory.

Display the electrostatic potential map. Recall that the colors "red" and "blue" depict regions of excess negative and excess positive charge, respectively, while the color "green" depicts regions which are electrically neutral. The former would be expected to enhance solubility in water while the latter would be expected to enhance solubility in hydrocarbons. Would you expect vitamin E to be soluble in cellular membranes? Explain.

2. Bring vitamin E radical onto the screen.

> Select "*vitamin E radical*" from the files in the "activities" directory.

From which atom has the hydrogen atom been abstracted? Examine the calculated equilibrium geometry of the radical to decide whether the unpaired electron (the radical site) is localized on this atom or if it is spread over several atoms (delocalized)? If the latter, draw appropriate Lewis structures showing the delocalization. On the basis of the calculated geometry, would you conclude that vitamin E radical should be especially stable? Elaborate.

In order to show the location of the unpaired electron, display the spin density. This depicts deviations from "perfect" electron pairing at different locations in the molecule. A spin density map limits the locations to those on the accessible electron density surface.

3. Display the spin density map for vitamin E radical.

> Colors near "blue" depict regions of maximum excess spin while those near "red" depict regions of least spin.

Is the map in accord with the calculated equilibrium geometry? Would you conclude that vitamin E radical should be especially stable?

Other compounds have been used as antioxidants. These include 3,5-di-*tert*-butyl-4-hydroxytoluene (butylated hydroxytoluene or BHT).

BHT

Does this satisfy the same requirements demanded of vitamin E? Is it likely to be as effective as vitamin E? Compare electrostatic potential maps and spin density maps to see.

3. Build BHT as well as the radical resulting from hydrogen removal. Obtain equilibrium geometries for both using the semi-empirical model, and request on electrostatic potential map for BHT and a spin density map for BHT radical.

> For BHT radical, you need to set **Multiplicity** inside the **Calculations** dialog to **Doublet**. To request a spin density map, specify **density** for **Surface** and **spin** for **Property** inside the **Surfaces** dialog.

When both have completed, examine the electrostatic potential map for BHT. Relative to vitamin E, would you expect BHT to be more or less soluble in a cellular membrane? Elaborate.

4. Finally, examine the spin density map for BHT radical. Relative to vitamin E radical, is the spin more or less delocalized? Would you expect BHT radical to be more or less easily formed (from BHT) than vitamin E radical (from vitamin E)? Elaborate.

41

Can DNA be Tricked?

Protons bound to heteroatoms in heterocyclic compounds are likely to be very mobile in solution, and where there are two (or more) heteroatoms, different isomers related by shifts in protons among the heteroatoms may be present in equilibrium. The situation is so common that these isomers have been given a special name "tautomers", and the equilibrium commonly referred to as a "tautomeric equilibrium". A simple and well known example involves 2-hydroxypyridine which in protic media is in tautomeric equilibrium with 2-pyridone.

2-hydroxypyridine   2-pyridone

The surprising fact is that the equilibrium actually lies in favor of 2-pyridone despite the fact that 2-hydroxypyridine is an aromatic molecule and would be expected to be very stable.

A much more important case concerns the four nucleotide bases used in the construction of DNA, adenine, thymine, cytosine and guanine. Each base incorporates several heteroatoms and each can give rise to several tautomers. The structure of DNA assumes the predominance of only one tautomer for each base (the one drawn in your textbook), which in turn hydrogen bonds to its "complementary base". Were any of the possible "alternative" tautomers present in significant amounts, the consequences could be catastrophic. In particular, the alternative might very well select an alternative complementary base leading to errors in replication.

In this activity, you will use HF/3-21G calculations to obtain energies for all "reasonable" tautomers (principal tautomer and all alternatives) for one (or more) of the nucleotide bases. This will allow you to say with confidence whether tautomeric equilibrium presents a real danger.

1. Build one of the nucleotide bases in its usual tautomeric form (see below). Use a methyl group to mimic the connection to the sugar-phosphate backbone in DNA.

cytosine   thymine   adenine   guanine

2. One after the other, build all the alternative tautomers for your selected nucleotide base (don't worry about including more than one stereoisomer for tautomers which incorporate imine functionality). Obtain equilibrium geometries for your full set of structures using the HF/3-21G model.

What is the energy of the alternative relative to the principal tautomer? What is its equilibrium abundance at room temperature (use the Boltzmann equation; see the essay *"Total Energies and Thermodynamic and Kinetic Data"*)?

> If you put both tautomers in the same document prior to calculation (**New Molecule** instead of **New** to start building the second molecule), you can use Spartan's spreadsheet to provide both the relative energy and the Boltzmann weight. Bring up the spreadsheet and *click* on the entry for the principal tautomer. For Windows, *click* on the header cell for an empty spreadsheet column, then *click* on the **Add** button at the bottom of the spreadsheet, select both **rel. E** and **Boltzmann Distribution** from the menu of items which appears and finally, *click* on **OK**. For Mac, *click* on the **Add** button at the bottom of the spreadsheet, and *drag* both **Rel.E** and **Boltzmann** from the menu of items into the spreadsheet.

Is the alternative likely to be present in sufficient amount to affect bonding in DNA? Elaborate.

Section E
Common Terms and Acronyms

3-21G. A **Split-Valence Basis Set** in which each **Core Basis Function** is written in terms of three **Gaussians**, and each **Valence Basis Function** is split into two parts, written in terms of two and one **Gaussians**, respectively.

6-31G*. A **Polarization Basis Set** in which each **Core Basis Function** is written in terms of six **Gaussians**, and each **Valence Basis Function** is split into two parts, written in terms of three and one **Gaussians**, respectively. Non-hydrogen atoms are supplemented by a set of single **Gaussian** d-type functions.

***Ab Initio* Models**. The general term used to describe methods seeking approximate solutions to the **Electronic Schrödinger Equation**, but which do not involve empirical parameters.

Acid. A molecule which "desires" to give up a proton.

Acidity. The **Energy** (**Enthalpy**) of the reaction: $AH \rightarrow A^- + H^+$. Typically given relative to a "standard" acid, A_sH, that is $\Delta E(\Delta H)$ for $AH + A_s^- \rightarrow A^- + A_sH$.

Activation Energy. The energy of a **Transition State** above that of reactants. Activation energy is related to reaction rate by way of the **Arrhenius Equation**.

Anion. An atom or molecule with a net charge of -1.

Antibonding Molecular Orbital. A **Molecular Orbital** which has a "break" or a "**Node**" between particular atomic centers. Adding electrons to such an orbital will weaken the bond while removing electrons will strengthen the bond. The opposite is a **Bonding Molecular Orbital**.

Arrhenius Equation. An equation governing the rate of a chemical reaction as a function of the **Activation Energy** and the temperature.

Atomic Orbital. A **Basis Function** centered on an atom. Atomic orbitals typically take on the form of the solutions to the hydrogen atom (s, p, d, f... type orbitals).

Atomic Units. The set of units which remove all of the constants from inside the **Schrödinger Equation**. The **Bohr** is the atomic unit of length and the **Hartree** is the atomic unit of energy.

Base. A molecule which "desires" to accept a proton.

Basicity. The **Energy** (**Enthalpy**) of the reaction: $B + H^+ \rightarrow BH^+$. Typically given relative to a "standard" base, B_s, that is $\Delta E(\Delta H)$ for $B + B_sH^+ \rightarrow BH^+ + B_s$.

Basis Functions. Functions usually centered on atoms which are linearly combined to make up the set of **Molecular Orbitals**. Except for **Semi-Empirical Models** where basis functions are **Slater** type, basis functions are **Gaussian** type.

Basis Set. The entire collection of **Basis Functions**.

Bohr. The **Atomic Unit** of length. 1 bohr = 0.529167Å.

Boltzmann Equation. The equation governing the distribution of products in **Thermodynamically-Controlled Reaction**.

Bonding Molecular Orbital. A **Molecular Orbital** which has strong positive overlap between two particular atomic centers. Adding electrons to such an orbital will strengthen the bond, while removing electrons will weaken the bond. The opposite is an **Antibonding Molecular Orbital**.

Bond Surface. An **Isodensity Surface** used to elucidate the bonding in molecules. The value of the density is typically taken as 0.1 electrons/**bohr**.[3]

Born-Oppenheimer Approximation. An approximation based on the assumption that nuclei are stationary. Applied to the **Schrödinger Equation**, it leads to the **Electronic Schrödinger Equation**.

Cation. An atom or molecule with a net charge of +1.

Chiral. A molecule with a non-superimposible mirror image.

Chiral Center. A tetrahedral atom (most commonly carbon) with four different groups attached. Two different arrangements ("stereoisomers") are possible and these are mirror images.

Chiral centers are labelled "R" or "S" depending on the arrangement of groups. Also known as a **Stereocenter**.

Closed Shell. An atom or molecule in which all electrons are paired.

Conformation. The arrangement about single bonds and of flexible rings.

Core. Electrons which are primarily associated with individual atoms and do not participate significantly in chemical bonding (1s electrons for first-row elements, 1s, 2s, $2p_x$, $2p_y$, $2p_z$ electrons for second-row elements, etc.).

Coulombic Interactions. Charge-charge interactions which follow Coulomb's law. Stabilizing when charges are of opposite sign and destabilizing when they are of the same sign.

Covalent Bond. A chemical bond which involves a significant sharing of a pair of electrons between the two atoms.

CPK Model. A molecular model in which atoms are represented by spheres, the radii of which correspond to **van der Waals Radii**. Intended to portray molecular size and shape. Also known as a **Space-Filling Model**.

Diastereomers. Stereoisomers which differ in the stereochemistry (R or S) of one or more (*but not all*) **Chiral Centers**.

Diffusion-Controlled Reactions. Chemical reactions without **Transition States** (or **Activation Energies**), the rates of which are determined by the speed in which molecules encounter each other and how likely these encounters are to lead to reaction. The combination of two radicals proceeds without **Activation Energy** and are examples of diffusion-controlled reactions.

Dipole Moment. A measure of the overall polarity of a molecule, taking into account differences in nuclear charges and electron distribution.

Electron Density. The number of electrons per unit volume at a point in space. This is the quantity which is measured in an X-ray diffraction experiment.

Electronic Schrödinger Equation. The equation which results from incorporation of the **Born-Oppenheimer Approximation** to the **Schrödinger Equation**.

Electrophile. An electron pair acceptor. A molecule (or part of a molecule) which desires to interact (react) with an electron-rich reagent or **Base**.

Electrostatic Charges. Atomic charges chosen to best match the **Electrostatic Potential** at points surrounding a molecule, subject to overall charge balance.

Electrostatic Potential. The energy of interaction of a positive point charge with the nuclei and fixed electron distribution of a molecule.

Electrostatic Potential Map. A graph that shows the value of **Electrostatic Potential** on an **Electron Density Isosurface** corresponding to a **van der Waals Surface**.

Enantiomers. Stereoisomers which differ in the stereochemistry (R or S) of all **Chiral Centers**. Enantiomers are non-superimposible mirror images.

Endothermic Reaction. A chemical reaction in which the **Enthalpy** is positive.

Energy(ΔE). The heat given off (negative energy) or taken in (positive energy) by a chemical reaction at constant volume. Quantum chemical calculations give the energy.

Enthalpy (ΔH). The heat given off (negative enthalpy) or taken in (positive enthalpy) by a chemical reaction. Enthalpy is commonly equated to **Energy** from which it differs by a (small) pressure-volume (PV) term: $\Delta H = \Delta E + P\Delta V$.

Entropy (ΔS). The extent of ordering (negative entropy) or disordering (positive entropy) which occurs during a chemical reaction.

Equilibrium Geometry. A **Local Minimum** on a **Potential Energy Surface**.

Excited State. An electronic state for an atom or molecule which is not the lowest-energy or **Ground State**.

Exothermic Reaction. A chemical reaction in which the **Enthalpy** is negative.

Force Field. The set of rules underlying **Molecular Mechanics Models**. Comprises terms which account for distortions from ideal bond distances and angles and for **Non-Bonded van der Waals** and **Coulombic Interactions**.

Frontier Molecular Orbitals. The **HOMO** and **LUMO**.

Formal Charge. A "recipe" to assign charges to atoms: formal charge = number of valence electrons - number of electrons in lone pairs - number of bonds (single bond equivalents).

Free Energy; *See* **Gibbs Energy**

Gaussian. A function of the form $x^l y^m z^n \exp(\alpha r^2)$ where l, m, n are integers (0, 1, 2 . . .) and α is a constant. Used in the construction of **Basis Sets**.

Gaussian Basis Set. A **Basis Set** made up of **Gaussian Basis Functions**.

Gibbs Energy (ΔG). The combination of **Enthalpy** and **Entropy** which dictates whether a reaction is favorable (spontaneous) or unfavorable at temperature T: $\Delta G = \Delta H - T\Delta S$.

Global Minimum. The lowest energy **Local Minimum** on a **Potential Energy Surface**.

Ground State. The lowest energy electronic state for an atom or molecule.

Hammond Postulate. The idea that the **Transition State** for an *exothermic* reaction will more closely resemble reactants than products. This provides the basis for "modeling" properties of **Transition States** in terms of the properties of reactants.

Hartree. The **Atomic Unit** of energy. 1 hartree = 627.47 kcal/mol.

Hartree-Fock Approximation. Separation of electron motions in many-electron systems into a product form of the motions of the individual electrons.

Hartree-Fock Energy. The energy resulting from **Hartree-Fock Models**.

Hartree-Fock Models. Methods in which the many-electron wavefunction in written terms of a product of one-electron wavefunctions. Electrons are assigned in pairs to functions called **Molecular Orbitals**.

Heterolytic Bond Dissociation. A process in which a bond is broken and a cation and anion result. The number of electron pairs is conserved, but a non-bonding electron pair has been substituted for a bond.

HOMO. **H**ighest **O**ccupied **M**olecular **O**rbital. The highest-energy molecular orbital which has electrons in it.

Homolytic Bond Dissociation. A process in which a bond is broken and two **Radicals** result. The number of electron pairs is not conserved.

Hybrid Orbital. A combination of **Atomic Orbitals**. For example, 2s and $2p_x$, $2p_y$, $2p_z$ orbitals may be combined to produce four equivalent sp^3 hybrid orbitals, each pointing to different corners of a tetrahedron.

Hypervalent Molecule. A molecule containing one or more main-group elements in which the normal valence of eight electrons has been exceeded. Hypervalent molecules are common for second-row and heavier main-group elements but are uncommon for first-row elements.

Imaginary Frequency. A frequency which results from a negative curvature of the **Potential Energy Surface**. **Equilibrium Geometries** are characterized by all real frequencies while **Transition States** are characterized by one imaginary frequency.

Infrared Spectrum. The set of **Energies** corresponding to the vibrational motions which molecules undergo upon absorption of infrared light.

Ionic Bond. A chemical bond in which the pair of electrons is not significantly shared by the two atoms.

Isodensity Surface. An **Electron Density Isosurface**. **Bond Surfaces** and **Size Surfaces** may be used to elucidate bonding or to characterize overall molecular size and shape, respectively.

Isopotential Surface. An **Electrostatic Potential Isosurface**. It may be used to elucidate regions in a molecule which are particularly electron rich and subject to electrophilic attack and those which are particularly electron poor, subject to nucleophilic attack.

Isosurface. A three-dimensional surface defined by the set of points in space where the value of the function is constant.

Isotope Effect. Dependence of molecular properties and chemical behavior on atomic masses.

Kinetically-Controlled Reaction. A chemical reaction which has not gone all the way to completion, and the ratio of products is not related to the relative **Activation Energies**.

Kinetic Product. The product of a **Kinetically-Controlled Reaction**.

LCAO Approximation. Linear Combination of Atomic Orbitals approximation. Approximates the unknown **Hartree-Fock Wavefunctions (Molecular Orbitals)** by linear combinations of atom-centered functions (**Atomic Orbitals**).

Local Ionization Potential. A measure of the relative ease of electron removal ("ionization") as a function of location.

Local Ionization Potential Map. A graph of the value of the **Local Ionization Potential** on an **Isodensity Surface** corresponding to a **van der Waals Surface**.

Local Minimum. Any **Stationary Point** on a **Potential Energy Surface** for which all coordinates are at energy minima.

Lone Pair. A **Non-Bonded Molecular Orbital** which is typically associated with a single atom.

LUMO. Lowest Unoccupied Molecular Orbital. The lowest-energy molecular orbital which does not have electrons in it.

LUMO Map. A graph of the absolute value of the **LUMO** on an **Isodensity Surface** corresponding to a **van der Waals Surface**.

Mechanism. The sequence of steps connecting reactants and products in an overall chemical reaction. Each step starts from an equilibrium form (reactant or intermediate) and ends in an equilibrium form (intermediate or product).

Merck Molecular Force Field; *See* **MMFF94**.

Meso Compound. A molecule with two (or more) **Chiral Centers** with a superimposible mirror image.

Minimal Basis Set. A **Basis Set** which contains the fewest functions needed to hold all the electrons on an atom and still maintain spherical symmetry.

MMFF94. Merck Molecular Force Field. A **Molecular Mechanics Force Field** for organic molecules and biopolymers developed by Merck Pharmaceuticals incorporated into Spartan.

Molecular Mechanics Models. Methods for structure, conformation and strain energy calculation based on bond stretching, angle bending and torsional distortions, together with **Non-Bonded Interactions**, and parameterized to fit experimental data.

Molecular Orbital. A one-electron function made of contributions of **Basis Functions** on individual atoms (**Atomic Orbitals**) and delocalized throughout the entire molecule.

Molecular Orbital Models. Methods based on writing the many-electron solution of the **Electronic Schrödinger Equation** in terms of a product of one-electron solutions (**Molecular Orbitals**).

Multiplicity. The number of unpaired electrons (number of electrons with "down" spin) +1. 1=singlet; 2=doublet; 3=triplet, etc.

Node. A change in the sign of a **Molecular Orbital**. Nodes involving bonded atoms indicate that a particular **Molecular Orbital** is **Antibonding** with respect to the atoms.

Non-Bonded Interactions. Interactions between atoms which are not directly bonded. **van der Waals Interactions** and **Coulombic Interactions** are non-bonded interactions.

Non-Bonded Molecular Orbital. A molecular orbital which does not show any significant **Bonding** or **Antibonding** characteristics. A **Lone Pair** is a non-bonded molecular orbital.

Non-Polar Bond. A **Covalent Bond** which involves equal or nearly equal sharing of electrons.

Nucleophile. An electron-pair donor. A molecule (or region of a molecule) which "desires" to interact (react) with an electron-poor reagent or **Acid**.

Octet Rule. The notion that main-group elements prefer to be "surrounded" by eight electrons (going into s, p_x, p_y, p_z orbitals).

Orbital Symmetry Rules; *See* **Woodward-Hoffmann Rules**.

Open Shell. An atom or molecule in which one or more electrons are unpaired. **Radicals** are open-shell molecules.

PM3. **P**arameterization **M**ethod **3**. A **Semi-Empirical Model** incorporated into Spartan.

Point Group. A classification of the **Symmetry Elements** in a molecule.

Polar Bond. A **Covalent Bond** which involves unequal sharing of electrons.

Polarization Basis Set. A **Basis Set** which contains functions of higher angular quantum number (**Polarization Functions**) than required for the **Ground State** of the atom, in particular, d-type functions for non-hydrogen atoms. **6-31G*** is a polarization basis set.

Polarization Functions. Functions of higher angular quantum than required for the **Ground State** atomic description. Added to a **Basis Set** to allow displacement of **Valence Basis Functions** away from atomic positions.

Potential Energy Surface. A function of the energy of a molecule in terms of the geometrical coordinates of the atoms.

Property Map. A representation or "map" of a "property" on top of an **Isosurface**, typically an **Isodensity Surface**. **Electrostatic Potential Maps**, **LUMO Maps** and **Spin Density Maps** are useful property maps.

Pseudorotation. A mechanism for interconversion of *equatorial* and *axial* sites around trigonal bipyramidal centers, e.g., fluorines in phosphorous pentafluoride.

Quantum Mechanics. Methods based on approximate solution of the **Schrödinger Equation**.

Radical. A molecule with one or more unpaired electrons.

Rate Limiting Step. The step in an overall chemical reaction (**Mechanism**) which proceeds via the highest-energy **Transition State**.

Reaction Coordinate. The coordinate that connects the **Local Minima** corresponding to the reactant and product, and which passes through a **Transition State**.

Reaction Coordinate Diagram. A plot of energy vs. **Reaction Coordinate**.

Schrödinger Equation. The quantum mechanical equation which accounts for the motions of nuclei and electrons in atomic and molecular systems.

Semi-Empirical Models. **Quantum Mechanics** methods that seek approximate solutions to the **Electronic Schrödinger Equation**, but which involve empirical parameters. **PM3** is a semi-empirical model.

Size Surface. An **Isodensity Surface** used to establish overall molecular size and shape. The value of the density is typically taken as 0.002 electrons/**bohr**^{3}.

Slater. A function of the form $x^l y^m z^n \exp(-\zeta r)$ where l, m, n are integers (0, 1, 2 ...) and ζ is a constant. Related to the exact solutions to the **Schrödinger Equation** for the hydrogen atom. Used as **Basis Functions** in **Semi-Empirical Models**.

SOMO. Singly Occupied Molecular Orbital. An orbital which has only a single electron in it. The **HOMO** of a **Radical**.

Space-Filling Model; *See* **CPK Model**.

Spin Density. The difference in the number of electrons per unit volume of "up" spin and "down" spin at a point in space.

Spin Density Map. A graph that shows the value of the **Spin Density** on an **Isodensity Surface** corresponding to a **van der Waals Surface**.

Split-Valence Basis Set. A **Basis Set** in which the **Core** is represented by a single set of **Basis Functions** (a **Minimal Basis Set**) and the **Valence** is represented by two or more sets of **Basis Functions**. This allows for description of aspherical atomic environments in molecules. **3-21G** is a split-valence basis set.

Stationary Point. A point on a **Potential Energy Surface** for which all energy first derivatives with respect to the coordinates are zero. **Local Minima** and **Transition States** are stationary points.

Stereocenter; *See* **Chiral Center**

Symmetry Elements. Elements which reflect the equivalence of different parts of a molecule. For example, a plane of symmetry reflects the fact that atoms on both sides are equivalent.

Theoretical Model. A "recipe" leading from the **Schrödinger Equation** to a general computational scheme. A theoretical models needs to be unique and well defined and, to the maximum extent possible, be unbiased by preconceived ideas. It should lead to **Potential Energy Surfaces** which are continuous.

Theoretical Model Chemistry. The set of results following from application of a particular **Theoretical Model**.

Thermodynamically-Controlled Reaction. A chemical reaction which has gone all the way to completion, and the ratio of different possible products is related to their thermochemical stabilities according to the **Boltzmann Equation**.

Thermodynamic Product. The product of a reaction which is under **Thermodynamic Control**.

Transition State. A **Stationary Point** on a **Potential Energy Surface** for which all but one of the coordinates is at an energy minimum and one of the coordinates is at an energy maximum. Corresponds to the highest-energy point on the **Reaction Coordinate**.

Transition-State Geometry. The geometry (bond lengths and angles) of a **Transition State**.

Transition State Theory. The notion that all molecules react through a single well-defined **Transition State**.

Valence. Electrons which are delocalized throughout the molecule and participate in chemical bonding (2s, $2p_x$, $2p_y$, $2p_z$ for first-row elements, 3s, $3p_x$, $3p_y$, $3p_z$ for second-row elements, etc.).

van der Waals Interactions. Interactions which account for short-range repulsion of non-bonded atoms as well as for weak long-range attraction.

van der Waals Radius. The radius of an atom (in a molecule), which is intended to reflect its overall size.

van der Waals Surface. A surface formed by a set of interpreting spheres (atoms) with specific **van der Waals radii**, and which is intended to represent overall molecular size and shape.

Vibrational Frequencies. The energies at which molecules vibrate. Vibrational frequencies correspond to the peaks in an **Infrared** and Raman **Spectrum**.

VSEPR Theory. **V**alence **S**tate **E**lectron **P**air **R**epulsion theory. A simple empirical model used to predict the geometries of molecules given only the total number of electrons associated with each center.

Wavefunction. The solutions of the **Electronic Schrödinger Equation**. In the case of the hydrogen atom, a function of the coordinates which describes the motion of the electron as fully as possible. In the case of a many-electron system a function which describes the motion of the individual electrons.

Index